Nobody's Perfect

Bill Bernbach and the Golden Age of Advertising

Also by Doris Willens

Lonesome Traveler—The Life of Lee Hays
Piano Bar (book and lyrics)
Spent (book and lyrics)

ISBN 1442135263 & EAN-13 9781442135260

Nobody's Perfect

Bill Bernbach and the Golden Age of Advertising

by

Doris Willens

CreateSpace

For the next generation

Ben, Liz, Kimmy, Jenny, Andrea and Nico

CONTENTS

◆ ◆ ◆

Introduction

"Well, what do you expect? The Renaissance lasted only 20 years."
—*Orson Welles*

This is the story of the single most influential advertising agency of the 20th century, and the single most influential advertising man, William Bernbach.

It is a story that he could not bring himself to write.

"Do it different" was his theme—a theme that later Apple Computer borrowed for its "Think different" campaign.

How he did it, how he helped his writers and art directors produce great advertising, runs through these pages.

But so too does a kind of Greek drama, a fable of profound human emotions—the wrenching relationships of fathers and sons, fears of betrayal and abandonment, and a promethian defiance of time and succession, the myth of the golden bough.

* * *

Nothing holds still. A company grows, or shrivels, or self-destructs, or is taken over, or takes over others. On Madison Avenue, another week, another merger. So what?

But the entire advertising profession felt an unparalleled sense of loss when, on a day in 1986, the name Bernbach was chipped off his agency's door—replaced by impersonal initials and new ownership. Since its birth in June 1949 and its exhilarating first ads for Ohrbach's apparel stores, Doyle Dane Bernbach had stood for challenging assumptions, breaking barriers, scorning the comfortable "dull but safe" approach of traditional advertising agencies.

This was the agency that rode to unprecedented glory, slaying the oppressive dragon of "hucksterism," and bringing back the grail of pride to advertising practitioners. The agency that proved that great work was what it was all about—not old school ties, or family connections, or country clubs, or bowing to every client whim, or shaving prices.

Its influence was anything but small and parochial. On the contrary, Bernbach and his agency changed the way America regarded the selling messages bombarding them daily. Where advertising had previously caused irritation, boredom, and even disgust, Bernbachian advertising touched and moved people in a whole new way. Unexpectedly, America entered into a love affair with advertising, which helped to fuel the unprecedented prosperity of the post-World War II decades.

The advertising created under Bernbach's great editorial eye influenced more than economics; it influenced cultural attitudes as well. "Think small" for Volkswagen helped change a generation's ideas about acquisitiveness. The Avis theme, "We're only Number 2. So we try harder," went into the language, a new way of looking at America's obsession with strivers and winners. And the poster campaign that started in the New York subways and became pin-ups on dorm and den walls across the country, "You don't have to be Jewish to love Levy's bread," in the words of one observer, "helped people feel comfortable with America's ethnic diversity in a way that any number of human relations commissions could not." All this while selling cars and rent-a-car service and rye bread.

The agency's influence was perhaps never more momentously registered than with a single commercial created for Lyndon Johnson's 1964 presidential campaign. A little girl plucks the petals of a daisy, innocently counting to ten. A military voice picks up, counting backwards from ten to the detonation of an atomic bomb. Although it ran as a paid spot only once, that anti-Goldwater commercial launched negative political advertising which, alas, has been with us ever since.

For better and occasionally for worse, Doyle Dane Bernbach made history. Its name remains a touchstone. The agencies that dominated the pre-Doyle Dane Bernbach industry—J. Walter Thompson and BBDO and Young & Rubicam and McCann-Erickson—underwent crises of their own, but all, eventually, took up the banner of creativity, and opened wide their doors to "ethnics" (meaning, then, to Madison Avenue, Jews and Italians), looking for the kind of talent Doyle Dane Bernbach had. New agencies would announce their philosophy to be that of Bill Bernbach, and their goal to become the Doyle Dane Bernbach of their time.

* * *

Every copywriter and art director in the business longed to work there.

Sometimes it seems that half of them did. Some called it the University of Bernbach—the training ground for generations of creative talent.

One needed only to walk through its corridors to sense the high spirits, the joy, the creative excitement, the passionate commitment to breakthrough work. In time, that would diminish; the same corridors filling with whispers about how the agency was changing, and with those whispers, a smell of fear and insecurity.

It was the good years that people remembered, before Doyle Dane Bernbach fell from grace, and disappeared into a new entity called DDB Needham Worldwide, Inc.

The industry mourned, and wondered how it had happened.

All the questions remained unanswered.

Books were promised. Seven, that I heard about from the DDBers who meant to write them. Others, perhaps, that I didn't hear about.

I had been in charge of the agency's public relations from 1966 through 1981, and remained on the payroll working half-time through 1984. I'd come to Madison Avenue via journalism—reporter on the *Minneapolis Tribune*, copy editor on the *Washington Post*, advertising news columnist on the *New York Journal-American*. The latter job gave me a kind of celebrity on the New York ad scene, and after four years of covering the news of the business, I moved into agency public relations. I stayed until my children grew up; then it was time to take risks. To work on theater projects, and perhaps books. I was commissioned to write a biography of a musician, and quit the agency.

I'd turned in my manuscript just two weeks before Doyle Dane Bernbach's eclipse. Then, ready to tackle another book, I decided to work on a biography of the agency, or of Bernbach himself—however many others might be planning to do the same.

Several of those others were copywriters; two had worked on the account management side of the agency. But one by one, the prospective authors dropped out of the run. The reasons they gave were varied. But as my own research went on, I began to wonder if there was something about the Bernbach/Doyle Dane Bernbach story that defeated all attempts at telling it—starting with Bernbach himself, who accepted a publisher's advance, and never produced the proposed book.

That something, I eventually concluded, had to do with images and reality. I came to believe that many a sleepless night troubled the lives of those who planned to write about Bernbach and his agency. Starting with Bernbach himself.

* * *

Maxwell Dane, who achieved national fame as Number Four on President

Nixon's "enemies list," thoughtfully answered all questions posed by the stream of journalists who interviewed him over the years. But he never stopped worrying that one day a Doyle Dane Bernbach book would be published that contained "all the gossip."

Such a book hasn't appeared and becomes less likely with the passage of time. *Some* of the gossip, however, does reflect the history of the agency's developing problems. Only those bits confirmed by two or more sources made their way into the story that follows.

* * *

"Tell me, kid, tell me what happened?" Ned Doyle, agency founder, 83 years old and frail with emphysema, asked the question again and again on the day that his name, with Dane's and Bernbach's, came off the door. His mind, lawyer-sharp, pondered the pieces of the story as he knew it—and nobody knew more about the goings-on of the agency than did Doyle.

After that, he lived in the hope that a book would be written, perhaps not so much about "what happened" as about the legend itself. Its title, he often told me, should be "Once there was a Doyle Dane Bernbach." The reference to Camelot was unmistakeable. And in that context, he wanted history to remember that the agency's name was *Doyle Dane* Bernbach. That Ned Doyle and Mac Dane were essential to the spirit, the philosophy, and the success of the company. That a biography of Bernbach alone would be misleading and incomplete.

In the last year of his life, Doyle unburdened himself of a story he hadn't told me before. That on the day of Doyle's retirement, in 1969, Bernbach exuberantly exclaimed to a trusted colleague, "Now, at last, it's MY agency."

Doyle told the story with a touch of irony and a dash of bitters. A man of flinty self-assurance, he tended to date the decline of the agency to his retirement.

He believed from the beginning that the heart and soul of an advertising agency is its creative work. So the fame of Doyle Dane Bernbach would inevitably rest with Bernbach. He just didn't believe that Bernbach could ever have made it without him.

* * *

From the beginning, Bernbach spoke, not of advertising, but of the art of persuasion. To persuade the consumer, the creators of ads needed to touch people's basic, unchanging instincts—their "obsessive drive to survive, to be admired, to succeed, to love, to take care of their own."

His disciples absorbed the lesson and produced unforgettable advertising. Because Bernbach kept so much of himself private, few realized how close to the bone his instructive and revealing words were. If they were at the heart of the art of persuasion, and the source of his agency's fabled rise, they also encompass the dark side, the primeval drives that would lead to the end of the Golden Age of Advertising.

* * *

"We walked in on the Monday after Bill died and we didn't see any change," one of Bernbach's associates recalled. Bernbach had died early on a Saturday morning, October 2, 1982, at New York Hospital, after a defiantly-secret, five-year battle with leukemia.

His colleagues saw no change because, they reassured themselves and one another, Bernbach had been only marginally involved in the agency's affairs for the past few years. He'd come to his office almost every day, despite the pain of his advancing (but never mentioned) disease, fastidious as ever in his impeccably conservative clothes, sitting alone at the round table that served as his desk, wasting away, consulted about very little, trying to ignore the worried huddles of executives that quickly broke up as he approached.

How much change, then, would his death bring about? Neil Austrian, the agency's chief executive officer, saw one immediate problem. The few clients who still asked, "Has Bill seen this?" were sometimes told "yes" when in fact Bill hadn't. His approval sealed their approval. What would happen now? For there wasn't another Bill in the wings. And in time, as one manager put it, "because the father that everybody was working for, seeking approval from, wasn't there, everybody began to push and shove," setting off tremors that would bring the temple down.

Might it have gone another way? Management authority Peter F. Drucker proclaims that "[an effective leader] knows that the gravest indictment of a leader is for the organization to collapse as soon as he leaves or dies. . . ."

In fact, nearly four years elapsed between Bernbach's death and the "big bang" mega-merger of 1986, the end of the old Doyle Dane Bernbach. One astonishing thing after another happened between the two events, obscuring the line that linked them. DDBers picked their favorite villains in those demoralized post-Bernbach years, but never stopped hoping the agency would regenerate. Finally, when it was all over, one heard the question, "Why didn't Bill anoint a creative successor before he died?"

The question was asked, again and again, by those I interviewed. Sometimes it had a ring of genuine bafflement. Sometimes it sounded like a prod in a direction I hadn't thought to explore. Eventually I saw the emerging outline of an answer, and it kept me awake nights.

* * *

I had expected to concentrate on the post-Bernbach years when I set out to research the story of the agency's fate. As Doyle Dane Bernbach's long-time PR head, I knew—or thought I knew—the territory. The drama that climaxed in the engulfing mega-merger had built after I'd loosened, then cut, my ties to the agency. My loyalties and friendships belonged to the "old" Doyle Dane Bernbach. The story I envisioned would require professional reporting and writing—and that was my training.

Everybody involved—past and present—wanted to talk about what had happened and their own theories of why. Especially to an old insider. It was a time of white hot fury that could not long be sustained. I tried to catch it on tape, at its peak, over the weeks that followed.

As I gathered material on the collapse, my Bernbach file folders grew fatter, and split into subdivisions, which in turn pushed out into new folders.

The story I had set out to research, for all its sensational disclosures, began to seem less compelling than the portrait building in my files. Who, in a year or two, would care about those last few years of betrayals and money grabs? The players in the final act would not long be remembered.

On the other hand, the advertising world would always remember Bill Bernbach. I began to mull the implications of that. Sleep became more elusive.

* * *

Ned Doyle to the contrary, everything pointed to a biography of Bernbach. Everything except my heart. I copied out the words of Katherine Anne Porter's biographer, who wrote of being emotionally disconcerted by "the uneasy sense, inhibiting rigorous investigation, that the revelations about her life constituted some cruel kind of exposure."

I supposed that Bernbach's spirit rested content with the final portrait of his legendary self. No one knew better than I how watchful he had been of his image. He kept its care entirely in his own hands. He dealt with the press as he chose. I handled the agency's public relations, not his, and my efforts to coordinate the two were not encouraged. He would pick up the phone and call the *New York Times* or *Advertising Age* and speak his mind on a sticky agency story, whatever strategy we'd hammered out with clients and lawyers. So, messy moments resulted for the agency posture. (The press, flattered by his calls, admired him more than ever.) So, we pulled our hair. It *was* his agency. And wasn't he the master in the art of communication?

And it *was* his image. And he was firm about what that should, and should not, encompass. He would talk to an interviewer with joyous excitement about advertising, about the art of persuasion. But an icy blue stare would cut off any attempts by the writer to get behind the ideas, to the man himself. Even a question about his work habits was over the line to Bernbach. If such reactions struck me as excessive, I quickly learned to accept them. He'd attained legendary status long before I came on the scene. He'd achieved that while relentlessly guarding his privacy. I might dare to "take him on" in some areas, but not in his determination to keep the "personal" from spilling into the press.

Yet one could never be sure just where Bernbach drew his lines. For example: as his 65th birthday approached, I proposed a gathering of all of Bernbach's creative offspring, past and present, the most remarkable collection of talent in advertising history. I could imagine no greater tribute. Nor a more powerful visualization of Bernbach's dominant impact on the industry.

Immediately, his closest associates assured me that he would never agree to inviting former DDB art directors and copywriters. What? Why not? Eyes rolled incredulously at my density. Surely I was aware of Bernbach's unforgivingness towards those of his people who had taken jobs with competitors, or started their own agencies. I had better leave it alone, they warned. I couldn't, so strongly did I feel about my proposal. I took it to Bernbach, who unhesitatingly approved—though he crossed a few names off the list I'd drawn up. The resulting event, a triumphant celebration, deserves a place of its own in this story, illuminating an unexpected passage in the fathers-and-sons saga of Bernbach's life.

The experience taught me that his closest associates had no more idea than I had of Bernbach's "off-limits." Yet that didn't stop them from trying to protect him. From . . . what?

* * *

Much later, I pondered the words of an old DDB copywriter, recalling the early years, musing that "Bill was very, very sensitive, and you never knew when you were going to step on a sensitivity. Not meaning to. You watched your words. Not with Ned, and Ned doesn't watch them with you. But with Bill, you weren't sure at what point he might become upset, so that made it less easy."

By then, I had learned a great deal more about the roots of Bernbach's sensitivities, and their entanglements with the image he had so carefully tended.

As the agency's fortunes changed, Bernbach had cause to worry about their effect on his own legend. The trial of his physical pain was made worse by concern about what would survive of what he had wrought. Yet he kept his private self sealed off. To hospital visitors in his final days, he would talk only about the agency and ads in production. Not a word about his leukemia. Not even to his sons.

He'd managed to get clear through life without giving away any more of himself than he'd intended. Why not let it be?

* * *

Perhaps because those who are legendary do not get the last word on their lives. They try. The Hemingways and Sartres and Hellmans, the Warhols and Frank Lloyd Wrights and Man Rays and Langston Hugheses, re-create themselves in the images they desire, and hope the best parts stick when biographers start the job of untangling truth from fiction.

And as Bernbach himself often told clients about advertising their products, "Nobody's perfect, and nobody's going to believe you if you claim to be." Still, the prospect roiled my insides.

I copied out another paragraph, this one from a *New York Times* Sunday Book Review article on Michael Holroyd's long-awaited biography of George Bernard Shaw. "To Shaw—who rewrote portions of the biographies that appeared about him during his life—this new work would seem a betrayal. 'When someone like Shaw is alive, he needs all possible protections,' Mr. Holroyd said. 'He needs sentimentality, prevarications, half-truths—which are necessary for all living people to get through all right. But when somebody dies, if we value them, we can then tell the truth about them insofar as that truth can be recaptured . . . If we have only lies and sentimentality as our picture of our heroes, we will be terribly misled as to what the facts of real life are, and being misled, I think we will become miserable.'"

* * *

And so, this is a story about images and reality, and how they affected the fate of the most celebrated agency in the Golden Age of Advertising, not so very long ago.

♦ ♦ ♦

1
Bernbach's Way

"I doubt whether there is a single agency of any consequence which is not the lengthened shadow of one man"—David Ogilvy

Bill Bernbach—5'7" tops, shirtsleeves rolled up, smoking—walked through the art bullpen, his extraordinary blue eyes scanning the promise and deficiencies of the ads-in-progress pinned on the cluttered walls, his raspy Bronx-tinged voice shouting out to the art directors whose offices opened onto the bullpen.

To one: "Can you get the picture bigger?"

At other agencies, they always asked, "Can you make the picture smaller?" No visual was ever too big for Bernbach.

And he'd call out to the writer.

"Can you make this line a little shorter?"

Or: "Throw out the whole first paragraph—why do you have to go through all that to get to the point? *There's* your point."

As he edited, the work in progress began to shape into another one of those Doyle Dane Bernbach ads that were setting Madison Avenue on its ear. The creative team watched the transformation in a state halfway between awe for Bernbach's editing genius, and resignation that the now-brilliant ad would, along its way to the outside world, become Bernbach's possession.

* * *

That was part of the bargain, said an old agency hand, years later. He deserved it, said another, he made it possible.

He opened their eyes and minds to new ways of looking at advertising. He introduced them to the integration of art and copy. He nurtured their idiosyncratic talents. And then—the final miracle—he took their work to the client and, with passion and conviction—sold it.

In the environment he created, they produced ads that were a strong fresh wind—open, sweeping, funny, involving. The rest of Madison Avenue was still stuck in the past, writing ads in "advertisingese." Product after product trumpeted as Amazing! or Most Amazing! or The Finest! Headlines proclaiming The Greatest!, The Most Fabulous Discovery Ever Made!, World's Favorite!, Best!, Most!, and the omnipresent So New!, So Different!

The illustrations that accompanied these puffing generalities often depicted users in one stage or another of "deep-down satisfaction," women sensuously stroking their fluffier towels, dreamily reclining on their cleaner floors, rapturously showering with their gentle-yet-more-effective soap.

That was advertising. In the words of one critic: "a too perfect marriage of the insignificant with the unbelievable."

Women, who had gone out into the world of factories and offices and the services during World War II, were streaming to the suburbs and a decade of trying to care about kitchen floors and fluffy towels. Very few actually felt the raptures expressed in the ads of that time.

* * *

Advertising became a big business around the turn of the century, with the rise of national magazines. Alert manufacturers foresaw that national advertising could vastly increase distribution and sales of their products. But the process took special skills and services. It required a writer to create a selling message. An artist to render the message in eye-catching fashion. Professional type-setting and illustration. A buyer to negotiate the purchase of space in each publication. On-time delivery of ad materials to meet publication deadlines. Thorough checking of how the ad reproduced, and insistence on make-goods where the quality was below-standard.

Inevitably, all these operations coalesced into advertising agencies. The agencies grew with American businesses.

Radio advertising, taking off in the late 1920s, greatly expanded the role of the agency. Copywriters could learn to write for the ear, and buyers of space in publications could learn time-buying. Then agencies entered the realm of programming, creating and producing shows on which clients with deep pockets advertised: the daytime soap operas and the nighttime favorites— among them the Maxwell House Showboat, the Kraft Music Hall, Lucky Strike Hit Parade, Jack Benny for Jell-O, Fred Allen for Sal Hepatica.

The post-war years brought the explosion of television, and new fields of expertise at agencies. Quickly, the agencies that created the big radio shows geared up to produce what America would watch—the Texaco Star Theater, the Goodyear Television Playhouse, the U.S. Steel Hour, the Kraft Television Theater. The big agencies got bigger.

When Doyle Dane Bernbach came onto the scene in 1949, the largest agency was J. Walter Thompson, handling a then-astonishing total of $130,000,000 in client billings. Young & Rubicam, second-largest, billed $92,000,000. BBDO, third with $87,000,000, was followed by N.W. Ayer with $79,000,000. Among the top ten, the smallest was Kenyon & Eckhardt, with $38,000,000. DDB's first-year billings of $500,000 barely made a blip in that league.

To break into the top ten, an agency needed top names on its client list. A big three soap company (Procter & Gamble, Colgate-Palmolive, Unilever). A great tobacco company (R.J.Reynolds, Philip Morris, American Tobacco, Lorillard). A major food producer (General Foods, General Mills, Quaker, Pillsbury). A big three car maker (General Motors, Ford, Chrysler). These were the big spenders, in print and broadcast, their slogans and jingles repetitiously drumming into the psyches of consumers.

Doyle Dane Bernbach's earliest clients were local retailers (Ohrbach's, Hess Department Stores), clothing manufacturers (Wear-Right Gloves, BVD underwear), and ethnic food products (Levy's bread, Hygrade all-beef kosher frankfurters). In Madison Avenue lingo, an agency with such clients was "Seventh Avenue," i.e.Jewish.

Such clients also meant that most of Doyle Dane Bernbach's earliest work appeared in newspapers and on bus and subway posters in just a few large cities—most importantly for the future of advertising, in New York, where most of the industry's writers and art directors worked, and watched, and took hope.

* * *

One day in 1949, a provocative ad caught the eye of *New York Times* readers."LIBERAL TRADE –IN," the ad, for Ohrbach's stores, announced. "Bring in your wife and just a few dollars . . . and we will give you a new woman." The artwork was big and bold. It showed a bouncy young man striding across and off the page, carrying (presumably out of Ohrbach's) a well-tailored young woman under his arm, the way you would lug an elongated gift box. Like the man, she was smiling. Unlike the man, she was stiff as cardboard. In fact, she *was* cardboard, a cutout.

Thirty years later, women's groups might have blasted the ad. But in 1949 it was ground-breaking—fresh and funny and different, and more than only advertising people were showing it to one another.

The look was new—the dominance of the photograph, and the way the man's stride burst through the page. The feel was new—the way the words and pictures worked together, each making the other funnier. The sound was new—words that real people used, colloquial English.

If it amused and entertained, it also sold, and hard. Its wit, after all, dressed up a very large promise: for a few dollars, you can look like a new woman. Rendered in humor and free of bombast, the claim seemed engaging, even credible.

The ad, and others in a similar vein for Ohrbach's, turned readers into friends, and friends into customers.

Copy by Bernbach, art direction by Bob Gage, the man some said to be "the unrecognized piece of Bill Bernbach."

* * *

You couldn't live in New York and be unaware of the delightful new ads popping up around the town. The bus poster with an elegantly-gloved hand pulling the stop-requested cord, and the words, "Stop the bus with your Wear-Right Gloves." Another poster for the same client, a standard "No Smoking" bus sign superimposed with a gloved hand fastidiously extinguishing a cigaret. The simple beauty of a brown paper bag of groceries against a white background, in a subway poster for Levy's bread.

Each was different from any commercial messages seen before, yet all bore marks of a shared heritage. Their source and their spirit were the teachings of William Bernbach.

Make your ad big, bold, simple. Only one really important central image or visual to an ad. If the reader has to stop and think what is meant, the ad is not effective. Size and beauty give you impact. Clutter on a page is inelegant, and distracts. Taste matters. A page gives off a "feel" the moment the reader turns to it. The page can say "quality" or it can say "schlock." Remember that the feel rubs off on the product. Everything on the page should say quality: the photograph, the type, the paper, the words.

The most powerful element in selling is an insight into human nature, knowing the compulsions that drive a person. An ad must touch those emotions. Hit 'em in the heart, in the gut, in the funnybone, but hit 'em somewhere. You won't touch them anywhere with a straightforward statement of your selling proposition. Knowing "the right thing" to say is only the take-off point. It's how you say the right thing that counts. Only artistry and imagery can bring your message to memorable life. The plots that served Shakespeare were old hat when he appropriated them as armature for his own work. His poetry and insights into human nature gave his plays everlasting life.

An ad should interrupt, startle, even shock the reader, else it will be lost in the torrent of messages and violent events of our times. It will sink into a morass unless you "do it different." Not just once in a while, but every time, in every ad, on every product.

If you do great work, we'll sell it. Don't worry about whether the client will accept it. If it's really great, we'll sell it. And Bernbach usually did, in the years remembered now as the Golden Age of Advertising.

* * *

Doyle Dane Bernbach opened its doors on June 1, 1949, exuberantly, joyously. "There was a spirit of high adventure," remembered Phyllis Robinson, who left Grey Advertising with Bernbach, Ned Doyle and Bob Gage, to become copy chief of the new agency. "We were out, and free, and no one was telling us how to make ads."

"We wanted it to be the kind of place where we would like to work," Doyle recalled. "An agency whose principles we could believe in. To be perfectly honest with the client. To give him the work we think he should have, provided it fit his goal. To be the experts in how to present the product to the public. Not to wonder what the client's wife is going to say about the advertising."

That, at the time, was uncommon. In post-war America, advertising was seen as a business fit only for the shallow and unscrupulous. The image had its roots in the 1930s, when books and articles began to expose worthless, wasteful—even dangerous—products, and the half-truths and outright deceptions used to advertise such products. Frederic Wakeman's best-selling novel, *The Hucksters*, only confirmed the public's most cynical view of the advertising business, and gave it a name.

To be sure, few clients were as tyrannical as the novel's Evan L. Evans, and not every agency ate dirt. But every agency and every client knew who had the power. Clients played on agencies' fear of losing business to make all kinds of demands, including, on occasion, women for the evening. Where one side holds the power, the other becomes adept at pandering and manipulation.

Doyle Dane Bernbach came onto the scene with a fresh vision. Talent to do great advertising is as rare as any other artistic talent. When an agency has such talent, the power balance shifts. Fear diminishes; the atmospherics change. And so does the moral climate.

Bernbach attracted and inspired and nurtured the talent. The readiness to dump troublesome clients was strictly Doyle's. Together, they formed the image of Doyle Dane Bernbach. The great work, and the guts! It was an image that would bring worldwide admiration. In time, many would charge that it was tainted with arrogance. Some saw it as an image that lingered long after the reality had changed.

* * *

The lights burned late in the 1800 square feet of Doyle Dane Bernbach's space at 350 Madison Avenue, a flight-and-a-half above the last elevator stop.

The original three creatives (Bernbach, Robinson on copy, Gage on art), and the new hires that soon came on board, were breaking the old rules, knocking the stuffiness out of advertising. Nobody wanted to go home.

"We were in love with our own brilliance," remembered Robinson, a woman of radiant intelligence. "We just loved to work. We thought we were so wonderful and clever; we would do three ads when one would do. In many cases, it made good advertising sense, refreshing the message. But often when it didn't make sense, when one ad could have run and run and run, we would make more and more because we loved to do them.

"We loved to feel the juices flowing and to come up with yet another clever idea. We were dazzled by ourselves, and I think that's part of what people came to think of as the arrogance of the agency. It wasn't arrogance. We were supremely confident. Cocky is about as strong a word as you could put on it. But supremely confident and enthusiastic and excited about our work, and I guess that was very new."

Bernbach showed the new hires how to work in copy/art teams. In other agencies, the copywriter wrote up all the words for an ad, then slipped the copy, with a sketch of a suggested layout, under the art director's door. That's how agencies wound up with ads that crowed "Most Fabulous Discovery Ever Made!" and illustrations of housewives mooning over their floors.

But when copywriter and art director began an assignment together, the room crackled with ideas. Copywriters suggested visuals. Art directors dreamed up headlines. Words and pictures worked together to make a third, bigger, thing.

Only after the client approved a sketch of the ad—headline, picture, and a grid of lines to show where the "body copy" would be—would body copy be written. "If an ad hasn't got enough stopping power without all the little words," said Bernbach, "no amount of talk is going to make people read it."

His creative people knew that Bernbach had no patience for writing "all the little words." Outsiders assumed he wrote many of the words, big and little. That misconception played a role in the image vs. reality story of DDB.

* * *

Bernbach, munching Hershey bars for energy, tossed ideas out to Bob Gage, who would be heralded by commercial artists as "the art director of the ages." Gage never said no to any of Bernbach's suggestions. He just sat there, bulkily, impassively, until one caught his fancy. Often he thought Bernbach's suggestions "corny." Like "SNIAGRAB," bargains spelled backwards, for Ohrbach's.

Bernbach's proposed headlines almost always embraced a visual idea. On his "Liberal trade-in" concept for Ohrbach's, he imagined "this man carrying his wife." "I thought it was corny," said Gage. "But then I did it in a way where she was stiff as a board across the page. And it looked good, you know?" (And it was pinned to bulletin boards all over town.)

Bernbach came up with an image for Flexalum window blinds as soon as he heard the company's problem. Women had turned off of blinds because the slats attracted dirt and were hard to clean. Flexalum used a special coating, but proclaiming "the amazing new discovery!" had no impact.

"Dirt bounces off like a ball," suggested Bernbach, and Gage's artwork showed just that: a ball bouncing off of a window blind. Bernbach and Doyle took the ad, by subway, to the company.

"They looked at the ad, and gave us the account," recalled Doyle. "We took a taxi back. That was our first presentation for a piece of new business."

A new Max Factor lipstick, "See Red," triggered the vision of a small drama. "They'll go mad over you when they 'See Red'" ran Bernbach's headline. On one side of the ad, two pre-yuppie men snarl in nose-to-nose competition for the voluptuous young woman on the other side. The ad long remained a favorite of Gage's. "The very situation that drew attention," he said, "also told the story of the product. There was a perfect integration of art and copy. In those days, particularly in cosmetic advertising, that was really new."

Bernbach was "the most visual" copywriter Gage ever worked with. So much so that Gage, in the mid-50s, "tried not to see Bill often, to prove I could do it without him."

* * *

The pause in the creation of a Doyle Dane Bernbach ad, between finding the concept and getting client approval, was Bernbach's cut-off point. He had no inclination to write "all the little words." The idea was the excitement. The body copy was drudgery. Phyllis Robinson at first, and later Judy Protas, finished the job.

* * *

The earliest clients were entrepreneurs, often first-generation Americans. They took chances and made their own decisions. N.M.Ohrbach taught the agency a thing or two about advertising ("I got a great gimmick. Let's tell the truth."). Others simply placed their faith in Bernbach ("If Bill says okay, then run it.").

If they were different from one another, they all had the same dream of achieving success, and the energy to work for it. Among the most memorable was Whitey Rubin, head of Levy's bread.

"He was always very interested in the advertising," Doyle related, "vitally interested in getting the best ads for his money. One time, excited about his campaign, he looked Bernbach straight in the eye, pointed his finger at him and said, 'Bernbach, I want you should write ads, that when a woman reads them, she'll think if she doesn't eat Levy's bread she wouldn't menstruate.' Bernbach didn't think he'd heard right. 'WHAT?' Whitey repeated his statement. Bill said, 'That's going to be a very hard ad to write.'"

Years later, when the agency had to deal with layers of brand managers at vast corporations, its principals looked back with nostalgia and gratitude to the old entrepreneurs who let Doyle Dane Bernbach do its best advertising.

* * *

Madison Avenue, the business, was a small and parochial place, gossipy, convivial. At the Art Directors Club, members buzzed with admiration for Bob Gage's graphic inventions. One such they termed "exploding the page." A woman soaring, the headline "Fly," the Ohrbach logo clinging to the edges of the page, the center stunningly empty.

At the Illustrators Club, Gage's name struck fear. Members worried that his powerful use of photography would set off an avalanche of imitation and render illustration out of fashion. Indeed, that happened.

Copywriters learned the name Bill Bernbach, and thought perhaps they could remain in advertising without losing their self-esteem.

At local bistros, the regulars at first spoke of "Ned's agency," Doyle being the only principal they knew. They snickered at the client list. So the ads made a splash. For local clothing stores and glove makers and Jewish rye bread. What did that have to do with selling cars, or airlines, or soap? Just a local phenomenon.

But the client list grew, the staff grew, the legend grew, the excitement inside the young agency built.

The new talent included Helmut Krone, Lester Feldman, Bill Taubin in art; Judy Protas, David Reider, Mary Wells, Paula Green in copy. Krone and Green would come up with "We try harder. We're only Number 2" for Avis. Taubin and Protas with "You don't have to be Jewish" for Levy's rye bread. Feldman with the lion prowling Wall Street for the Dreyfus Fund. Reider with Utica Club's "Sometimes I wonder if it pays to make beer this way."

None of them was a name before coming to DDB. So perhaps it was not surprising that in the early years the press described all the work as "Mr. Bernbach's ads." What came to bother some creatives was Bernbach's apparent encouragement of that term, and the way his superb editing skills led to an ownership position in the credits for their campaigns.

◆ ◆ ◆

2
The Private Sector

"At the heart of an effective creative philosophy is the belief that nothing is so powerful as an insight into human nature, what compulsions drive a man, what instincts dominate his action, even though his language so often camouflages what really motivates him." —Bill Bernbach

Years later, when presidential advisers and leaders in the worlds of art and science and finance sought his help in matters of persuasion, Bernbach would sometimes say, but only to a trusted friend, "Can you believe all this is happening to a little Jewish boy from the Bronx?"

It was a question for the good times, the great times, expressed with a joyous sense of wonder. This was the private Bernbach, revealing for a moment the core of his self-image.

Publicly, Bernbach gave away as little of himself as possible. David Ogilvy, Bernbach's life-long rival for the esteem of the industry, revelled in his past, publishing books filled with provocative personal anecdotes, gleefully disclosing such details as his propensity to create ads while "at stool."

"The Showman," Bernbach contemptuously (and privately) called Ogilvy for these displays. His final put-down: "Name one creative person ever to emerge from under Ogilvy." Publishers waited in vain for Bernbach to write his own personal anecdotes.

Early in my tenure at the agency, I innocently asked Bernbach, for an in-house publication, if he had ever considered writing fiction. "No, never," he replied, rather sternly. Ever the pursuing journalist, I followed up with, "Why do you think that is so?" He drew himself up and responded, "I have no sores to squeeze." The subject was closed.

I would remember those words often in later years.

* * *

"Playing it safe can be the most dangerous thing in the world," Bernbach counseled advertisers, "because you're presenting people with an idea they've seen before, and you won't have impact."

Bernbach was the great proponent, the philosopher of risk-taking in advertising. Mainstream agencies and major clients pooh-poohed that approach until Doyle Dane Bernbach's remarkable results with "doing it different" could no longer be denied.

Yet in his own life, Bernbach felt comfortable only with the familiar. He took the same route to work each day. He requested the same suites in the same hotels on business and personal trips. He ate at the same restaurants, the Algonquin Hotel's Rose Room for many years; later the Four Seasons and "21." When the agency moved to a new building, he ordered his old office replicated, even to the extent of having the floor torn up and re-installed in his new quarters.

With fame and growing fortune, he evolved a style of dressing that would never change. Soft-sculpted suits in shades of grey. Unvarying blue shirts, custom-made by London's Turnbull & Asser. Navy blue silk foulards discretely patterned with dots or dot-sized diamonds in red or white. "The corporate cravat," a *New York Times* style writer called such ties, in an article titled "Tales That Ties Tell."

"Dots," the slightly-tongue-in-cheek article asserted, "are the most conservative pattern of all, favored defensively, by those nervous about being thought low, drunken or cynical . . . by those whose fiduciary honor must be thought beyond question. . . ."

Bernbach's conservative and consistent style of dress expressed outwardly his traditionalist values as husband and father. "Square," in the opinion of those colleagues who didn't, as he always did, rush home to their wives and children after work. But that square devotion seeped into the marrow of the agency, inducing the feeling that a corporate family loyalty would last forever.

* * *

"Rules are made to be broken," Bernbach often urged the faint of heart, creative people who got stuck in conventional wisdom, or clients who balked at accepting ads too strong for their tastes.

Did it signify that the philosopher of iconoclasm in advertising should wrap each day in the comfort of the tried and true? The question didn't arise because Bernbach's passion for privacy had kept his image focused entirely on his *ideas,* not on his habits.

And why not, really? His philosophy, not his personal life, is what changed advertising. But the gap between philosophy and his lifestyle, it will perhaps be seen, provide space for misconceptions and misunderstandings that would contribute mightily to the ultimate fate of Doyle Dane Bernbach.

* * *

When they met as co-workers at Grey Advertising just after World War II, Ned Doyle saw Bill Bernbach as "a nice little guy, very creative, with gold-rimmed glasses, and on the scared side."

One supposes that Bernbach saw Doyle in a bright, heroic light. Doyle, then 43 and ten years Bernbach's senior, had returned from the Pacific theater of operations as a captain in Marine Corps Aviation, having had to talk and battle his way into the service after being rejected for his age.

Bernbach would always look up to war heroes. His own war service had lasted but two months. At his induction physical, his pulse raced so fast that the doctors thought he had "taken something." They sent him to the infirmary and kept him for several days, long enough for any "something" to wear off. His pulse continued to race at the same alarming speed, 148 beats per minute. The examiners decided that rate might be normal for him, and shipped him to boot camp. An examining doctor there soon shipped him back home, certain he wouldn't survive training.

Later, his official biographies would cover that period with a brief phrase about Bernbach's "stretch in the U.S. Army."

Not until the last year of his life did Bernbach respond to an interviewer's question about his wartime experience. Then Bernbach said ". . . they found out about me in Washington. The guy who ran public relations, General somebody in Washington, found out I was at Fort Eustis, and he sent for me. But I had gotten out a day before he sent for me, because I had some kind of fast heartbeat or something, and I was too old, to be honest."

He was 31 at the time.

* * *

More than his service record attracted Bernbach to Doyle. He had a keen mind, honed at Fordham Law School, and the Irish gift of keeping a table in laughter. From his mother's side, Doyle had inherited a German kind of rough, no-nonsense honesty. He dealt straight. And most wonderfully, he propounded a then-rare view of advertising—that the heart of an agency is its creative work.

Bernbach never lost his skinny-little-city-kid admiration of jocks, and Doyle shone in that area too. Sports fans remembered him as star quarterback for Englewood High and for Hamilton College.

Doyle's unshakeable self-confidence must also have appealed to a Bernbach ruffled by events of the previous ten years. After Hamilton, Doyle had moved easily into a job as magazine space salesman, attending Fordham Law School at night. He passed the bar in 1931, only to find entry law jobs paid $10 a week. He earned $75 selling space. He opted against a career in law.

The Great Depression, which scarred so many lives and psyches, scarcely scratched Doyle. He kept moving up, in big jobs on big magazines, in Chicago and New York, jobs that glittered with days and nights of entertaining. He seemed to know half the clients and agency men in those cities, and they all enjoyed his stories and his insights into the business. Women adored him; they were bees to his honeysuckle. In the parlance of the time, Doyle was "a man about town."

* * *

Doyle was also a risk taker, a man who loved new, different, chancy. When he came out of the service, he wanted to try something different—working on the agency side of business. Grey Advertising hired him, at 43, to be an account man. He soon attracted Grey's copy chief, Bill Bernbach.

Bernbach took to dropping into Doyle's office in the late afternoon, wired with excitement about having "just created the greatest ad ever made." Doyle quickly saw that Bernbach "was really something," definitely worth taking a risk on. He also sized up the copy chief as unworldly, and unaware of the rest of the world of advertising.

Bernbach sought Doyle's approbation, but had no patience with tales of the industry. What did the past have to teach? Every day was a fresh beginning! Every assignment had the potential of turning out "the greatest ad ever made!" Why bother with the history of advertising? The very *idea* of advertising was too limiting, too narrow gauge. Bernbach saw the business instead as the art of persuasion, and took energy not from other people's ads, but from the writings of biologists, physicists, mathematicians, philosophers, biochemists, sociologists, even jazz musicians. There lay insights that could change the future of advertising.

It was the future that would help erase some of the pain of the past.

* * *

A small story, having to do with Bernbach's birthdate, August 13. Those who told me the story heard it from Bernbach many years later. The scene (in one version) was an Ohrbach's board meeting. Or (another version) a birthday party for N. M. Ohrbach. No matter. At every event he attended, Ohrbach was the center of nervous attention, an imperious huge bear of an entrepreneur. He was, at the time, the agency's most important client, the man who'd made it possible for Doyle and Bernbach to open their own agency by promising them his business. In that sense, he was the man who begot Doyle Dane Bernbach.

At the gathering, Ohrbach, born under the sign of Leo, asked the group for their birth signs. Geminis, Scorpios, Cancers . . . as the signs rattled off, Ohrbach stood prouder and prouder, surely the only Lion in the room. Until Bernbach's turn. Ohrbach appeared stunned when he heard Bernbach's birth date. He peered scornfully down from his great height, and said, *"You're a Leo?"* As much as to say, "you've just ruined the image of a Leo."

Bernbach was reminded of the episode in 1969, on the agency's 20th anniversary. A special issue of the *DDB News* carried a feature on the birth signs of the ten board members. Only Bernbach was a Leo.

The finding delighted Bernbach. Now he could relate the Ohrbach story with special relish. Ohrbach's words must have seared at the time; down-putting words from the man to whom Bernbach's agency owed its birth. He'd long since proven his worth to N. M., and to his real father, too.

* * *

Bill Bernbach was born in the Bronx in 1911, the fourth and youngest child of Jacob and Rebecca Bernbach, immigrants who arrived from Russia and Austria at the end of the 19th century.

Jacob, like N. M.Ohrbach, was a large man with a large sense of himself. His talent as a designer of coats and suits enabled him to afford an apartment for his family in the Grand Concourse's flagship building. He dressed with his own sense of style, favoring vests with white braiding, which struck some relatives as peacockery. He had his portrait painted; it hung alone and patriarchically in the living room.

For all that, Jacob could quake before Rebecca, a tiny, simian woman who terrified her family with bodeful reflections on her health, and threats that she would surely die if they acted against her will. In her kosher kitchen she prepared only the bland food she could digest. The children picked at their food and looked underfed.

But there were other forms of nourishment in the Bernbach household. Music and art. Minna, the oldest child, and Bill, twelve years her junior, studied piano with devotion and talent. Harry, two years younger than Minna, played the violin with a love that lasted through his lifetime. Graham, two years younger than Harry, sketched and dreamed of becoming a great painter.

Friends and neighbors marveled at the young Bernbachs' talent, their ambition, their vitality. One remembered Bill at the age of 12, taking a girl cousin by the hand and running her over to meet his piano teacher, all the while enthusiastically selling her on the importance and pleasure of music.

While Jacob spent his days making a living in the great city's garment district, and the children were busy playing and learning, Rebecca tenaciously clung to the traditions of the Old World, insisting the family conform to them. Thus, none of the children should marry before the first-born daughter. But the years passed and beautiful Minna did not marry. Suitors she had a-plenty; all were rejected as beneath her. Harry watched the process with alarm. He finished his education, started a career as a tax lawyer and wanted to marry. Rebecca swore she would die if he married ahead of Minna.

Minna never married. In 1927, Harry did. Bill, 15 at the time, could not have failed to observe that their mother, for all her threats to do so, did not die. Still, Harry had married within the faith. Rebecca could bend enough to accept his defiant act.

But it was faith that had sustained her ancestors and her people against centuries of hatred and violence. She and Jacob had left the heart-in-the-mouth threats of physical terror back in Europe when they came to the golden land. She had never envisioned the possibility of one of her own children succumbing to a different kind of threat to her faith: intermarriage.

Bill would do that, years into the Great Depression.

* * *

Jobs were in scarce supply when Bernbach graduated from New York University, in 1933 with a Bachelor of Commerce degree according to NYU's records, or in 1932 with a Bachelor of Arts in English literature according to his biographical material. Eventually, through a family connection, he was hired to run the mailroom of Schenley Distillers.

The Twenty-first Amendment to the Constitution had been ratified on December 5, 1933, repealing Prohibition. Ex-bootleggers turned into distillers. At the young Schenley company, headquartered in an elegant mid-town brownstone, Bill wrapped bundles of "The Merry Mixer," a promotional brochure of cocktail recipes much in demand across wet-again America. A young Hunter College graduate, Evelyn Carbone, addressed the labels, often glancing up to see if Bill had, as he often did, re-buried his head in a book. She loved his passion for books, seeing him as a kindred spirit in a coven of bootleg-era survivors. Not that she meant to stay long at Schenley's; she meant to return to Hunter for a master's degree in French.

Evelyn in no way resembled the golden girls on whom Bill got crushes in school days. Her beauty was a quiet, dark Italian kind. Not in a sensuous way. Evelyn radiated a sweetness, a shyness that won all hearts. Bill fell in love, and forever. Evelyn brought him home to her large, warm, voluble family.

Rebecca asked questions as Bill prepared to leave on Sunday for dinner in Brooklyn with the Carbones. He couldn't lie. When she learned the truth, Rebecca flung herself on the floor and screamed. Why was he trying to kill her? He knew that marrying a *shiksa* would kill her. Bill protested that this was just a dinner, not marriage. No, who goes clear to Brooklyn for just a dinner? It could only end in her death.

Sunday after Sunday, the awful scene was repeated. Bill dreaded and loathed these frenzies. They triggered within him a lifelong dedication to decorum, civility, "nice" behavior. But at the time, all he could think to do was cut back on his weekly visits to the Carbones. Even every other week strained his ability to endure his mother's storms. None of this altered his love for Evelyn.

Rebecca's anger only calcified as the years of courtship went on. Meanwhile Bill and Evelyn talked of marriage and worried about their finances. They continued in low-paying jobs at Schenley. She had moved out of the mailroom, to receptionist in the import division, where managers made frequent use of her fluency in French and Italian. Bill worked for Schenley's board chairman, Grover Whalen, as (in Evelyn's words) "office boy—but several steps up from that." Though the job paid little, it had compensating factors.

Whalen was "Mr. New York" in the press, famed for his many civic activities. He'd been hired by Schenley's tough and shrewd owner, Lewis Rosenstiel, to bring instant respectability to the business after Prohibition. Whalen's friendships ranged from mayor and cardinal through celebrities and pols and newsmen on all levels.

At Schenley's, Whalen quickly spotted the quality in the mailroom kid from the Bronx, and moved him onto his turf. Bernbach's brightness and inexperience brought out the paternal in Whalen. He instructed Bill on the fine art of tipping. He took Bill along on a not-so-necessary business trip so that the young man would have his first airplane ride. He invited Bill and Evelyn to accompany him to celebrity-laden events. A prominent Catholic, he understood the pain that religious differences could create. He encouraged the young lovers to follow their hearts.

* * *

Once Bill brought Evelyn to dinner at his brother Harry's house, where their father Jacob would be. The brothers hoped that when Jacob met Evelyn, he would respond to her gentle *zieskeit*, her sweetness, and would take up the cause of their union. But through the entire meal, Jacob refused either to look at Evelyn or speak a word to her. Evelyn sat rigid, stricken with terror.

Bill saw he would have to chose. In 1938, he and Evelyn went to a justice of the peace and were married.

Despite all of Rebecca's scenes, Bill's marriage did not kill her. But something almost as dramatic and fateful followed. Rebecca, vengeful as a Greek fury over what she perceived to be rejection, betrayal and religious violation, instructed Jacob on what he must do.

And so, in the Orthodox tradition, Bill Bernbach's father declared that his son was dead.

Accounts gained from 1949 through 1960:

Barton's Candy
Book of Knowledge
Broxodent
Buxton leather goods
BVD
Chemstrand
Clairol
Coffee of Colombia
Cole of California swimwear
Dreyfus Corp.
El Al Israel Airline
Flexalum blinds
General Mills
Hess department store
Hygrade Foods
Israel Tourist Office
Lane Furniture
Levy's Bread
Max Factor
Necchi-Elna
Ohrbach's apparel stores
Olin Mathieson
Philip Morris Alpine cigarets
Polaroid
Rheingold Breweries
Schenley
Tom McAn shoes
Utica Club Beer
Volkswagen
Warner foundation garments
Wear Right Gloves
Wedgewood

♦ ♦ ♦

3
The Golden Age of Advertising

"An idea can turn to dust or magic, depending on the talent that rubs against it."—Bill Bernbach

"Every period has its own special group, like the Algonquin Round Table. I think for now, we're it." The comment was expressed matter-of-factly at a gathering of the agency's creative people in the Plaza Hotel at the end of 1959. For then, and the decade that followed, they had reason to believe they *were* it, fellows of Bernbach's round table, in the Golden Age of Advertising.

In 1956, the *New York Times* reported that Doyle Dane Bernbach "has had a pattern of success rivaled by few in the Madison Avenue field. In 1958, *Time* magazine noted that the agency's billings had "shot up to $20 million— and the growth of its reputation has been even more spectacular." In 1959, a *Newsweek* article said that the agency "has been piling up new clients almost without trying . . . In fact, most of Doyle Dane's new clients have sought out the agency themselves after they were attracted by advertising that Bernbach describes as the 'interrupted idea—something unusual enough to stop you, make you look and listen.'"

The clients won in the 1950s were still the little guys, or products in trouble, or experimental brands (Alpine cigarets for Philip Morris), or newcomers to their field (Polaroid) or to this country (Volkswagen). The top advertisers still went to the top ten agencies, which were bigger than ever. J. Walter Thompson hit $250 million in billings in 1960, and BBDO was a close second with $234.8 million. The smallest of the 1960 top ten, Foote Cone & Belding, billed $99.6 million. But Doyle Dane Bernbach was coming along fast, reaching $46.4 million in 1960. And doing it, not with slogans and jingles and advertisingese, but with breakthrough work that came to symbolize advertising's Golden Age.

The agency's copywriters and art directors—known collectively as "the creatives," a term they disliked but never shook—shared in discovery, adventure, invention. They were in the right place at the right time. They were the envy of the industry. At Doyle Dane Bernbach, the very atmosphere seemed to expand talent. Egged on by Bernbach to be better and better, they flourished in the excitement of it all, learning from one another, knocking themselves out to astonish one another with their inventiveness. Competitive they were, in that sense, but also supportive, encouraging. They ran through the halls, calling out to all to come look at what so-and-so had done.

It was a time of "waves crashing, and the moon over the mountains," in the words of one who'd been there.

They invented new looks, new attitudes, new approaches. A cautionary "you can't do that, it's never been done that way," uttered by a cameraman, a photo-grapher, a type shop owner, or an account man, would elicit a "why not?" from the creatives.

Greatest of all the stars of Bernbach's round table were the legendary art directors, Bob Gage and Helmut Krone.

No one had ever seen an ad anything like Krone's early campaign for Polaroid. The page was all but filled with a close-up of a deeply lived-in face: Louis Armstrong, Georgia O'Keeffe, a sad clown. In a sea of the vacuous faces that illustrated ads of the time, they could not have been more riveting. A mere six lines of copy quietly introduced a new, sharper-image Polaroid film. No headline, no logo; high readership, strong response.

Krone on Volkswagen, a new kind of car ad, the Beetle perched in limbo. Honest in its total lack of pretension. Free of Detroit's traditional "borrowed elegance"—the columned mansion in the background, the beautifully-gowned woman in the foreground. And with its plain look, the revolutionary message, "Think small."

Krone on Avis, creating a new look by turning the Volkswagen format (large space for picture, one- or two-word headline, small block of copy) inside out. For Avis, the picture became very small; the headline and type very large.Its message turned ad boastfulness inside out, finding virtue in being "only No.2."

Gage, meanwhile, moved from print to television commercials. He scorned the look and feel of what he saw on the air. Shot by Hollywood cameramen, with Hollywood lighting and Hollywood draperies, they reflected, to Gage, a movie point of view. Gage sought an advertising point of view, and achieved it by hiring top-rank New York photographers to shoot his commercials. The rest of the industry would soon follow Gage.

Many of the techniques later taken for granted began with Gage. Stop-motion commercials, which he invented for Chemstrand nylons. Vignettes, for American Airlines' "Business traveler" campaign. Quick cuts, for Jamaica Tourist's "Contrasts" campaign ("It has mountains, it has beaches . . . it's mysterious, it's obvious . . . it's hot, it's cool . . ."). Copied and copied and copied.

Commercials hadn't tried to touch viewers' hearts before Gage and Phyllis Robinson began selling Polaroid through love.

"When Bob saw 'West Side Story,' he was knocked out by the song 'Maria,'" recalled Robinson. He sang it all day in the office—Maria, Maria, Maria. 'I clocked the song,' he told me. 'It's three minutes. If Leonard Bernstein can make people cry in three minutes, we can do it in a minute.'"

And they did. A mother and father, proud and shaken as they leave their little boy in sleep-away camp for the first time. An adoring father with his sleepy little girl on a Central Park horse carriage ride at the end of a happy day at the zoo. Weddings and farewells and homecomings. Each moved viewers' emotions in 60 seconds, a third of the time for Bernstein's "Maria."

Since then, we've seen weddings and farewells and homecomings for wines and soft drinks and deodorants and insurance and cars and chemical companies and . . . you name it. Some are good indeed. But none has ever packed more warmth and love in a minute than Gage and Robinson's early commercials for Polaroid.

* * *

"You knew you were in a very special place," recalled Paula Green, who went on to open her own agency. "You were always aware of that. And it was a matter of wanting to be very good."

The great work rolled out. The classic "torn ocean" ad for El-Al Airlines. The unforgettable "cat" ad for Ohrbach's. ("Has Bill gone crazy?" asked N.M. Ohrbach. "Who will get that a cat smoking a cigaret is supposed to be a catty woman? Well, if Bill likes it, okay.") The elegant and witty ads for Chivas Regal. ("Give dad an expensive belt.") Juan Valdez picking coffee beans one at a time for Coffee of Colombia. The delights of "Tummy Television" for Sony. The hilarious "sock dance" for Burlington Mills. The stunning prisms of hair colors for Clairol. The dramatic "We want you to live" campaign for Mobil. The unending appeal of the Volkswagen ads. The gorilla banging an American Tourister suitcase against his cage, trying without success to damage it. The Cracker Jack commercials featuring the funny, touching Jack Guilford. The important anti-nuclear ads ("Dr. Spock is worried") for SANE. And on, seemingly endlessly, on.

These days, ads are tested for overnight recall. Doyle Dane Bernbach's ads are remembered decades after they ran.

* * *

Bernbach supervised it all, through the Golden Age. And so these were often called "Mr. Bernbach's ads." Traditionally, ads were credited to their agencies, almost never to staffers. Agencies worried that talent would be pirated if names became known, and so copywriters and art directors worked in anonymity.

But these were not "Doyle Dane Bernbach ads," they were "Mr. Bernbach's ads. That was something else again. Bernbach's children, indoctrinated with the importance of artistic talent, had egos of their own. Insiders began to speak of "love/hate" feelings among the creatives for Bernbach. They loved him for fathering their growth. They needed his approbation. ("We did it to see Bill's eyes light up," Gage said.) They feared his disapproval of their work. They resented their work becoming his. They wondered if they'd have to leave home to prove they could do it without him.

* * *

"The nice little guy . . . on the scared side" that Ned Doyle had met at Grey grew into an industry legend. He was "the man who launched the creative revolution on Madison Avenue," the patron saint of creatives, the hero who feared no clients.

Such acclaim inevitably affected the atmospherics. Bernbach considered his role as a leader.

"You have to learn to be arrogant," he instructed Gage, who struck him as too comradely and direct with those he supervised. "You can't do this job if you're not arrogant."

And: "If you feel a creative person is getting out of line, thinking he's just too great, when he shows you his next piece of work, even if it's terrific, tell him you're not quite sure of it."

He knew how to play his children, how to keep them aware of his authority. He also knew how to pick them up when they felt down, and how to make them feel he was on their side, even when he wasn't.

"If you do great work, we'll sell it," he had told them again and again. Again and again they had brought him work they thought was great, that the client wouldn't buy. An oft-repeated scene in Bernbach's office went like this:

Creative team (defiantly in love with their proposed campaign): "The client doesn't like it. We think it's terrific."

Bernbach (studying the stats): "My God! This IS terrific!" (He beams approbation; the creatives beam gratitude.) "We'd better get the account man up here." (Creatives nod, expecting the account man will be told to say to the client, "Take this or else.")

Account man arrives. (Women rarely ran accounts in those days.)

Account man: "The client agrees it's terrific. But they don't like certa things about it and they're not going to buy it."

Bernbach: "Well, they're wrong. This is terrific." (Creatives sit taller.) "What *is* it the client wants?" (Account man gives specifics.) "Oh, is that so?" (To the creatives): "I don't see how you can do better than this, but maybe you can. Think about what they're thinking about. I'll bet you can come up with an even better idea."

Exit creative team, on air, eager to get back to the drawing board, to "do it" for Bill, to show him he's right about their ability to come up with something even better.

That was part of his genius, motivating them to *want* to go back to the drawing board after the client rejected their babies. Contrary to legend, Bernbach never believed in shoving work down a client's throat. He knew well that his creative people, in their stretch to "do it different," frequently went clear off the wall.

"What is it we're trying to do here?" he asked the team, before he looked at their boards. And then, "Is this a smart way to sell the product?" They had continually to be set on the right track, and reminded that advertising was about selling, not about cleverness.

"Do it different" had its exceptions.

"Don't change something good," Bernbach instructed. Antique Bourbon came to the agency with an old slogan, "If you can find a better bourbon, buy it." Said Bernbach to the client, "I'm not going to touch that. It's a great line."

Also: "If you have something important to say, say it." Don't be cute when you could be giving the reader significant new information about a product."

Bernbach confided to copywriter David Reider that, in his shirt pocket, he kept a slip of paper with three words, "Maybe he's right."

The client? The account person? The other guy? A lesson on the flip side of arrogance? A lesson for them, or for himself?

* * *

Like one's real father, Bernbach wasn't always patient and protective and homiletic. On bad days, days when he learned of an account in trouble, he'd be tight-lipped, agitated, angry, icy, harshly critical.

Even on good days, creatives entered his office with trepidation, anxious about how he might react to their boards.

"It was terrifying," said Paula Green, "because you wanted so desperately for him to like what you did. And you were terrified he wouldn't like it . . . not terrified of him, but of his disapproval. That's very parental. Teacher/

parent. When there's a teacher you adore . . . The only thing that could really upset me was his disappointment in me.

"You were aware of his special reputation. So it wasn't that we needed psychoanalysis; it's that we were in a very particular situation. You learned to look very hard at your work before you showed it to Bill. And to ask yourself, where is he going to find holes? You became your own greatest critic. What's Bill going to see? Where's the hole? Where's the problem? You learned by anticipating, knowing that he had such a sharp eye for a weakness in an idea of a campaign."

Roy Grace, who became one of the agency's top art directors, remembered showing Bernbach some boards when he began working on the Volkswagen account in 1963. Bernbach studied them and said, "Whenever you show a VW, it should be either very large or very small on the page." Grace nodded and asked, "Why? Bernbach looked at me steadily with cold blue eyes for about 15 seconds. I never asked him Why again."

Grace came to love being with Bernbach.

"He was the world's greatest audience. There was no fooling him, no bull-shitting him. He would be infuriated if you opened with, 'The client loved it.' If the work was good, his little feet started dancing. It was like bringing an enormous present to a little kid. If the work wasn't good, beware. He turned icy, he could cut you up, or he could just be indifferent.

"He could take things apart and tell you the how of them. He had an understanding that everything has to be reduced to its simplest form, and then expanded on. He could look at a piece and in a flash know if it was 'there.' The ultimate compliment was, 'You know how good this is? I'm going to put it on my reel.'"

"With Bill, God bless him, you never, never, never, never knew," mused Bill Taubin, one of the agency's Hall of Fame art directors. He and copywriter David Reider loved a line they came up with for El Al. The Israeli airline made all its flights at night. Well, then, it would be "The only fly-by-night airline." Congratulating themselves on their idea, they took it to Bernbach.

"He said, and I'll never forget his reaction, 'Are you kidding?'" End of meeting.

An art director still fresh from a mainstream agency, listened to Bernbach critique his boards, and then, pencil poised to make notes, asked, "What do *you* want, Bill?" Bernbach froze. What he wanted was people who could come up with fresh ideas of their own, time and again. The question ended the A/D's career at Doyle Dane Bernbach.

* * *

The Art Directors Club gave Bernbach a special award in 1959 "for his impatience with the trite and usual, for proving that boldness and originality in art direction are successful selling tools, for working with art directors and encouraging them to grow creatively. . . ."

On the agency's tenth birthday, *Advertising Age* ran an article that opened with these words:

"Of all the ways an agency can win fame and fortune for itself and its clients,there are two most frequent: the sheer weight of advertising; the impact of advertising. For Doyle Dane Bernbach . . . there's no question but that the freshness, originality and piercing quality of most of its advertising has done the trick. . . ."

Bernbach and his agency dazzled the press throughout the Golden Age of Advertising:

"Now even the most ardent skeptics have to admit that the 'Doyle Dane Bernbach approach' works. . . ."—*Art Direction*, January 1, 1960.

"DDB's inventive campaigns have not only won the agency a blue-chip roster of 40 clients but something even harder to come by: the admiration of the ad industry. . . ."—*Newsweek*, June 8, 1964.

"The 'hot agency' of 1964 was Doyle Dane Bernbach."— *New York Times*, January 11, 1965.

"This agency stands as one of the powerful forces in photography today. . . ."—*Photography Annual*, 1966.

"It is quite possible that the effect of DDB is as culturally significant as that of, let us say, writers such as Mickey Spillane, Kerouac, Ernest Hemingway, or artists such as Paul Klee, Andy Warhol, George Bellows— even if the motifs are more commercial. . . ." — *Advertising Age* columnist Stephen Baker, November 1, 1965.

"The only great school for copywriters is Doyle Dane Bernbach—it's the Harvard Business School of copywriters and a great institution which Bill Bernbach started. . . ."—*Madison Avenue Magazine*, November, 1968.

Some of his early colleagues remembered Bernbach as "a sweet, unassuming guy before he started to believe his press notices." But how could such press notices not have had an effect?

The adulation added to his aura. People walking into his office—clients, staffers, politicians—would enter nodding vigorously, and their heads kept bobbing while Bernbach talked.

"I've seen people come into his office and literally tremble," said Roy Grace. "The sheer size and scope of what he represented was so enormously powerful and attractive."

How could he remain modest and unassuming, when statesmen sought him out for advice?

President John F. Kennedy, looking ahead to his 1964 re-election campaign, said to his brother Bobby, "Get me the agency that does the Volkswagen advertising."

How could he remain modest and unassuming when proposals were floated to establish a "Bill Bernbach Academy of Advertising," perhaps stimulated by the *Madison Avenue* magazine comment?

Bernbach introduced the idea to Ted Factor, the agency's West Coast head, as they drove from Monterrey to San Francisco on business. The agency's creatives would double as teachers. The Academy would bring more income and even wider fame, Bernbach excitedly told Factor.

"Are you serious?" asked Factor. "There'll be people all over the country with diplomas saying they're Bernbach graduates. That will water down the value to a client of having Doyle Dane Bernbach as his agency."

Snapped Bernbach, "Anyone can find a negative."

"He really wanted it," Factor recalled. "But I never heard another word about it after that."

In time, there were people all over the country who had learned from Bernbach. And that did water down the value of having Doyle Dane Bernbach as one's agency. But it also improved the quality of work turned out by agencies everywhere.

♦ ♦ ♦

4
Past Imperfect

"It's a rule of human nature that a man wants to be admired."
—Bill Bernbach

As Bernbach's reputation grew, so did requests for interviews and biographical material. Very little in his past seemed to him worth reprising. Bernbach loved elegance, beauty, tastefulness. He insisted on quality in every element of an ad, quality that would rub off on, and burnish, the image of the product.

Not that one could create a silk purse out of a sow's ear. On the contrary, "the magic is in the product," he preached. But one made choices, along the way, of what to include, and what to omit, in presenting the product to the public.

The beauty of advertising was control. The media ran the ads given them, in the space or time purchased. The power to shape perceptions was yours.

Life itself was rather messier. One had somehow to acknowledge the past. Editors and reporters didn't simply print what one gave them. They might accept an unwillingness to discuss the personal, but they insisted on a full-scale review of a subject's professional background.

Bernbach did what many others do. He put the best possible spin on the available material.

* * *

Some of the available material Bernbach wished he could excise, including his most significant pre-DDB job, copy chief of Grey Advertising. "Couldn't you just refer to it as 'another agency?'" he would suggest to an interviewer. The Grey connection made him visibly uneasy, possibly because of Grey's reputation when he worked there, as the prototypical "Seventh Avenue" agency. Or perhaps because of the contempt he professed to feel for Grey management's values and standards.

"Whenever I had to make a management decision," Doyle cracked more than once, "I thought of what Larry Valenstein would do in that situation, and then did the exact opposite."

Yet Grey's founders, Valenstein and Arthur Fatt, had *discovered* Bernbach, working in a tiny retail promotion subsidiary. They'd recognized his talent and pushed him forward fast, proud and supportive of his work. Fatt, especially, regarded him almost as a son. Bernbach's leaving surprised and devastated him—a reaction not unlike Bernbach's when creative stars left *him*. None of this intense personal connection was I aware of until after Bernbach's death. I had worked at Grey in the early '60s. I remembered how Fatt would turn ashen at a mention of Bernbach's name.

Breakaway agencies are a fact of business life. Not often do their origins enter the realm of the unmentionable.

The intensity of Bernbach's desire to bury the Grey connection, the contempt he felt towards the founders, suggests something deeper than business. An aftershock, perhaps, of the father/son temblor in his personal life. With Grey, Bernbach did the abandoning. That's easier to do if you tell yourself that the "father" deserves what he's getting.

* * *

The industry memory of Doyle Dane Bernbach's origins in Grey trailed off and in time evaporated, what with the total lack of family resemblance to keep it alive. Doyle Dane Bernbach would be seen as rising from a sea of boiling creativity, life-sized and pure and radiant as Botticelli's Venus. How much more aesthetic if Bernbach could begin his own story with the birth of Doyle Dane Bernbach, when he began to emerge as the person he wanted to be.

* * *

The business with his parents, for example. In some families, time leads to forgiveness. Perhaps Bernbach hoped his parents would come to accept Evelyn and rescind their dire, old-country response to his marriage. He didn't doubt that, whatever their disappointments, parents come through for their children in times of need.

At the end of the 1930s, Bernbach found himself in need. Jobless, and with no jobs available for which he had experience, he asked Jacob for financial help to see him through. Jacob, prodded by Rebecca, refused. The hurt of the first rejection was now compounded by anger, outrage, humiliation. The slender thread of hope for reconciliation snapped. His parents had forsworn him when he married. Now he forswore them.

Lesser traumas have upended stronger psyches. Bernbach swallowed his anger and, looking back later from the pinnacle of success, could claim, and perhaps believe, that he "had no sores to squeeze."

* * *

The parents/son split resolved one potential mixed-marriage problem: Bill's and Evelyn's children would be raised in the Catholic church.

Evelyn's large and embracing family—parents, six sisters and a brother—had a healing effect on Bill. He loved to sit at the long dining room table on a Sunday and share their warmth, the good talk, the heaps of tangy Italian dishes. He overcame the old habit of picking at his food. He filled out some, and stood straighter. Even when he'd metamorphosed into a legend in the world of advertising, his happiest kind of Sunday afternoon was dinner with the Carbone family.

But that was private, and never part of the projected public image.

* * *

His five or six years at Schenley had to be covered in his biographical material. It was a long stretch, his first job after graduating from New York University, and not exactly image-enhancing. Simply, then, he distilled the half-decade experience into a single anecdote that ends with his writing his way out of the mailroom and into the advertising department. The listener, or reader, assumes Bernbach continued writing Schenley ads until he left the company. Evelyn, who was there, shook her head when asked about Bill's ads for Schenley.

Bernbach related the story of his interview for a copywriting job at the William Weintraub agency in 1940.

"I said, 'Well I have no experience.' He [Weintraub] said, 'Then why don't you just write me a letter, telling me why you should have this job.' I said, 'I don't know why I should have the job; I don't even know if I'm equipped.' He said, 'Why don't you write the letter anyway?'" Bernbach did, and got the job, his first in an advertising agency, without a portfolio of ads to show Weintraub.

* * *

Grover Whalen, who had plucked the promising young man out of Schenley's mailroom and helped shape him socially, took Bernbach along when he became president of the 1939 New York World's Fair. (Whalen gets no mention in Bernbach's biographies.)

In a bureau that handled public relations functions, Bernbach wrote brochures, articles, a booklet about the history of fairs. He wrote short speeches for Whalen. Perhaps greetings and comments for visiting celebrities. That may have been the source of his basic anecdote about his Fair job.

"I ghosted speeches for a lot of prominent people—for governors, mayors, a lot of prominent people." The anecdote was quoted in many interviews. Once, however, while Bernbach was visiting Hawaii, a reporter for a local newspaper pressed for elaboration. Which governors, mayors, prominent people? she asked. If he turned his icy blue gaze on her, he didn't succeed in squelching the subject. She wrote:

"Bernbach's introduction to the advertising business came as a ghost writer for a string of politicians whom he refused to name."

In summing up his career trajectory, Bernbach usually went from the Fair to the Weintraub agency. "I thought it might be a good idea to ghost for some products instead of people. It might be lucrative and it might be very interesting," he said more than once.

In fact, a year passed before Weintraub hired Bernbach. A year without a job. Evelyn brought home her small pay from Schenley, where she'd stayed on as a receptionist. Wives' pay never covered living costs then. That was when Bernbach asked his parents to help, and when they refused.

Desperately needing work, Bernbach took on a free-lance assignment that must have come through a Schenley acquaintance still friendly with the old bootleg bunch. Bernbach would do promotion on a new product, Talkavision, which an underworld character named Yermie Stern hoped would elevate him to the world of legitimate business.

News of the assignment alarmed a Schenley executive who cared about the young couple. "This is serious stuff," he warned Evelyn. Talkavision was sponsored by mobsters, including Three Fingers Brown. Bill had to get the hell away from those people, fast. Why hadn't she told him things were that bad? He'd see what he could do for Bill with the head of Schenley's ad agency, Bill Weintraub.

And so, at 30, Bernbach entered the advertising business.

* * *

The year of unemployment blipped out of Bernbach's history, never to be mentioned in interviews or biographies. It wasn't quite a total loss, however. One of Bernbach's most effective stories came out of a Yermie Stern incident. The story concludes with Yermie's anger when an associate phones to explain why he can't attend an important meeting.

"Son of a gun," says Yermie. "Everything happens to me. His father died."

Yermie's reaction perfectly illustrated Bernbach's most basic belief about the art of persuasion:

"Everyone feels he is the center of the universe . . . Nothing interests him as much as himself. You begin to communicate with him, you get his attention, when what you say has value for him." Bernbach found value in the most unexpected places.

Much later, his colleagues would whisper about Bernbach's obsessive concern with money. A family friend saw it from another perspective—as a morbid fear of poverty rooted in his frightening jobless year.

* * *

At Weintraub, Bernbach met the first great influence on his work in advertising—Paul Rand, the agency's head art director. Though Rand was only 27, he was already known as one of the nation's best graphic designers. Art magazines ran cover stories on this striking young apostle of European modern, Bauhaus, Le Corbusier. With playful and witty images, Rand made memorable such products as Dubonnet wine, Airwick, El Producto cigars, Lee Hats. Nobody could mistake Rand ads. He *signed* them, as an artist does his paintings—a privilege granted no other advertising art director before or since.

Rand's ads were *visual ideas*, with little or no copy. In American advertising, words were prime. Not just "Amazing!," "Finest!" and the like, but also verbal ideas fashioned into slogans and themes that became part of America's pop heritage in the years between the two world wars.

"I'd walk a mile for a Camel." "You'll wonder where the yellow went." "Not a cough in a carload." "Sal Hepatica for the smile of health." "A skin you love to touch." "The penalty of leadership." "They laughed when I sat down at at the piano." A great copywriter could make an agency's fortune. Art directors, on the other hand, merely rendered the copywriters' verbal ideas.

Rand was on a different plane, and Bernbach was eager to learn from him. Soon the two young men were lunching together every day at Gluckstern's deli-restaurant in the West 40s, Bernbach absorbing lessons that Rand, delighted by Bernbach's interest, happily dispensed.

"It's possible to do good work and also be effective in the marketplace," Rand would say. "The fact that most ads are lousy has nothing to do with the marketplace; it has to do with the fact that people are lousy."

Rand would speak about the need for an ad "to hold its own in a competitive race," about arresting visual images, about avoiding artistic tricks, about solutions that stem from the product. Few American designers were working this way, but "other guys were doing it in Europe."

Bernbach came to Weintraub, Rand told me, as "a public relations guy who knew nothing about art, or advertising art." When he left a year later, he had absorbed enough from Rand to prepare his ascent to patron saint of advertising art directors.

* * *

Bernbach mentioned Rand often in later interviews. His was the one name from Bernbach's pre-DDB years that he could speak with pride. The *New York Times* would call Rand "one of the most influential and fascinating designers of our time." As early as 1941 he'd been described as "a painter, lecturer, industrial designer, advertising artist who . . . [is] an idealist and a realist, using the language of the poet and the business man." He designed logos for IBM, Westinghouse, ABC; taught design at Yale University; published brilliant books on design theory.

In his earliest mention of Rand in print—a 1953 interview—Bernbach stated that Rand "did for the advertising artist what Beethoven did for the musician; he actually liberated him."

But as the years brought more and more acclaim to Rand, Bernbach's memory of their early friendship shifted in emphasis. The image became that of two young men starting on an equal level of experience, with Bernbach emerging as the innovator and as a factor in Rand's books.

"There [at Weintraub] I got the integration between copy and art, which I innovated. I helped Paul with some books he was writing, and we integrated our copy and art like it wasn't done before."

Rand, a man not easily stirred to rancor, never forgave Bernbach for such comments. "Everything has already been done," Rand quoted the 12th century philosopher Maimonides.

"The integration of copy and art had been done in Europe for *years* before. Imagine taking credit for something like that!" As for his classic book, *Thoughts on Design*, Bernbach had read the manuscript, but "didn't so much as change a word." What especially rankled Rand was "the myth that Bernbach taught me everything I ever knew about advertising."

* * *

In later years, Bernbach *did* teach many young creative people everything they ever knew about advertising. And he did popularize (if not innovate) the integration of art and copy. If Rand liberated the advertising artist, Bernbach liberated the creative process.

Bernbach was to advertising what Freud was to healing, wrote one of his best-known alumni, the flamboyant art director George Lois. "He encouraged artistry and imagery in an industry that sang the praises of walking a mile for a Camel and still rejoices over a jerk squeezing Charmin."

He also encouraged advertisers to use a touch of self-deprecation, perhaps humor at one's own expense, to disarm consumers. And yet his own story, as he told it through the years, had not a trace of self-deprecation or humor. Each experience had been re-cast and heightened to make it worthy of inclusion in his life story.

So it is with the autobiographical material of other famous men. But Bernbach's uneasiness with the reality of his past would matter to the future of Doyle Dane Bernbach.

Account Gains and Losses, 1961-1965

In:

1964 Democratic Presidential campaign
American Airlines
Avis Rent a Car
Bankers Trust
Bulova Watch
Burlington Industries
Continental Insurance
Cool-Ray sunglasses
Cracker Jack Co.
Crown Zellerbach
General Foods
Gillette Company
H.J. Heinz
International Silver
Jamaica Tourist Board
Joseph E. Seagram
Lees Carpets
Lever Brothers
Mobil Oil Corp.
Occidental Life
Ocean Spray Cranberries
Quaker Oats
Sony
Uniroyal
WTS-Pharmacraft

Out:

General Mills
Philip Morris
    (Alpine cigarets)
Schenley
Utica Club Beer

♦ ♦ ♦

5
Cashing In

"But it is pretty to see what money will do."
—Samuel Pepys

Ned Doyle loved the thought of telling troublesome clients to go to hell. He fantasized exotic ways of doing so.

"You go to a hardware store and buy a power mower," he instructed Ted Factor, on the phone from the Coast with a string of complaints about client Ernest Gallo, the winemaker. "Put it in the back of your car and drive to the winery. When you get there, shove it up his ass and turn on the power."

Bernbach blanched. Doyle, like his real father, had lost his love and respect. In his devil-may-care style, Doyle would put his feet on the most majestic boardroom table and swear like the old Marine he was. Bernbach needed civility, niceness, good manners. Doyle embarrassed him.

Doyle worried him, too, with his eagerness for face-offs with clients. Despite the myth, Bernbach had an almost morbid fear of losing clients. Not that he pandered to them, or gave them what they asked for. On the contrary, he would throw out finished ads that the client had approved, if he considered the work unworthy. He returned from vacation in the mid-60s and killed a pool of new client-approved commercials for Rheingold beer, although the agency would have to "eat" the very substantial production costs. The commercials were parodies of operas, a stupid way, in Bernbach's opinion, to sell beer.

But in the way he led creatives to "think about what they (the clients) are thinking about, he pursued harmony, not confrontation. Bernbach transmuted "the client's wrong" into "the client's right" day after day, year after year, while his legend as a heroic contender against insensitive advertisers grew—along with the agency's reputation for "arrogance." Young creatives who never met Bernbach would continue to invoke his name as the champion who would have fought for their rejected campaigns.

Yet, from the beginning, Bernbach's founding partners marveled at the intensity of his anxiety about client departures.

The first client split was at Doyle's insistence, when the Necchi-Elna sewing machine company gave its television advertising to another agency, asking Doyle Dane Bernbach to keep print.

"You can't handle an account like that," Doyle told the client, and his partners. "You become a special pleader for one medium over another, and that's untenable." Necchi-Elna represented a fourth of the young agency's billings.

The deed done, the founders went to dinner. Doyle, expansive in his victory, drank rather than ate. Mac Dane ordered lobster and went vigorously at it. An ashen Bernbach watched him, incredulously.

"How *can* you?" asked Bernbach, pushing away his own plate in his distress.

Dane shrugged and continued cracking lobster claws. "You win some, you lose some," said he.

Neither forgot that dinner. To Bernbach, Dane's hearty repast revealed surpassing insensitivity to loss. Dane remembered the night as his first glimpse into the depths of Bernbach's fears and insecurities about matters Dane considered ordinary business comings and goings.

* * *

Some saw Doyle Dane Bernbach as the lengthened shadow of three men in one, indivisible. "As much one person as three men can be," wrote an admiring journalist in 1959.

"Do you think you know me well enough to refer to me by my first two names?" Bernbach would ask anyone who referred to the agency as "Doyle Dane."

The three men had flipped a coin to settle the order of their names in the agency title. After which, according to agency legend, Bernbach said, "Nothing will ever get between us, not even punctuation."

Walking into a room together, the three never failed to surprise people seeing them for the first time. They were shorter than average—although Bernbach and Doyle each felt he was considerably taller than the other. The three were older than expected for new celebrities. (Bernbach was 38, Dane 43 and Doyle 47 in the year the agency began.) They looked, as a trio, more like subway commuters from the outer boroughs than the founders of a Cinderella advertising agency.

"The most unassuming, unprepossessing men you can recall ever having encountered," in the words of a 1959 magazine profile.

Joe Daly, the first account man to become a vice president of the agency, remembered his reaction on meeting them: "*Those guys* are Doyle, Dane and Bernbach?"

* * *

Dane had plenty of experience with business wins and losses as head of his own small agency. A lucky break changed his destiny. Doyle and Bernbach had enlisted Herb Strauss, one of Grey's best account men, as third partner in their planned breakaway agency. Grey's owners, getting wind of the plot, persuaded Strauss to stay by promising him the future presidency of Grey, a promise they kept. Their efforts to keep Bernbach and Gage from leaving failed.

When Strauss pulled out, Dane pushed in, through his old friendship with Doyle, who had hired him as advertising promotion manager of *Look* magazine before the war. They had remained tennis partners in the years since.

Dane offered a valuable asset—a going agency, incorporated and accredited by the media—which he would submerge into a new company. Doyle proposed the union to Bernbach, who would agree only if Dane accepted half the number of shares the "senior partners" would receive. After all, said Bernbach, they were bringing in the talent and the big account (Ohrbach's). Doyle relayed the condition to Dane, who reflected for several days. The condition galled. But to reject it would hurt no one but himself, depriving him of a chance to break out into a promising new agency, an agency with a vision, with talent (Bernbach, Gage and Robinson) to realize that vision, and with a front man (Doyle) who knew everyone in town. Dane accepted.

Their names coalesced into one. But any impression that the three men had some kind of bond based on equality was strictly illusory.

The intensity and complexity of feelings between Doyle and Bernbach never ensnared Dane. Nobody viewed him as a rival. Neither glamour nor artistry emanated from his sensible presence. "Benign accountant" was the phrase some used to describe his looks. Bernbach, out of Dane's hearing, called him "the shopkeeper." And indeed one could imagine him behind a neighborhood store counter, wearing a hardware apron, peering benevolently over his glasses, knowing every customer's names and family problems.

Like Bernbach, Dane led a life of utter rectitude, faithfully riding the subway home to the wife he married in 1939, and their only child, Henry James Dane. Unlike Bernbach, Dane loved physical exertion, playing a dogged game of tennis, and spinning on Rockefeller Center's ice rink at noontime. Unlike his partners at the start, Dane had always made time for community and political activities. Doyle looked on Dane's work for "good causes" with his usual jaundiced eye

"Where've you been, Mac?" he'd asked when Dane returned to the agency at an off hour. "Agency business or obituary business?"

All three partners would amass impressive obituary material in the years ahead. And public service would become one of the splendid hallmarks of the agency.

Another, of equal importance, was the agency tradition of caring for the welfare of its people. The source and guardian of that vital tenet was the accidental partner, Maxwell Dane.

* * *

Dane watched Bernbach grow less dependent on Doyle, "a father figure Bill really leaned on in the early days," as Bernbach "achieved more prominence and gained more self-confidence."

Bernbach must have seen the shift differently, a result of his disappointment with Doyle's behavior, rather than his improving opinion of himself. Doyle gave him problems, inside the agency as well as with clients Doyle was eager to dump.

Bob Gage told a story about showing Doyle his finished artwork for a Max Factor ad. "I had Helburn shoot the photograph, and I loved the girl, and the artwork was beautiful. Here's the way the conversation with Ned went: 'Bob, this is just beautiful. Really beautiful.' So I picked it up and started to walk out, and he said, 'But isn't she cross-eyed? Here, let me take another look at it.' He did, and then said, 'She's a cross-eyed bitch!'

"So I decided never to show Ned another piece of work like that," Gage related, laughing at the memory, and loving Doyle, "just a sensational man," nonetheless.

One day soon after, Bernbach came into Gage's office and confided that he'd "had it out with Ned."

"What do you mean?" asked Gage.

"I told Ned the creative decisions are mine. He has nothing to do with the creative. And Ned finally agreed."

The anger, and courage, that propelled Bernbach into such a scene might be deduced from the almost total absence of other such scenes in Bernbach's life. He would remain silent when most deeply hurt or disappointed. The atmosphere would cloud over; the offending person could feel Bernbach's brooding unhappiness. But words were rarely spoken.

In this case, the outcome of the scene with Doyle seemed to surprise

Bernbach."That Ned is really something," he said to Gage a few weeks later. "He means what he says. He's never interfered since."

* * *

In subtle and not-so-subtle ways, their relationship continued to change. Doyle felt the loss of Bernbach's former admiration. He drank more. Inevitably, that inflamed Bernbach's feeling that Doyle was betraying him.

"I think Bernbach was always worried about me because of my drinking," Doyle said in 1977, when he and I began an oral history project. "He didn't know when I might fall in the gutter, but he never criticized me."

Instead, Bernbach swallowed his anger and assumed more of Doyle's responsibilities. By 1960, when Nancy Underwood became Bernbach's secretary, the agency's perception of Doyle was that he "didn't work."

Bernbach, by contrast, worked demonically to cover the bases. Underwood logged 200 calls to Bernbach's office on a single, record-setting (but not by much) day. He tried to return every call, in addition to reviewing every ad, even trade ads, for every client. Many of the calls were from advertisers, eager to talk to the hot agency about handling some of their business. Underwood screened calls before bothering Bernbach with them. Doyle, more and more, was left out of the loop.

"Is this about new business?" Underwood would ask. If so, a second question followed. "Do you have an agency now?" Whether yes or no, she asked the third and most vital question. "How much do you intend to spend?" She had the authority to tell the caller, if the figure was too low, that she was sorry, but the agency didn't handle accounts of that size. She soon convinced Bernbach to give her the names of some smaller agencies for referrals, "out of sheer good manners."

How many advertisers with small budgets but great potential slipped through the cracks no one knows. The scenario could only have played out in an agency so explosively successful and so unskilled in management techniques as Doyle Dane Bernbach in the '60s.

Presentations to potential clients were nothing more than Bernbach showing agency ads out of "the black box," a leather presentation case, and telling the story behind each. Underwood would stock the black box, selecting ads she deemed relevant to the advertiser's business. Bernbach would ask her, when he picked up the case, what she'd put in this time.

The presentation was informal, unrehearsed, impressive, especially with the bloated sales results Bernbach over-enthusiastically appended to each story. Fine for the go-go, expansive, risk-taking '60s. New business poured in, spreading the warm feeling that the good times would go on forever.

But Bernbach began to complain to a confidante that he constantly "ended up doing the whole job, making all the decisions."

"Bill didn't feel that Doyle and Dane were especially important," Dane mused several years after Bernbach's death, "except maybe at keeping the agency sound financially. I think he viewed me, especially, in that category. That it could be the most successful agency, but be broke. Half in jest, half not in jest."

* * *

Client Jack Dreyfus, head of the Dreyfus Fund, gave them a new perspective on their agency. They could sell shares to the public.

"He used to say, 'You've got a goldmine here! It's ten times earnings!'" Doyle recalled. "We didn't know what the hell that meant. So when that was interpreted into dollars, what the shares would bring on the market, we thought, 'My God, a third of that for each of us is over a million dollars!' Who the hell had a million dollars around here? Joe Daly was wearing the same goddamn suit he'd worn for five years."

The Dreyfus Fund didn't handle public offerings. Doyle explored the idea further with Mark Appleman, who lived across the hall from him on East 19th Street, and worked in investor relations for Francis I. duPont, a brokerage house that did handle public offerings.

Wall Street and Madison Avenue had little interest in one another at that time. How could a service business operate in a fishbowl? Would clients look at the necessary disclosures and conclude that their agencies' salaries and profit margins were too high? Would they then insist on shaving fees? Would the revelation of who had how many shares breed discontent in agency management ranks? How much attention would management divert from client business to the care and feeding of financial analysts and shareholders? What of the costs of annual meetings, annual reports, proxy statements?

The arguments against going public were formidable and daunting. They did not, at the time, include a fear of takeovers, presumed unthinkable in a personal service business.

Still, going public seemed to make sense for Doyle Dane Bernbach. Two of the founders were aging. If they retired, or died, they or their estates would get only the book value of their shares. And that was very much lower than estimated market value, given the rapid growth and promise of the dynamic young agency. Accountants and lawyers studied the numbers and actuarial tables and gave their blessings. Doyle's neighbor won the underwriting job for duPont.

Doyle Dane Bernbach had achieved fame by doing the unexpected for clients. Now it was doing the unexpected for itself. Its trek to Wall Street made big news. Not that it was the first agency to go public. Two years earlier, the small and sassy creative agency headed by two Bernbach alumni, Papert Koenig & Lois (Julian Koenig and George Lois teamed on some of the earliest

Volkswagen classics), had shocked Madison Avenue by putting its shares on the market, thereby reinforcing the belief that anyone could sell anything in the go-go '60s. (PKL, dubbed "Stillman's East" after the then-famous gym because of fist fights among its principals, didn't survive the economic shake-out of the '70s.)

A year after PKL's plunge, Foote, Cone & Belding went public. This was a weightier matter. But though FCB was larger, well-established, and respected, its base was Chicago, which cast a remoteness to the act. Now came Doyle Dane Bernbach, with the substance missing from PKL, the proximity FCB lacked, a reputation for trend-setting, and Maxwell Dane, who marshaled impressive statistics to prove to the investment community the essential stability of large advertising agencies. He paved the way for the J. Walter Thompsons, Interpublics, Ogilvys and Greys to sell their stock to the public, with consequences that long reverberated in the industry.

* * *

When they rode back uptown on an August day in 1964, the founders carried a check for $6,270,890.40, made out to "Maxwell Dane, as agent for shareholders." Fifteen times earnings! Since they still owned 75 percent of their stock, the transaction seemed like a miracle.

Of that sum, $1,602,468 went to Doyle. A like amount was shared by Bill and Evelyn Bernbach. Dane and his wife got $929,466. After the three founders, the largest sum went to Bob Gage, $539,071. Then the star account man, Joe Daly, with $494,859. A big drop to the next level: $293,596 for Ted Factor, and $239,308 for Eddie Russell, a contender with Daly for the aging Doyle's job. The next drop was even steeper, down to $79,414 for Phyllis Robinson. Among the other creatives, art director Bill Taubin got $76,140; Helmut Krone, $65,988; copy chief David Reider, $47,588; copywriter Jack Dillon, $30,456; copywriters Paula Green and Bob Levenson, $15,863 each.

"Very few people shared the stock, when you stop to think about it," in Joe Daly's opinion. "Very few. Doyle, Dane, Bernbach, myself and Gage. The rest? Forget it." Inevitably, the event induced a Balzacian fascination with money in a place previously focused entirely on the creative product.

Doyle swore that Dane had dragged his heels on a public offering, worried that his lesser share would be noticed by the press. It wasn't.

Dane attributed the resignation of the agency's marketing maven, another contender for Doyle's job, to his shock on comparing the number of shares he'd been given to those of Daly and Russell.

Bernbach received calls from DDBers running foreign offices, hurt that people without bottom-line responsibilities had been rewarded, while they, who labored to create profits for the home office, had been overlooked.

High-level creatives approached Dane with gripes about "how come so-and-so got that much, and I only got . . ."

On every level, DDBers marveled at the Wall Street magic that overnight had made their leaders millionaires. Some began to dream of opening their own agencies.

* * *

Bernbach and Doyle remained equal shareholders after the 1964 offering. Not so after a second public offering of agency stock in 1966. Bernbach sat that one out after a market downturn forced the underwriters, unable to defer the announced event, to offer the stock at a price Bernbach thought too low. Doyle didn't like the price either, but took a more philosophical view, which he expressed to the underwriters in typical Doyle fashion.

"When I go see a whore, I expect to get fucked."

Still, Doyle participated in the offering, reducing his holdings and leaving Bernbach, who didn't, with some 16 percent of the agency stock, by far the largest block.

* * *

Going public "suddenly put a substantial amount of cash in the founders' hands," recalled a lawyer involved in the event, "so that they could begin living like the successful people they were."

Bill and Evelyn Bernbach moved from Bay Ridge, Brooklyn, to one of Manhattan's most striking apartment buildings, the United Nations Plaza. Mac Dane bought a co-op on Park Avenue and 67th Street. Doyle remained in his East 19th Street penthouse apartment, but bought and sold several summer residences, a research firm, and a basketball team. Joe Daly moved into a world he'd longed to enter—buying, breeding and racing horses. Ted Factor began collecting antique automobiles. Bob Gage later recalled that the stock sale enabled him to feel "like I had some money, which was a good feeling."

The agency's biggest guns had been rewarded. The smaller guns settled for stock options and the hope that the share price would keep going up.

* * *

In time, going public came to be seen by many as perhaps the single most important event in the eventual decline of the agency. "It's not an unmitigated blessing," conceded Mac Dane, two decades after the event. Understating, in his trademark style, Dane cited the deadliest result of going public for a service business: "You become a little more interested in your bottom line."

True, the agency became mesmerized by its bottom line. But the later perception among the creatives that going public ended DDB's willingness to say "take this campaign or else" to balky clients, does not hold up. Bernbach never said "take this campaign or else" to a client.

♦ ♦ ♦

6
Talking about Writing

"It is not every question that deserves an answer."
—Publilius Syrus, *Maxims*

Bill Bernbach was all too visibly uncomfortable. His visitor, Denis Higgins, a senior editor of *Advertising Age,* scribbled a note. He would afterwards write that Bernbach had regarded him "with the manner of a man who is being grilled by an auditor from the Internal Revenue Service and who in his heart knows he is innocent." An acute observation.

Bernbach's anxiety surprised Higgins, for the occasion marked a singular honor. Bernbach had received recognition as an industry immortal with his induction into the Copywriters Hall of Fame. Now came the ritual Hall of Fame interview, to run in the most important publication in the field.

"WILLIAM BERNBACH Talks About How He Writes Copy," the headline would read.

The year was 1965 and Doyle Dane Bernbach was the idol of the industry. Its founders were not only famous now, but rich, after selling a portion of their stock to the public. Every creative person in the business would sift Bernbach's words, seeking nuggets of inspiration that might help their own careers.

But Bernbach had no desire to discuss the particulars of how he wrote copy. He was ready with a testy answer to Higgins' first such question.

"I remember those old *Times* interviews where the interviewer would talk to the novelist or short story writer, and say, 'What time do you get up in the morning? What do you have for breakfast? What time do you start work?' And the whole implication is that if you eat corn flakes at 6:30 in the morning, and then take a walk and then take a nap and then start working and then stop at noon, you too can be a great writer."

Higgins was taken aback. Most admen savored questions about how they did what they did. Later in the interview:

"Q. I wanted to ask you briefly about your own habits.

"A. (laughter)

"Q. Why are you laughing?

"A. I'm laughing because you are going to habits again as if that were the answer.

"Q. No, it's not the answer. I realize it's not the answer. What I mean by habits—when you did write body copy, were you your own editor, even though you were the boss?

"A. Yes, sure, absolutely.

"Q. And you don't need an outsider, a third man to edit you?"

Bernbach ignored the follow-up question and talked instead about editing others. Higgins couldn't play prosecutor; he went on to other questions, asked with increasing irritability.

All writers need editors. Why this puzzling insistence that he, Bernbach, did not? Altogether, the interview elicited very little about how Bernbach wrote copy, and finally, Higgins figuratively threw up his hands and asked Bernbach to name his favorite among the ads he had turned out through the years.

Said Bernbach: "Well, you know I started with the Ohrbach campaign myself. And I did the Ohrbach ads personally for about 17 years running. So I have a deep affection for them. I did the cat ad, for example. You know the one I mean. . . ."

* * *

Everyone in the business knew the cat ad. The one cattily headlined, "I found out about Joan," spoken by a tabby who peered from under a fashionable hat, suavely clenching a long cigaret holder in its mouth.

A little-known story about the cat ad may illuminate some of the puzzling aspects of the Copywriters Hall of Fame interview. The ad ran in March 1958 issues of newspapers in New York, Newark and Los Angeles—Ohrbach's turf. Hundreds of readers wrote to request copies, a rare event in those days. *Time* magazine reported that "the greatest compliment came from Madison Avenue, where admen paid their respects by posting the Ohrbach's ad on their own bulletin boards." *Time*'s story ended with one adman's view, "A masterpiece."

Alas, *Time* credited only one of the ad's creators. "Produced by the

Manhattan ad agency of Doyle Dane Bernbach, Inc. and written by a 35-year-old bachelor girl named Judith Protas. . . ."

Bernbach saw red. Protas had warned the *Time* reporter to be careful about credits, because Bob Gage and Bill Bernbach, "the head of this agency," had created the concept. Only afterwards had she written the body copy. What did *Time* care about credits and egos? *Time* aimed for tight stories with every fact either informative or entertaining. Protas' age, sex and marital status made the delicious bitchiness of the copy more fun. Says the cat about Joan:

"The way she talks, you'd think she was in *Who's Who*. Well! I found out what's with *her*. Her husband owns a bank? Sweetie, not even a bank *account*. Why that palace of theirs has wall-to-wall *mortgages*! And that car? Darling, that's horsepower, *not* earning power. They won it in a fifty-cent raffle! Can you imagine? And those clothes! Of course she *does* dress divinely. But really . . . a mink stole, and Paris suits, and all those dresses . . . on *his* income? Well, darling. I found out about that too. I just happened to be going her way and *I saw Joan come out of Ohrbach's!*"

A quarter of a century later, and Bernbach dead, Protas still felt the sting of his fury about *Time*'s story. The nation's premiere news magazine rarely considered ads worthy of editorial coverage. They'd written up the cat ad as a "masterpiece" and failed to attribute it to Bernbach, who thought of it as his own. The concept, not the body copy, gave an ad its life force.

"He never forgot, and I don't think he ever forgave," Protas recalled in 1983, "because it was one of the big explosive successes of the agency."

Two weeks after naming Protas as the ad's writer, *Time* ran a story titled "Adman's Adman." It trumpeted the growing success of Bernbach and his agency. On his work for Ohrbach's, it noted that "he stressed sophistication instead of price with the eye-catching illustration and a minimum of copy that later became his trademark. (See Bernbach's recent cat ad. TIME, March 17). . . ."

Somehow, Bernbach had convinced *Time* to make good its earlier lapse. Almost certainly, the hand of the magazine's business side reached out to the editorial offices. Editors do not soon forget such incidents. Still, Bernbach had won his point. (Gage was used to being left out of the credits and didn't much care, having a strong sense of his worth and no ego problems.)

So ended the cat ad story. Or did it? In 1962, *Time* sent out phalanxes of reporters for a landmark story on the advertising business. The cover of its October 12 issue featured photographs of twelve agency executives. Each represented "an advertising philosophy or technique that has helped to make the industry what it is and seems likely to shape its future."

David Ogilvy was there, and Leo Burnett. Fairfax Cone and Marion Harper. So were Robert Mondell Ganger and Henry Guy Little, names not widely known even then. Bernbach, who more than anyone was shaping advertising's future, did not appear on *Time's* cover. Was it a deliberate omission? This time, no protesting telephone calls could repair the damage. One can't remake a *Time* cover.

* * *

The image of Bernbach copywriting almost everything produced in the early days by the young agency was bolstered by press reprints of what they identified as "Bernbach's ads." And they *were* Bernbach's ads, either in concept or in shaping. But beyond the headlines, he did very little writing, even before the founding of Doyle Dane Bernbach.

Bob Gage: "He used to do the headlines with me, and the concepts with me, and then he would let Judy Protas write the body copy. He'd go back up to his room. He never wrote body copy. Only on rare occasions."

What about back in the days when Gage worked with him at Grey Advertising? "I'm sure he wrote something, but I don't know. He got bored with it after the headline."

Doyle: "Hank Hunter of Olin Mathieson told Bill the company was going to shorten its name to Olin. They would need an ad. Bill said, 'I've got the ad. "Call me by my first name."' Hunter said, 'Bill, you're crazy. You should take the assignment back to your office, give me fifty other names, tell me this is the one you suggest, and charge me $50,000. . . .'"

"What idiot changed the Chivas Regal bottle?" moaned the copywriter assigned to the account. "That's the headline!" pounced Bernbach, and another classic ad was born.

From Helmut Krone's wastepaper basket, Bernbach fished wads of crumpled papers and beamed upon spreading open a sheet with the words, "We're only Number Two. So we try harder."

What did it matter if Bernbach did or did not write much beyond the headlines? To advertising history, it matters not at all. In attempting to understand Bernbach, it signifies.

* * *

The sense of unease among his closest colleagues grew along with his collection of press notices. They pondered his need to take credit for so much that others helped create. They wondered what drove him to portray the quality of his writing when pushed, as in the Higgins interview, as above and beyond the need for an editor—a claim no other writer would make. They saw that the more his image became that of "writer," the pricklier became his sensitivities.

A few in the upper reaches of management placed bets on whether he would ever finish the book he spoke of writing. But that's a later chapter.

Account Gains and Losses, 1966-1969

In:	Out:
Alka-Seltzer	Avis Rent a Car
American Tourister luggage	Barton's Candy
British Travel Association	Broxodent
Buitoni	Buitoni
GTE	Buxton leather goods
Hills Bros. coffee	French Gov't Tourist Office
Jack-in-the-Box	General Foods
Kitchens of Sara Lee	Lane Furniture
Lehn & Fink	Lowrey Organ
Life Magazine	Manpower Inc.
Manpower Inc.	Mead Johnson (Metrecal)
Mead Johnson (Metrecal)	Ocean Spray
New York Racing Association	Parker Pen
Parker Pens	Pfizer
Porsche Audi	Rheingold Breweries
Stroh Beer	Thom McAn shoes
Warner Lambert	Warner foundation garments
	Whirlpool
	WTS-Pharmaceutical

◆ ◆ ◆

7
The Guy with the Bulging Muscles

"Nearly all men can stand adversity, but if you want to test a man's character, give him power."—Abraham Lincoln

There's nothing that says an advertising agency should become an established institution. Helmut Krone believed that companies should self-destruct after 25 years. The exciting, fresh ideas don't often come out of institutions.

Bernbach and Doyle walked out of Grey because they wanted to do advertising their way, not to start a company that would sprout multi-national subsidiaries and listings in the daily stock tables. Their way meant superior ads to Bernbach, and gutsiness to Doyle. Coming in to work everyday, and doing it. Beyond that? Well, . . .

"Did we ever sit down or did we ever think that as of a certain date a Doyle, a Dane, a Bernbach, would have to give up the reins to someone else and who would it be?" Doyle reflected in an oral history interview. "We never did that, and dammit, we should have."

Neither Doyle nor Bernbach was likely to believe that others could fill their growingly-legendary shoes. And perhaps the entangling underbrush of their rivalrous father/son relationship, its thorns scratching memories of an older hurt, inhibited open talks about the fraught subject of succession.

Then too, orderly management methods seemed contrary to the essence of the sensationally-successful young agency. Whence came the magic of its great work if not from the riotous high spirits, the trusting freedom? Can magic be institutionalized?

Moreover, things kept happening so fast—the new campaigns bringing new glory and a constant stream of new clients—that nobody had time to look back at the clients who streamed out, or ahead to the future of the most-admired and fastest-growing agency in the business.

No, nothing says an advertising agency should become an established institution. But a big agency has big clients, and big clients have multi-national offices and multi-layers of management. If the agency wants to stay big, it tries to provide the stability and service of an established institution.

Doyle Dane Bernbach burst into the top ten agencies in 1965, in tenth place with $130 million in billings. J. Walter Thompson, BBDO and Young & Rubicam held the top three spots, but the ground was rumbling under the old agencies. DDB had beaten out BBDO for the important American Airlines account in 1961. Unlike the small and troubled clients of the agency's first decade, American was a great and successful airline. H. J. Heinz, Uniroyal, Mobil Oil and Lever Brothers quickly followed American into Doyle Dane Bernbach, all expressing their admiration for the agency's Polaroid and Volkswagen work. Advertisers across the country were showing dissatisfaction with the creative output of their own agencies, and asking their account people to bring them ads with "the Doyle Dane look."

Moreover, the giant agencies had been losing a significant advantage, as the booming television networks elbowed them out of control over programming. And as costs skyrocketed, fewer advertisers could afford to sponsor regular shows of their own. "Specials" were devised as a less burdensome alternative. Shared sponsorships became more common, eventually leading to "buying spots" on certain kinds of programs—sports, or news, or daytime, or prime time. If an advertiser did not need an agency to create programs, why not choose an agency that produced outstanding ads and commercials? The established agencies beefed up their creative departments.

* * *

Ned Doyle later said that he had wanted Doyle Dane Bernbach to stay small, to be "a Tiffany," and that Bernbach wanted big, "a Macy's." Dane said simply, "If you stop growing, you die."

There was no putting the growth genie back in the bottle. The questions now had to do with change, and whether a top ten agency could keep on doing the knock-out work of a sassy newcomer, and whether big clients *wanted* knock-out work.

Jay Chiat said of his own booming young agency some years later, "Let's see how big we can get before we get bad."

No one at Doyle Dane Bernbach was thinking that way.

* * *

Joe Daly had many things going for him; the most powerful being his absolute hold on the Polaroid account.

Somewhere in mythology wafts an image of Polaroid's creative genius, Dr. Edwin Lane, working in mutual admiration and productivity with the creative genius of his advertising agency, Bill Bernbach, to produce a glorious success story. Not so. The only Land-Bernbach encounter Polaroid people recall was a "devastating meeting" in 1973 about the Lawrence Olivier commercials for the SX-70 camera.

"It was big people trying to impress each other with name-dropping," said a client participant. That vein running out, Land handed Bernbach his camera and asked him to look through the view-finder. Bernbach took the camera gingerly, as though he'd never seen one before. He studied it a moment, then held it up to his eyes. Instead of the view-finder, he peered into the lens. "We all died," our source said, "Land lost all respect for Bernbach because of that."

Daly brooked nobody's intervention in his running of the Polaroid account. His aura projected the message that, if badly crossed, he would walk, with Polaroid, Bob Gage and Phyllis Robinson, to open his own agency. Could he have? Nobody knew for sure. But the possibility had to haunt Bernbach. Often he wished, and occasionally he tried, to move Daly aside. He couldn't, until the end.

Meanwhile, Doyle Dane Bernbach's account staff absorbed the lesson—familiar at old-line agencies, but unexpected in this idealized and iconoclastic place—that winning control over a big and profitable account was 1) possible at the agency, for all the puffing about creative work being everything, and 2) the route to invulnerability and fortune, whatever one's imperfections.

Joe Daly personified that.

* * *

He was smart, gutsy, forceful, quick, attractive, egotistical, so bursting with life that his job and a family of seven children couldn't begin to absorb his energy. Daly womanized brazenly, though with consideration for consequences at the agency.

"I had a standing rule," Daly said years later, "which I have kept all my life. 'Never put your prick in the payroll.'"

On the other hand, stewardesses on American Airlines, one of Daly's major accounts, and the scrubbed blond demonstrators at Polaroid conventions were among Daly's favorite targets. Clients, watching this, were not especially amused. Daly "lost stature" at sales meetings and conferences, said former Polaroid client Ted Voss, long after.

Daly's wife vented her anger one night by piling all his suits into a bathtub and running steaming hot water until they shrank beyond salvation. Like Doyle's wife, and for similar reasons, Daly's wife eventually gave up on him. Womanizing and heavy drinking. A world apart from the loyal family devotion of Bernbach and Dane.

* * *

Art director George Lois, encountering Daly in 1960, described him as "a tough-looking bird with a military crew cut . . . [whose] muscly arms bulged in his short-sleeved shirt." Daly—younger, taller, more conventionally handsome than Doyle—often lost out to Doyle in their approaches to women at out-of-town sales meetings. Decades later, Daly still spoke with awe about the way women responded to Doyle.

"He'd go up to a woman and say, 'Hey, you,' and POP! I tell you, that guy was very, very wicked with women."

Here was another rivalry, this one between men cut from the same cloth. City tough, Irish competitive, brainy, cocky—the stuff of dazzling courtroom lawyers and super pols, or, in other times, of argonauts and astronauts. "Star quality," admirers said.

Both men swaggered when they walked, Doyle burdened by his outsized football shoulders, Daly with the intriguing limp of a dashing war hero. Daly had joined the Navy in 1940, after graduating from Fordham University, and trained as a fighter pilot. Stationed on the carrier Enterprise, he'd fought at Midway and Guadalcanal, risen to the rank of lieutenant commander, won the Navy Cross, the Air Medal and the Purple Heart.

War heroes and jocks. The kinds of men Bernbach looked up to, felt drawn to—until they let him down. Daly could have been a younger version of the Doyle that Bernbach had admired and envied. Not surprising, then, that Doyle never stopped resenting Daly's replacing him, any more than Daly ever stopped feeling competitive with Doyle's legend.

* * *

Everybody agreed that Daly ran accounts brilliantly, devising superb tactical ideas, orchestrating on his clients' behalf the best agency talent.

"You want to know the single most important reason for Daly's greatness as an account man?" a close co-worker asked. "Very simply, it's that every one of his clients has always known that he would never put the agency's interests ahead of theirs."

Would he show greatness as an agency leader? That question never got asked. There were other candidates, men with different virtues and abilities. They might, of course, have turned out worse. But in Doyle's opinion, "Joe did more to crack the place up than almost anybody."

* * *

Daly brought a Manhattan glamour to the accounts he ran. Chemstrand moved into the agency late in 1952, with a budget of $1 million, far larger than any other client. The company made fibers, Chemstrand nylon and Acrilan. These were bought by mills, which spun them into fabrics for apparel makers, or into blankets and carpets for retailers. In short, the target was the trade. Anywhere else, the advertising would have been placed in trade media. Not at Doyle Dane Bernbach, and not under Daly. They took a product three stages removed from the consumer and turned it into a consumer product.

Daly: "We felt Chemstrand had to go to the consumer, and then merchandise their consumer advertising to the mills, to the cutters, and through to the retailers."

That they did with a string of news-making television specials. With Daly at the controls, Princess Grace of Monaco agreed to star in her first TV special. Elizabeth Taylor, who had declined all previous proposals, agreed to do Chemstrand's second special: "Elizabeth Taylor in London." (She asked Daly to rub her back when it went out of whack in her hotel room.) Chemstrand's third was "Sophia Loren in Rome," another superstar's first TV appearance. (Loren and Daly lunched in the back seat of a limo, on one of the hills of Rome.) Judy Garland made her comeback on a Chemstrand special.

So heralded and glittering were the events that mills and cutters readily sold all their Chemstrand fabrics (identifiable to consumers by Bob Gage-designed tags) to retailers *before* each special went on air.

Daly's tactics, often copied since, were unique then. And their impact, in these days of celebrity overexposure, is not likely to be equaled.

* * *

Daly orchestrated a different kind of TV excitement, live action demonstrations, for Polaroid when the half-million-dollar account came to the agency in 1954.

"We bought only shows where we could do live commercials," related Daly, who wrote the early copy and stayed at the studios to oversee the presentations, "because at that time it was still a great gimmick that the picture developed in 60 seconds. For a one-minute buy we'd usually get about three minutes of talk by the show host. We were the first sponsors on the Steve Allen show, on the Johnny Carson show. Gary Moore, Jack Paar—any show we could do live. We did live commercials at football games with cheer-leaders and coaches. We did them at Grand Prix races with the race stars.

"The excitement and suspense were, What if the picture didn't come out? What a gutsy thing Polaroid was doing, leaving itself open to failure on live TV."

At first, the agency had a protective shot ready to slip to the show host if he bungled. Daly said, let's go cold.

"The point became that with a Polaroid picture at least you *know* when you miss, and you can take the picture again. Once, Gary Moore made a bad goof. He got gunk all over his hands, and his reaction was, 'Yuck.' So the next week we brought a little eight-year-old girl on. And when Gary started to do the commercial, she went up to him and said, 'You made such a mess of it last week, let me show you how to do it. It's so easy.' And she took the picture. It was wonderful."

For ten years, Polaroid did live shows. Every demonstration produced tension, drama, suspense, and ultimate success. Simultaneously, the agency's print ads for Polaroid said "quality, quality, quality." Polaroid sales soared; Polaroid's budget at Doyle Dane Bernbach soared. For client and agency, a great American success story.

Green-eyed competitors put down the agency's contribution with comments such as, "Oh sure, it's easy with a unique product like a Polaroid camera." (Or a Volkswagen car.)

But Polaroid had an agency before Doyle Dane Bernbach, the Boston office of BBDO. Tacky ads in undistinguished magazines portrayed the camera as a kind of party trick. (And other small cars popular in Europe made little impact in the U.S.)

Polaroid's then-marketing head gave "fifty percent of the credit to the product and fifty percent to the way DDB bought and executed time." The client-agency relationship was the strongest, soundest, and one of the most profitable for DDB during most of the 30 years it lasted. Its end would help precipitate the agency's downfall.

Meanwhile, it was a helluva power card for Daly.

* * *

Ex-Navy pilot Daly was a natural to supervise the American Airlines account when it landed at the agency in 1961. With Polaroid and Volkswagen, American would become one of DDB's three most profitable accounts. But it never settled in as comfortably as Polaroid and VW. Often the press reported that the airline was eyeing other agency suitors, on the verge of leaving DDB. Remarkably, the airline remained on board for 20 years, and then the agency did the resigning. But through the years, the airline's restlessness unnerved Bernbach, undermined his trust in Daly, and nearly led to the sale of the agency in 1974 (see chapter titled "William and Mary").

One example of Daly's strategic thinking and quick action for American: When Chet Huntley, NBC's esteemed news anchor, announced his retirement, Daly got on the phone to network contacts, pumping for information, laying plans to snare Huntley as a spokesman for the airline. A respected newsman turn flack? It seemed unthinkable in those halcyon days. Nothing was unthinkable to Daly. He pressed, and harnessed Huntley's authority and presumed journalistic objectivity into the service of American Airlines. It was, at that time, an unprecedented coup.

A revealing aside about the American Airlines account: Daly and Bernbach each believed the account stayed at the agency for only one reason— himself.

* * *

While Daly scored triumphs for his clients, Doyle sat in smaller client meetings, working the *New York Times* crossword puzzle and barking, "Let me know when you get to something important."

Doyle, like Bernbach and Dane, had signed a five-year employment contract as part of the agency's going public. So he was wired in until 1969. His title was executive vice president, in charge of account services. He probably considered himself in charge of backbone.

Bernbach, fretting about Doyle's idiosyncrasies, found a way to outmaneuver him. He would give his own title, agency president, to an account man, who in a leap would be over Doyle. The number one account man, hands down, was Daly.

So on January 1, 1968, Joe Daly became president of Doyle Dane Bernbach. In that role, his notices were far less compelling than the raves he drew as an account man.

Said one DDBer a few years later: "If Joe Daly was president of the United States, his first interest would be Polaroid."

♦ ♦ ♦

8
Bernbach's Book

"Between the idea and the reality . . . Falls the Shadow"—T.S.Eliot

The secrecy, the heartache, the pretense, the disappointed expectations that would fester in the gap between image and reality are most visible, perhaps, in a scan of the episode known as "Bill Bernbach's book."

In 1966, David Ogilvy's book, "Confessions of an Advertising Man," reached the best-seller list. A few years earlier, Ted Bates chief (and Ogilvy brother-in-law) Rosser Reeves had scored with a book titled "Reality in Advertising." The public seemed intrigued by the subject of advertising. Which adman would be next to gain best-sellerdom?

In the late '60s, a major publisher approached former *New York Times* advertising news columnist Walter Carlson with an offer to write a book with, for, or on Bill Bernbach or the glamorous Mary Wells. Carlson instantly opted for a book on and with Bernbach.

Bernbach listened with interest to Carlson's proposal on his role in bringing a Bernbach book to publication. Carlson was gentle and modest, but also reassuringly professional. The 20-year veteran of the *Times* had written often and admiringly about Bernbach and the agency in his column. An unsigned essay on advertising in the *Encyclopedia Britannica* 1967 Yearbook—an encomium to "the Bernbach school"—turned out to be a Carlson product.

The concept had appeal. Less work for Bernbach. And Carlson wrote well. Importantly, he was outside the agency. Bernbach could not have asked an agency writer to do what Carlson was proposing. That could diminish his stature within the agency, or raise the collaborator to an unwanted plateau.

Lawyers joined the discussions. Carlson's hopes ran high. The potential for great prestige as Bernbach's co-writer, and for large and long-running royalties, was dazzling. Bernbach's thoughts were running on a different track.

Years later, Carlson recalled that the deal collapsed over percentages of royalties. Knowing he'd do more than fifty percent of the work, he asked for half of the royalties. Bernbach balked.

Possibly. Nobody ever described Bernbach as openhanded with money. But a lawyer involved in the negotiations had a different memory—that the talks fell apart not on money, but on credits. At the very least, the ex-*Times* man wanted the words "as told to Walter Carlson" under Bernbach's name. Not in small type somewhere inside the book. In readable type, on the book's cover.

Possibly Berrnbach had imagined the project as pure ghost writing. Journalists did that for famous people in those days, silently, and for a small percentage of the royalties or, more usually, a set fee. Nary a trace of their hand would be found in the books they had ghosted. Bernbach may even have planned to mention Carlson's name in the acknowledgements. Something along the lines of, "Thanks, too, to Walter Carlson, without whose help in pulling together material. . . . etc."

The man who fought *Time* magazine to wrest full credit on the Ohrbach cat ad was not likely to accept another man's by-line on the cover of his book. But Carlson (whose wife happened to be a hard-digging trade reporter) was told the problem was the money. Negotiations ended.

Carlson felt the disappointment deeply. Bernbach's colleagues felt nothing. They had no idea, then or later, that the talks had been going on.

* * *

Bernbach signed a contract of his own with Harcourt, Brace, Jovanovich, accepting a then-generous advance of $10,000. He put the money into trust funds for his sons.

No ghosts haunted the scene this time. This was Bernbach, making a commitment of his own, signing, taking the money, stashing it into his children's future. Such a process has a momentum of its own, creating an illusion that the job is already half under one's belt.

Bernbach fairly danced with joy as he told his colleagues about the contract with the fine and famous publishing house. Privately, a few felt doubts from the onset. They saw Bernbach as a great editor and great conceptualizer. "A headline is an *idea*," said one. "It's not *writing*."

"What happens in the other 29 seconds?" Bob Gage once asked when Bernbach offered an idea for a 30-second commercial.

What would happen to the hundreds of blank pages for a book?

"He'll never write it," whispered one of his associates to another.

"Oh yes he will," responded the other. "He would hate to return a hunk of money like that."

* * *

Bernbach exhuded confidence about the project.

"How's it going?" he'd be asked.

"Just great. I'm getting a lot down," he buoyantly answered.

* * *

Contracts mattered mightily to Bernbach. The promise of a contract would entice him into negotiations to sell his agency to his former employee and glamorous competitor, Mary Wells, in 1974. When those talks ended, his fears were eradicated by a 10-year contract from Doyle Dane Bernbach (see chapter titled "Fathers and Sons"). The explosions of relief and exhilaration set off by that contract would strike some as excessive, given that it *was* his agency.

By that time, Bernbach had experienced two decades of fame, and the admiration of the industry. But fame and admiration do not necessarily overcome the self-doubts of earlier years. Success can also stir concerns about one's worthiness, about being found to be less than one's image.

A contract confirmed one's worthiness. The Harcourt, Brace, Jovanovich contract showed that the world beyond advertising believed in him. And that strengthened his belief in himself.

* * *

The years slipped by. "How's it coming?" one of the lawyers on the deal asked every six months. "Just great," Bernbach responded with enthusiasm.

Ned Doyle kept asking, too, until the day that Bernbach told him, still with enthusiasm, that his editor at the publishing house had informed him that "Mr. Jovanovich was going to handle him personally."

"I figured," said Doyle, after Bernbach's death, "that meant the editor had thrown up his hands. I stopped asking."

The editor wanted what editors always want: revealing anecdotes, fresh insights, a bit of self-revelation—a reader's money's worth. Instead, Bernbach gave him material pulled together by his two secretaries out of his basic stump speech, his guest lectures to business classes, the 3x5" cards on which he noted his thoughts about the art of persuasion, and relevant quotations from others. Theory, ideas. Increasingly familiar to the industry, and without the personal recollections that would bring ideas to vibrant life.

The editor returned the material as unacceptable. Bernbach fell into a slough of despond, made up of his insecurities. The editor asked off the project, but the contract remained in force, and Jovanovich himself stood ready to shepherd a new manuscript from Bernbach.

None came forth.

* * *

Bernbach didn't tell his colleagues about the rejected manuscript. Instead he sounded a positive note—Mr. Jovanovich was going to handle him personally. His transparent face showed how little he would appreciate further questions on how the book was going. Now his colleagues were left with another Bernbach area of sensitivity, another subject on which they had to monitor their words.

Through the '70s, the agency acutely felt the lack of a Bernbach book to attract new business. The whispers of doubt on the management floor grew more agitated.

"Why doesn't he write the bloody book?"

"Did he ever write an ad?"

* * *

Neil Austrian, who solved many of the agency's problems in the '70s by facing them, broke into Bernbach's silence about the book with the suggestion that a writer be hired to help "finish" it.

"It would be terrific for the agency if we could get the book that you've been writing out while you're still actively involved," opened Austrian, proposing a woman author he'd met as a candidate to "help you get this book written."

Austrian: "Bill pulled his glasses down and looked over them at me and said, 'You want *her* to write words in *my* book?' And that ended the discussion. Bill absolutely refused any help. In essence, I was told to stay out of it."

The strange game continued, Bernbach holding on to the promise of "*my* book," and his colleagues pretending to believe he was writing it.

* * *

Bernbach did in time accept help, from a source under his control insofar as terms, division of labor, and implications were concerned. Had he accepted Austrian's offer to put a ghostwriter on the agency payroll, the news would have trickled out. Someone else's words in his book? Unthinkable.

Bernbach's friend Brendan Gill, the *New Yorker* magazine writer, had a happier suggestion. Bernbach didn't need a ghostwriter. He needed someone to help him get his own words on paper. Gill's 28-year-old son Michael could conduct a series of interviews that would evolve into the long-awaited book.

And so a new phase got under way. Michael Gill came often at first. Bernbach's secretaries would transcribe the tapes of each session for the young writer, who hoped to shape them into a book. But as the transcribed interviews piled up, they came to resemble the material rejected by Harcourt, Brace.

The intervals between interviews grew longer. In time and in secret, the new attempt faded out. But true to the pattern found in Bernbach's life, no one—not his sons, not top agency management—could say after his death whether or not Michael Gill was actually writing Bill Bernbach's book. They would check and learn that Michael Gill wasn't. They then renewed his involvement, but the project came to naught.

* * *

Bernbach never stopped believing he would somehow write his book. In the final months of his battle with leukemia, he lunched one day at the Gloucester House, across from the 50th Street entrance to DDB's headquarters, with client Bruce Gelb, entertaining him with anecdotes about the early years of the agency.

"What great stories, Bill," said Gelb. "You should put them on tape."

Replied Bernbach, "Well, I'm including some of them in my book."

* * *

As his illness progressed and pain sometimes kept him from going to the office, Bernbach made plans to work on his book at home. A roll-top desk and files were set up in his United Nations Plaza apartment.

He completed a page of dedication that would eventually become the dedication of "Bill Bernbach's Book," a $50 coffee-table book written by copywriter Bob Levenson and published in 1987 by Villard House, a subsidiary of Random House. (The Bernbach family had returned the Harcourt, Brace advance to regain ownership of the material.)

One paragraph in the dedication stands out as Bernbach, not as an advertising man, but as a citizen of the world.

". . . What happens to society is going to affect us with ever-increasing rapidity. The world has progressed to the point where its most powerful force is public opinion. And I believe that in this new, complex, dynamic world it is not the great book or the epic play, as once was the case, that will shape that opinion, but those who understand the mass media and the techniques of mass persuasion. The metabolism of the world has changed. We [in the communications field] must ally ourselves with great ideas and carry them to the public. We must practice our skills in behalf of society. We must not just believe in what we sell. We must sell what we believe in . . ."

"Bill Bernbach's Book" gives the reader brief histories of the agency's major accounts, "a bit of biography" on Bernbach, and many of Bernbach's best-known aphorisms, sprinkled through the handsome pages of classic Doyle Dane Bernbach ads and commercials.

Its publication put countless noses out of joint among the copywriters and art directors who had worked on the ads, none of which carried the names of their creators. Said one: "Levenson wrote the book exactly the way Bernbach would have done. With no credits."

* * *

"The funny thing," reflected Bob Gage a few years after Bernbach's death, "is that Bill could never write a book. He had a speech. That's what he wrote—the speech."

"The speech," as we shall see later, had a modular format. Parts got added and subtracted as needed over the years. A segment he added in 1978, by which time he knew he had leukemia, and always included thereafter, seems especially poignant against the backdrop of his failed efforts to put himself into a book.

"I came across a prayer in a wonderful book by the eminent poet W. H. Auden called 'A Certain World' in which he collected the pieces that he most enjoyed reading in his life. *He felt that such a book would convey the kind of man he was far more accurately than his autobiography could. For no man, he too understood, could be completely objective about himself.* [Author's emphasis]

"The [Auden] book was divided into different subjects, and in the section on 'prayers' there was this one by St. Augustine: 'Dear Lord, make me chaste and continent, but not just yet.'

"I can't think of a more vivid example of the uphill, if not the impossible, battle that reason and logic have in the final conduct of a man."

Ostensibly, the point of the segment is St. Augustine's plea, which never failed to trigger the laughter of self-recognition among audiences. But what, in fact, do the italicized lines add to the audience's appreciation? Bernbach the editor excised superfluous lines.

Far from being superfluous, those lines, I believe, carried a message from the deepest corners of Bernbach's heart: Autobiographical writing will not be forthcoming from me, friends. But in any case it would not have done the job. You will discover more of the man I was through the kinds of men I admired and read and so often quoted in my speeches: Albert Einstein, Aristotle, John Maynard Keynes, Sir Kenneth Clark, James Watson, biologist Albert Szent-Gyorgyi, philosopher Henry Byerly, sociologist Daniel Bell, Artur Rubinstein, Thelonius Monk. Remember me in that company.

Account Gains and Losses, 1970-71

In: Out:

Avianca   Alka-Seltzer
Boise Cascade   Boise Cascade
Korvettes   Gillette
Lehman Brothers   International Silver
National Liberty Corp.   Lehn & Fink
O.M. Scott   Monsanto (Chemstrand)
Schick Safety Razor   New York Racing Association
Terminix   Occidental Life
United Virginia Bankshares

◆ ◆ ◆

9
New Faces

"We have two requisites for people working at Doyle Dane Bernbach. Number one, they have to be nice people. And number two, they have to have a lot of talent. I'm sorry for the nice guy who doesn't have talent, but that's bad for my business. And I don't give a damn how much talent the son-of-a-bitch has. I don't want him. Life's too short." —Bill Bernbach

As the turbulent '60s came to an end, Doyle Dane Bernbach found itself, for the first time in its celebrated young life, losing more business than it was gaining. The agency had been perfect for the unruly, energy-releasing, do-your-own-thing '60s. A corporate flower child, defying convention with love and an open heart, the agency shrugged off encrustations of The Way Things Were Always Done.

Not that the agency worked to shape itself to the anti-establishment times. More likely its engaging counter-culture messages ("Think small," "We're only number 2," "You don't have to be Jewish") gave impetus to the tradition-breaking '60s. Doyle Dane Bernbach was '60s back in the stiff-necked '50s. Ahead of its time, its work dominated the advertising of the '60s.

What corporate attitude could better have suited the Age of Aquarius than Bernbach's exhortation to "do it different" and his belief that "rules are meant to be broken? (Too often forgotten was his admonition, "never do so at the expense of selling.") But where once Doyle Dane Bernbach was the only agency that knew "how to do it," other shops now were at least trying.

The stunning success of DDB's campaigns (imagine the glow of a Volkswagen or Polaroid or Avis client, at board meetings and cocktail parties!) forced mainstream agencies to strengthen their own creative line-ups, often with pirated DDBers, as valued old clients requested a "DDB look" for their ads.

Creative talent was in demand everywhere. New agencies sprang up, some headed by DDB alumni, Bernbach's children, showing they could cross the street by themselves. Bernbach, deeply disturbed by defections, repeatedly made the point that a DDB writer or art director is not a DDB writer or art director at another agency. A transplanted flower does not grow the same way in different soil. (See chapter, "The Basic Stump Speech.") To be sure, Doyle Dane Bernbach remained the cynosure, the mother church, the seat of the founder of creativity as religion, the best place to work. But no longer the only place to get good work.

Management hadn't quite taken that in. Nor did they grasp the import of the backlash that was gathering force in a nation tired of revolution, tired of hairy young people, tired of older people who didn't make them behave. Or a business world tired of equating "no rules" with "liberating," ready to respond to parameters (whatever *that* meant), to every kind of copy testing, to any set of catchy rules ("24 ways to improve whatever").

The times they were a'changing, but Doyle Dane Bernbach was not.

* * *

Then-creative director Bob Levenson recalled it as a time for the agency when "strange was good."

A commercial for Thom McAn shoes featured a young man locked in his bedroom, stroking a shoe, a slightly-demented expression on his face. His mother, peering through the keyhole, shouts, "Irving, are you in there with the shoes again?"

An Alka-Seltzer commercial set in a cafeteria centered on an apparent psychotic whose wild-eyed presence disturbs the digestive system of another customer, not to mention that of the viewer.

Black-clad, barefoot peasant women swarm on a middle-east desert in a Lever Brothers commercial, chanting exaltations of idolatrous gratitude to a giant box of detergent, whose short-lived name was Hero.

A Volkswagen bus sits, inexplicably, in the living room of Mr. Average Guy. We know he's Mr. A. G. by the way he slurps his soup. The doorbell rings. An elderly couple, strangers to Mr. A. G., tell him they've come from "such a long way" to see the bus. He admits them, and the camera follows on a tour of the vehicle's interior.

"There was a sort of 'Don't worry, all you creative lunatics, you just keep doing what you're doing, and we'll take care of the account guys, we'll take care of the clients. You just be as bananas as you can possibly be,'" Levenson recounted. "And it raised a generation of people who, because we buffered them from some ugly day-to-day realities, weren't accustomed to them when they had to face them."

In fact, not facing ugly day-to-day realities was a way of life at the very top at the agency.

Ned Doyle told a story that supported his own casual attitude towards complaints about the agency's shortcomings:

"One day Bill Howard, advertising director of Macy's, arrived late for lunch with a few of us. 'Sorry,' he said, deadpan, 'but Macy's won't open tomorrow.' He waited for our shock, then broke into a grin. 'If everything I heard this morning is true, Macy's can't possibly open tomorrow.'" Of course Macy's opened the next day, and as far as Doyle was concerned, so would Doyle Dane Bernbach. Thriving businesses have a momentum of their own. If one stopped to analyze and try to fix things, one might disturb the vapors that in some mysterious way created the magic.

Why tamper? The good news had always outweighed the bad news. A dip in the new business chart would soon right itself and point back in its historic direction—up. After all, the decade was ending with two of the agency's Alka-Seltzer commercials, "Bride's first meal" and "Mama Magadini," the undisputed favorites of the year. Their punch lines, "Poached oysters?" and "Mama Mia, that's-a some spicy meatball!" became part of the language.

So what if creative teams, in their eagerness to achieve similar smashes, sometimes landed in the swamp of "strange is good"? They weren't faulted for trying. The only sin at Doyle Dane Bernbach was playing it safe.

* * *

Strange people began turning up on the agency payroll. Seat-of-the-pants hiring judgments were presented as *faits accompli* to DDB's thoroughly professional, increasingly frustrated, personnel department.

A man named Dmitri arrived with some fanfare to head a special creative service. He claimed kinship with the Russian nobility, his family having been driven out by the bolsheviks, he said, "from St. Petersburg, the former name for Moscow." Didn't he mean Leningrad? Dmitri waved off the query. His work performance wasn't much better than his Russian history, and Dmitri soon vanished.

A young man called Kevin was hired to set up a music operation in the creative department. He was, a dozen wide-eyed staffers told me, the composer of two current pop hits—"Jean," the theme song for "The Prime of Miss Jean Brodie," and "Flying on a Jet Plane," Peter, Paul and Mary's top-ten record. The Uniroyal account group, mightily impressed, had commissioned Kevin to compose music for a commercial.

Whoa! I knew enough about music royalties, from having written lyrics for children's recordings, to have an idea of the money that would roll in to the composer of two pop hits. Kevin looked too seedy to be rolling in royalties. I walked across Fifth Avenue to Record World and checked the credits on "Kevin's songs." "Jean," it turned out, was written by Rod McKuen, and "Jet

Plane" by John Denver. Hearing this, the agency's general manager shrugged, "But maybe he has talent." The agency's lawyer, on the other hand, shouted, "Get him out of here, and tear up his Uniroyal music! How could we ever believe he composed it?" Kevin left quietly.

Dmitri and Kevin are worth mentioning only as egregious examples of the careless way the creative department was hiring in the '70s. Hiring mistakes happen everywhere. It's almost impossible to determine how much job-seeking writers, art directors or TV producers actually contributed to the portfolios of their ads and commercial reels. But total credulity about claims that *are* checkable bespeaks sloppiness or hubris. In the case of Kevin, a messy lawsuit against Uniroyal and other clients he "composed music" for, might have resulted.

Few DDBers remember Dmitri or Kevin. Many would remember the strange new faces brought in by top management. For these, in time, would erode the confidence of the troops in their leaders, damage the agency's image, and lead to payroll cuts that hurt the innocent.

* * *

To head a languishing subsidiary, Joe Daly made a seat-of-the-pants offer to Arvin Spelvin (not his real name), after hearing him spoken well of by former McCall's editor Herbert Mayes.

Enter Spelvin, short and demanding, spouting orders for expensive office equipment and furnishings. That seemed rather cheeky in a place known for its plain, pipe-rack, shirtsleeve environment. Soon enough word spread that Spelvin was "a bit of a kook." Well, many creative people are, thought Dick Kane, the agency's personnel director.

"Being a bit of a kook," said Kane, years after the episode, "doesn't necessarily mean he's not good for the agency, but it's kind of a red flag for somebody in my position." He called a trustworthy contact at Spelvin's former agency—one of the oldest, largest and most respected on Madison Avenue.

Kane: "I got an earful. They were ready to send him to prison. One of the worst people. Kickbacks, everything. They'd found out one day and fired him. And we picked him up."

On hearing the bill of particulars, Daly withdrew his support. Exit Spelvin. His memory, however, survived, as Exhibit A in juicy agency gossip about management's weird personnel decisions.

* * *

Far more puzzling was the sudden appearance early in 1970 of a tall, heavy-set, perspiring stranger we'll call (for the sake of his survivors) Edward J. Sewell. Daly had hired him, without a word to Personnel, as senior vice president in charge of acquisitions, a slot for which Personnel was vetting highly-placed candidates.

Sewell had two items on his agenda on the first day of his employment. One brought him to my office—a press announcement. On paper, his credentials looked strong. Twenty years with a Wall Street banking firm, the last eight as president. Board member for a number of prominent companies.

So why was this man sweating? And why did he keep harping on his wife's social connections in Washington, D.C.? He showed no interest in how or whether the *New York Times* or the *Wall Street Journal* would play the release—only in what the *Washington Post* would do with it. An extraordinary priority, given his career to date and his mission for the agency. Something was awfully askew here.

His second concern brought him to Dick Kane, via Mac Dane, who alerted him that Sewell was "very interested in our medical coverage."

Kane: "Mind you, I expected a superstar. We'd been looking for a top level person for that job. Someone with the qualifications to become president of the agency. He walks into my office and I could see he was frightened to death. I shook his hand. It was like sticking your hand in dishwater, it was so wet and so limp. I really thought he was ill."

Sewell would talk about nothing but medical coverage. When they finished, Kane called the Wall Street banking firm that had employed Sewell for 20 years. The head personnel officer told Kane that Sewell had been out of the bank for a year. He refused to tell Kane why Sewell left. Kane determined that no one from Doyle Dane Bernbach had bothered to run even the most cursory check on Sewell.

"How the hell did we hire this guy?" a senior vice president griped to Kane a few weeks later.

"Your guess is as good as mine," shrugged Kane.

"I was on a plane with him," the senior VP related, "and he broke out in a nervous sweat and went absolutely crazy because he was expected to open some doors to somebody we wanted to do business with. I told Daly to get this guy out of here before he ruins us."

Sewell did not venture forth again on behalf of the agency. He sat in an office on the management floor, his door tightly shut, counting off the days until the end of his year's employment contract, protected by medical benefits.

The phrase "nervous breakdown" attached itself to the Sewell episode. Since no one ever knew him, the words were spoken, not in sympathy for the man, but rather to bolster the bizzareness of Exhibit B.

* * *

Skipping slightly out of sequence, I recall the arrival, in December 1971, of a sniffish man, slender and tight and patrician in elegantly-tailored three-piece suits of European origin. He peers through his spectacles as a Prussian would through a monocle, with a disdainful air. Perhaps he is looking down his nose at the raffish environment of the agency. The art director with uncombed blond curls cascading over his Mickey Mouse T-shirt. The circulating, bra-less secretary in the city's shortest hot pants. The aging TV producer sporting Indian beads and cowboy boots, discussing the sexual proclivities of auditioning actresses. The sea of beads and jeans and gold chains and Abercrombie & Fitch fishing bags. Oh, lost, and by the wind-grieved shore!

Here, to help Doyle Dane Bernbach reap new business, is Oscar Lubow, a person of renown in the industry. A former principal in weighty research firms—Daniel Starch & Staff, C. E. Hooper Inc., The Public Pulse Worldwide Inc. One-time head of business development for Young & Rubicam. A man trailing advanced education degrees and military honors.

Lubow is Bernbach's idea. Daly has no choice but to go along, for the agency's new business record is deteriorating scarily under his presidency, and Bernbach's wind is up.

Bernbach allows Lubow the title of Assistant to the Chairman, himself being chairman. What Bernbach will not allow, in his concern about image, is a peep about new business activities. He wants no rip in the industry vision of Doyle Dane Bernbach beating off advertisers clamoring for admission.

So Bernbach comes up with positioning Lubow in two primary roles: "government relations in the U.S. and abroad," and "forward planning of agency structure and services, both here and abroad."

"Who's our guy in backward planning?" I ask Daly when I'm alone with him in his office.

"You just organize the press conference," he growls.

"Not I," I state, surprising myself with my cool, this being my first face-off with Daly. (I reported to Mac Dane until he retired in November 1971.) "Lubow's here for new business. If we make fools of the press, they won't forgive us."

Daly stares at me. He has, I realize, never until this moment considered that a company spokesperson might resist a management decision. I also realize that this is a man used to getting his way, a man who believes in selling above all, truth being subjective in any case. I figure ours will be a short-lived relationship, but I don't blink. Finally, Daly pulls himself out of his chair and disappears into Bernbach's office. Long minutes later, he returns.

"Okay, forget the press conference. Just put out the release."

The release is only marginally less awful than a press conference. But I am stunned at having won any part of this battle, and I give in to the rest. I put out what Bernbach wants said, in quotes attributed to him. I feel I have just lost my professional virginity. I also sense that I have passed a test of sorts with Daly. In the years ahead, I will win some and lose some, but Daly will never fail to listen.

When the Lubow news hits the street, phone calls pour in to Ned Doyle and others, the general import being that Doyle Dane Bernbach should expect from Lubow large expenditures and minimal results. Doyle chides Daly on the hiring. Daly repeats Lubow's claim to have brought in $80 million in new business for Young & Rubicam. Doyle shrugs and bets Daly that Lubow won't bring in a single piece of new business in the year ahead. Daly doesn't see how he can lose. He takes Doyle's bet.

* * *

What followed was a comic opera. Lubow traveled the country in first class, issuing weekly "Summaries" on a new agency form emblazoned "CONFIDENTIAL—REPORT OF NEW BUSINESS CONFERENCE—CONFIDENTIAL." Down the left-hand margin, in splendid cloak-and-dagger style, ran the warning words, "PLEASE READ AND DESTROY." Each "summary" was a list—of corporate executives and their companies.

"Had Oscar contacted these people, was he planning to—or what?" scribbled Ted Factor, the puckish head of DDB's profitable and prestigious Los Angeles office, member of the agency's powerful executive committee, confidante of Bernbach, and newly-elected "Western Advertising Man of the Year."

If Factor asked the question mischievously at first (he'd had calls about Lubow's hiring too), the tone changed to panic when a Lubow "summary" came out listing six important prospects in Factor's own territory: Bank of America, Dole, Del Monte, Castle & Cooke, Levi-Strauss, and Sunsweet Growers. Lubow didn't respond to Factor's urgent queries about what, if any, contacts had actually taken place. Factor called Daly.

"Do you know how foolish and disorganized his do-it-yourself operation could make us look? Like the right hand doesn't know what the left hand is doing. . . ."

Factor to Daly, in a confidential memo: ". . . I will need information on calls made in the West, so that future contacts will be conducted in such a way that the right hand of DDB will seem to know what the left hand is doing. . . ."

Daly memo to management supervisors and domestic office heads on new business procedures: "We all recognize that it is increasingly important to coordinate our total contact with new business prospects so that the left hand of DDB knows what the right hand is doing. . . ."

Left hand and right remained uncoordinated. Factor never learned what Lubow was doing in his territory, or anywhere else.

* * *

Agency gossip had by now picked up on some of the unusual expenditures of the "forward planner." Since a new business department had never been needed in the past, minds were boggled by Lubow's ordering of hundreds of reels of agency commercials. What did he do with them?

Ted Factor found an answer on his desk one morning. A DDB-L.A. account man had received a letter from an old friend, an executive of a large California company. Gleefully, while shedding written crocodile tears, Factor forwarded the letter to Daly.

"Please tell your new business bloodhounds to lay off," the writer began unceremoniously. "Our account is not up for grabs. If and when it ever is, I will tell you . . . Quite frankly . . . your New York office's overture to R— would be laughable if it weren't so pathetic. First, he received a can of film in the mail. No advance warning that it was coming. Nothing to explain what it was. Or what to do with it. It just appeared—and so became an imposition.

"Others, of course, reviewed the film and found it was a selection of DDB's spots. The only trouble was that the reviewers were so ticked off at the imposition on their time, plus the ham-handed, mysterious method of delivery, that even if the stuff had been exceptional, they'd have played hell liking it. . . . [Two weeks later] R— got a note from one Oscar B. Lubow which announced that he was to receive a complimentary copy of a drug study done for Governor Rockefeller a couple of years ago. How nice. Just what the hell is he supposed to do with that? How is it relevant to peddling our product? DDB? Oscar Lubow? Governor Rockefeller?

"R—'s comments on that letter will remain privileged. But I assure you they were pertinent. As I say, do yourself a favor: tell 'em to lay off. . . ."

Daly promised Factor he would "shoot Oscar down."

* * *

Doyle watched the calendar run out on Lubow's first year at the agency. Not a single piece of 1972's new business could be traced to his activities. Doyle never stopped reminding Daly of their bet. If Daly lost, the chiding would go on forever.

Daly called in Lubow, who had remained un-shot down, and pressed him for something, anything, in the way of new business. Lubow then brought forth a minnow. The Bank of the Commonwealth, a Detroit bank, would happily name Doyle Dane Bernbach as its agency. But its billings were below the agency's minimum. And servicing a small Detroit account from New York could only cost the agency money.

So? This wasn't about profitability; this was about ego.

On December 18, Doyle Dane Bernbach announced a new account,

Detroit's Bank of the Commonwealth. Daly collected his $100 from Doyle. Doyle knew he'd been snookered. He didn't care about the $100, but he did care about what the new account said about the state of the agency's new business efforts. The incident added to Doyle's growing perception that Daly wasn't the leader Doyle Dane Bernbach needed.

* * *

Daly kept getting "all kinds of hollers about Oscar from all around." When Lubow's contract ran out, he "resigned to pursue other business interests." Daly's staff memo said Lubow had "completed his assignment." Management was "pleased that he will continue to be available to DDB for consultation in the months ahead."

The troops shook their heads and wondered, as did Factor, about "the cost, both in dollars and *esprit*."

* * *

Of far greater financial consequence was the impulsive hiring, late in 1970, of Ross MacLennan as successor-in-residence to Maxwell Dane.

"When we hire someone for the mailroom," personnel head Dick Kane wearily told Dane on learning the news, "we do a more thorough job of searching out, and referencing, than with this person who could well be the next president of the agency."

"I know," said Dane, "but Daly wants him."

The agency had, in fact, commissioned the prestigious management consulting firm of Booz, Allen & Hamilton to do a top-level search for Dane's successor. But Daly had jumped to hire MacLennan on reading in the morning *New York Times* that he was leaving Ted Bates after 20 years because he'd lost out on the presidency. Booz, Allen rolled its corporate eyes, filed its carefully-screened candidate list, and collected its $50,000 fee.

MacLennan's experience at Bates covered finance, international, and acquisitions. What better could Booz, Allen find? MacLennan even *looked* good, apart from teeth that didn't quite seem to fit his mouth. A kind of middle-age, heavying-up Clark Kent. Pleasant, mannerly, unflappable . . . a gentleman. Certainly nice, and maybe even talented.

But different, too. He decreed the removal of the agency's client list from the quarterly report to stockholders. "I don't want Wall Street to think of Doyle Dane Bernbach as an advertising agency," he said, as though that made perfect sense.

He was breathtakingly honest about his conviction that "one had to use people and organizations for one's personal ends." His own goal, he told a colleague, was to amass $4 million by a date certain.

He came up with ideas for management compensation that had never been imagined. One inventive proposal would have had the agency pay college tuition for children of key executives. (A big thumbs down from Internal Revenue on that one.)

He could be disarmingly, and fatally, casual on business decisions. Thus, he rejected the need for a CPA audit before buying an Oklahoma group of double discount stores, Trade Mart, later described as "garbage on shelves." Said MacLennan, "If you can't trust a person you're doing business with, you shouldn't be doing business with them."

MacLennan's trust ranged far and wide; important acquisitions received little or no supervision. (See chapter titled "William and Mary.") This, as time went by, would prove disastrous to the agency, resulting in the loss of millions of dollars, which led to the loss of many jobs.

When at last MacLennan "resigned" from Doyle Dane Bernbach, with generous and grossly undeserved severance pay, he joined the actuarial firm he'd given the agency's pension business to. Perhaps in gratitude, the firm gave him the title of president, a good salary, and all the time he wanted to manage his international real-estate holdings.

Joe Daly thanked MacLennan in a staff memo "for his wholehearted commitment to DDB during his years with us."

DDBers who knew the real story gagged.

♦ ♦ ♦

10
Family Interlude

"For creative people, rules can be prisons"—Bill Bernbach

Spring of 1972 brought forth a new honor for Bernbach and his agency. A full-scale retrospective of Doyle Dane Bernbach's work, sponsored by the Parsons School of Design, opened in the Time-Life Exhibition Center, the first time that one agency's work had been the subject of an art show in New York. Large blow-ups of Bernbach aphorisms were juxtaposed dramatically with austerely-mounted ads, the whole radiating importance and beauty.

Bernbach himself received Parsons' Diamond Jubilee award "for his creative contributions to the graphics communications industry and for his influence on the development of so many outstanding talents in the industry."

All through the preparations and to-do related to the tribute, Bernbach seemed distracted, fidgety. Something other than business problems was bothering him.

* * *

More important to Bernbach than any tribute was a family event that took place in the spring of '72. John, Bernbach's 28-year-old son, spirited his two children from the Park Avenue apartment of his wife Robin, flew them to France, and refused to bring them back to her.

The aftermath unfolded in sensational coverage in the *New York Post.*

Robin tried to get the children back. She sued John for divorce, charging adultery. John sued Robin for divorce, charging adultery. French private detectives, hired by Robin, testified that John had spent overnights in a Paris apartment with Jane Bush, co-respondent in Robin's suit. Jane, British and beautiful, was the divorced wife of a former friend of the young Bernbachs, and mother of two children.

To substantiate his charges of Robin's adultery, John's lawyer called a young clothing store executive who told the court about a night he'd spent with Robin. He also said, according to the *New York Post*, that he and John were currently getting along "very well, and we're considering going into business together." The judge concluded that his testimony was "unworthy of belief," and Robin won her suit.

None of this, at the time, appeared to have anything to do with John's father's advertising agency.

But it turned out to have everything to do with John's going onto the payroll of Doyle Dane Bernbach's Paris office. He'd been there for four months before Joe Daly heard about it.

* * *

Among the observations that Bill Bernbach wrote onto his 3x5" file cards was this: "What makes a man successful—single-mindedness, an energy, an ego that makes him dominate—is so often the very thing that makes for a tragic relationship with his own family, especially a son brought into the business."

I came upon the card after Bernbach's death, when, working part-time at the agency, I was putting together a booklet titled "Bill Bernbach said . . . ." I could find no reference to the card's origin, nor any trace of its use in Bernbach's speeches or articles. Yet he kept it until the end, and the cards that he kept were those that had resonance for him.

The possibility is that Bernbach, in writing down those words, was thinking of some of his old clients—colorful, strong-willed entrepreneurs from the old country, whose sons never had the same gut feeling for advertising as had their fathers. It may never have occurred to him that John's unexpected emergence within Doyle Dane Bernbach struck others with similar force. Bernbach had that capacity: to exempt himself from an unpleasant concept, or from a policy that no longer suited pressing problems.

"To take care of one's own." How often Bernbach referred to this basic, unchanging instinct, this "obsessive drive."

So there was John, fled to Paris, living with the divorced wife of his old friend, trying to keep his children out of reach of the United States domestic law. But the French government limited foreigners to visits of four months, unless they could prove they had "good reason to remain." What better reason than a job?

John needed help.

Bernbach considered the agency policy against nepotism. He remembered his own father's refusal to help him, because of the "shame" of his intermarriage. How did that shame compare with the embarrassment of lurid headlines in the *New York Post*? He could wish they'd never happened, but they wouldn't alter his feelings about his son. Without family loyalty, the world would spin out of control. John loved Jane. John loved and wanted his children. Bernbach's own grandchildren! What good was an agency policy (*his* agency) that stood in the way of his family's well-being?

And so Bernbach scrapped the rule, picked up the phone, and called the head of the Paris office. John went onto the payroll. Bernbach neglected to mention his action to his colleagues in top management.

* * *

Doyle Dane Bernbach's founders staunchly believed in the policy of no nepotism. Their sons—Bernbach's two, Doyle's two, Dane's one—grew up understanding that they could not expect to find jobs, even summer jobs, at the agency.

"We always knew that we couldn't go into Doyle Dane Bernbach," Paul Bernbach recalled many years later, when his brother had risen to president of the mega-merged DDB Needham Worldwide. Paul, who went into law and real estate, had never considered advertising as a profession. "I suspect that on an unconscious level I would not have wanted to expose myself to comparisons with my father," he reflected.

Not so John, who clearly reveled in being a Bernbach in the European offices of Doyle Dane Bernbach. Watching him in action during international meetings, high-level agency people soon dubbed John "the playboy of the Western world."

"You'd go to a meeting, all the general managers," recalled one. "John would be there. He was sort of a secretary—he'd take notes. At the end of the meeting, everybody would have something to do, to follow up on. Everyone except John. John would say, I can't do that because I've got to have lunch with somebody in Paris, or in Rome tomorrow, and dinner in Athens the night after that, and then I'm going to Cannes. It began to rub people a bit."

John tooling around Europe in his Ferrari, John at Orly airport with a deck of Concorde tickets in his jacket, John never still long enough to return phone calls—the portrait built.

* * *

Inevitably, word of John's hiring reached *Advertising Age*. What made the report interesting to Don Grant, the reporter who covered the agency, was DDB's widely-known and esteemed anti-nepotism policy.

Grant called me, and I called Bernbach, to work out some "language" to respond in the most favorable possible way. Instead, Bernbach said firmly that he would telephone Grant and talk to him "to try to keep the story out" of the publication.

The story stayed out. Years went by before John's name finally appeared in the trade press, and by then he'd been with the agency for so long that reporters simply shrugged and ran the news of his promotion in Europe without comment.

I never learned what Bernbach said to Grant to keep the story out. But Grant, and *Advertising Age,* were responsive to the argument that personal news didn't belong in the trade press. Perhaps Bernbach convinced Grant that John would remain on the payroll only until the lawsuits were resolved. Perhaps Bernbach actually intended to go that route when he chose to ignore years of agency policy and take care of his own.

* * *

John married Jane. The court gave Robin custody of the children—though when they grew up, they favored spending time with John and Jane. John took on new responsibilities at the agency. He worked to live down the playboy image. When he met the agency's new worldwide management team in 1974, he offered to resign, realizing that the situation was "delicate."

"If my presence is an embarrassment to you, I'll get out," he volunteered. His offer was not accepted, unsurprisingly. The new managers would hardly have wanted to start their reign by letting the owner's son go.

In the years that followed, John's role in Europe grew in importance and effectiveness. Reports of John's accomplishments muted some of the grumbling back in New York. Not all. Doyle and Dane had no interest in agency slots for their sons, but found it nonetheless galling that Bernbach should sweep aside long-standing principles to rescue his high-living son.

Well, didn't Bernbach always say that rules are meant to be broken?

Account Gains and Losses, 1972-73

In:	Out:
Avis Rent a Car	British Tourist Association
Bank of the Commonwealth	Cool-Ray
Celanese	Cracker Jack
Hammond Organ	Kitchens of Sara Lee
Madison Labs	Korvettes
Ponderosa System	Lees Carpets
Procter & Gamble	Lever Brothers
Ralston Purina	National Liberty Corp.
Tropicana	Transamerica
	Warner Lambert
	Whirlpool

♦ ♦ ♦

11
The Revolting Creatives

"The time to stop a revolution is at the beginning, not at the end."
—Adlai Stevenson

"The second creative revolution," a wag called the uprising of November 15, 1972. It was an event soon forgotten, worth recalling chiefly as a reminder of how different Doyle Dane Bernbach was from all other advertising agencies.

Just a week earlier, Richard Nixon had won his second term as President of the United States in a crushing landslide that seemed to bury America's tolerance for youthful rebellion. That didn't upset DDB's hairy young creatives nearly as much as the news, on the morning of the 15th, that creative stars Roy Grace and Evan Stark were leaving to become partners in a small, existing agency of little consequence.

Work stopped cold. Copywriters and art directors gathered in small groups in hallways, offices, screening rooms. Roy and Evan now! They ticked off the names of creatives who had previously left—lured by the glamour (and higher salaries) at Wells, Rich, Greene; by the potential of power (and higher salaries) at mainstream agencies; by the ego satisfaction (and higher salaries) of joining smaller agencies as name partners. Once upon a time, DDB creatives routinely rejected offers of more money to remain at Camelot. Was it still Camelot?

Ah, that was the real question. The gathered groups swapped perceptions of leaks and cracks that could bring down the walls of this legendary place. The agitation level rose with every hour. A bad time for department head Bob Levenson to be in London on business.

Unhappy workers in every company huddle and gossip. But they do it out of management's sight. At Doyle Dane Bernbach, the creatives flocked to a "town meeting," called by an anonymous memo, right there in the company cafeteria, at 4 o'clock in the afternoon.

What did they think an advertising agency was, anyhow? Athens in Fifth Century BC? The Berkeley campus?

* * *

In his 26th floor office, Bill Bernbach, a copy of the anonymous memo in hand, placed a transatlantic call to Levenson.

"You'd better come back here and look after your department," warned Bernbach in icy tones, "because you've got trouble."

How to deal with the unruly event? The natural response of a company leader would presumably be to turn up at the meeting, take questions, offer reassurance—especially in the absence of the department head. Bernbach, doing that, would have disarmed them at once. He knew well how they worked for his approbation. He'd clipped a comic strip in which the hero, Pogo, expresses what Bernbach did every day of the year: "They come in and I give them a pat on the head and they go out happy."

But that was one team at a time. Master and disciples. Guru and acolytes. Father and sons. Long ago, he'd walked the halls and popped into creative offices, shepherding works in progress. As the agency grew, he'd withdrawn into his office, still guiding much of the work, but now the acolytes made the pilgrimage to his sanctum. They'd slip into the black leather armchairs around his circular wooden table. Five chairs were alike. The sixth had a higher, throne-like back. That was Bernbach's.

With his keen visual sense, Bernbach had found furniture that symbolized a perfect combination of authority and Camelot. Here he felt in control. For all his fame and honors, he never grew comfortable speaking to large groups, even of his own people. Even in good times.

And now, the creative department was going off half cocked. If Bernbach felt betrayed when one of his "children" abandoned him for another agency, what did he feel on learning of this mass disturbance?

He could not bring himself to acknowledge the appalling event, to validate it by his presence. This was Levenson's department, Levenson's responsibility, Levenson's problem. Bernbach remained in his office, brooding.

* * *

The 19th floor Eatery, a place with all the ambiance of an Iron Curtain country cafeteria, filled up with sober-faced creatives. In typical DDB style, the doors remained open and employees from other departments wandered in and out, buying coffee and snacks, wondering what the hell was going on, some staying to find out, since no one was in charge to ask them to leave.

That ensured agency-wide dissemination of whatever was said at the meeting.

Perhaps nothing would be said. With no one in charge, no one rises to open the meeting. It's one thing to bitch about the agency in halls and offices; quite another to stand up and be counted by the great old art directors and undoubted Bernbach loyalists, Bob Gage and Helmut Krone.

An embarrassed silence. Finally, a sensible and talented young copywriter, Jane Talcott, stands up. It is time, she says, to ask why so many creatives are leaving, to see if something can be done to stop the outflow. This is the occasion to speak up.

Others then rise, in each case preceding their gripes with ameliorating words: "This kind of meeting could only happen at Doyle Dane Bernbach; if things went badly at J. Walter Thompson, no one would care enough to call a meeting. But. . . ."

Or: "I love Doyle Dane Bernbach, I want to stay. I *want* to want to stay, but. . . ."

But things weren't like the old days. Good work was being done. But not as good as formerly. Maybe because management was running scared, and account men looked for "safe" ads to sell to balky clients.

"Maybe I myself haven't produced brave new concepts worth fighting for," concedes a young art director, with a watchful eye on Gage and Krone, "but the general atmosphere discourages me from trying. Management doesn't seem as willing as in the old days to fight."

And where was the famous old sense of excitement. the shouting in the halls to come see an incredible new ad? Where the helpfulness and encouragement of the old days, the chances to learn from the agency greats?

Someone asks Bob Gage what he thinks. Gage lumbers up and in his slow baritone, socks it to them. He'd come to listen and perhaps to help. But having heard them out, he thinks the real problem is that they aren't working hard enough. They aren't producing advertising that measures up to Doyle Dane Bernbach standards.

Krone follows him up. "I'll tell you what I think. It's hard for me to say this, but I think the trouble with Doyle Dane Bernbach is its creative department. You're all coddled. When did anyone ever come downstairs and blame you when we lose an account? You're not the ones who are on the line, it's the account men. At least once a week, an account man will say to me, 'Helmut, I need your help.' And I know what he needs. He's not getting good enough ads from his creative team.

"I'd like to dispel the myth of 'the old days.' The old days were tough. There were lousy clients, like Max Factor, and ads that were due tomorrow and a client who didn't know what a good ad was. But we worked. And we did great ads in spite of the client. Nobody around here is trying to do a new page. I . . . I can't go on. This has me too upset."

Now the young rebels wilt, chastised by the old giants. The meeting breaks up; what else is there to say in an open meeting? Back in their smaller huddles, they try to assess the possible effects of the "town meeting." What would Gage and Krone tell Bernbach? Presumably, they'd tell him the same things they'd said at the meeting. That the real problem was the creatives not doing good enough work.

That was about the last thing the anxious copywriters and art directors had expected to come out of their brief rebellion.

* * *

"There is no fire, Bob," Krone reassured Levenson by telephone the next morning. "There's no reason for you to fly back. Believe me, it was not that kind of meeting."

I'd come to Krone's office to suggest an article that would further the process of dispelling the myth of "the old days." It might be done for a trade magazine, or at the very least for the agency's in-house publication.

"Excellent idea," agreed Krone.

"I'll need some other examples, not just Max Factor."

Krone thought a long moment. Then: "But I used the only example I had."

The myth of "the old days" remained un-dispelled.

* * *

"Helmut is full of shit," said Bert Steinhauser, another of the agency's top-of-the-line old art directors. "This place *has* changed. They've all sold their souls."

* * *

I needed some words about the meeting, in case the press called. Bernbach, his voice tight with anger, said to check back later; he wanted to hear from Bob Gage first. An hour later, the anger had vanished, replaced by a benign calm and Buddha-like smile. Bernbach distilled for me an official bottom line on the uprising.

"It was a good meeting, it wasn't a bad meeting. It was low key. The fact that Evan and Roy are leaving is just another indication that other agencies come to us when they're looking for talent. That says a lot for us. They always have and they always will. That's all right. We've always grown our own and we've got plenty more that we're growing right now. . . ."

The words proved unnecessary. The trade press was too busy covering the hard news of Grace and Stark departing to chase after soft rumors of a more general malaise.

* * *

What had Gage said to bring about such a remarkable turnaround in Bernbach's attitude towards the meeting? By happenstance, Gage and I arrived early for an awards luncheon at the Plaza, and we sat at the agency table, talking about the "town meeting."

"The subtext of that meeting," said Gage, "the unspoken underlying complaint, was that some creative people have been teamed with mediocrities. And they're worried that they are considered mediocrities by extension. The agency hasn't weeded out mediocre people. That's the real problem. The mediocre people have to be cleared out."

That was the subtext? Well, Gage would grasp underlying complaints that would fly right past me. But I could see how Bernbach's agitation had been calmed. Now he could write off the uprising as the work of mediocre people, hired in the scramble for talent during the wild growth years of the late '60s, not good enough to be called Doyle Dane Bernbach creatives. Not his children at all. This was Levenson's problem. Levenson was added to the list of people who had let Bernbach down.

* * *

Behind closed doors, an agency old-timer sat me down and offered a different subtext to the Eatery meeting.

"Nothing's happening here. A president is supposed to bring in new business. That's really what all the problems are about. When you don't have new business, people can't move up, and when they can't move up, they become discontented. In fact, business has been going out, so the work has shriveled. That means the top creative people stay on the remaining accounts; the people below have less and less to do.

"We need a new president."

In time, there would be a new president—and four more after him, all in a period of eight and a half years.

* * *

Bob Levenson returned from Europe and called the creatives back to the Eatery for a follow-up meeting. He spoke to their fears that "all the good people are leaving."

"Good people have been leaving for years. Where do you want to start? George Lois and Julian Koenig. Mary Wells. Paula Greene. Ron Rosenfeld. Len Sirowitz. Sid Myers. Helmut Krone [who had left and since returned] And those are only the ones who started their own agencies! . . .

"Now look at what those who left accomplished. Except for Mary and maybe George at his best, the accomplishments were really minimal. And I'll say this with Helmut right in this room: the best of Krone at DDB was, and is, a lot better than the best of Krone at Case & Krone. There's something in the air here. Paula, Ron, Len were all better here. . . ."

Doyle Dane Bernbach was still the best place. Talk to some of the people who'd left for other agencies, and they'll tell you the same thing.

Some things needed improving. A new creative management supervisory system would help get good work through. "And I assure you that we are starting to be a lot less patient with mediocrity."

Creatives who felt they weren't getting enough work should "put together all the stuff you're proud of, whether it got produced or not. So we will know you better and know your work better and we'll know your ability to do great work better.

"This is not a vindictive thing. It is not a purge, or punitive, or anything of the kind. It's something we probably should have been doing all along." (The insecure suddenly felt more insecure.)

Levenson wound up with promises of higher salaries, which "I must tell you, were in the works before your spontaneous, impromptu meeting."

"Yeah, sure," muttered more than one skeptic.

* * *

The creatives had risen to cry "something's going wrong," and the response had been, "if so, it's the creatives."

"Do great work, and the business will come," Bernbach often said.

Doyle Dane Bernbach still won the most awards, still had the reputation as the top creative agency. The stars who had never left—Gage, Phyllis Robinson, David Reider, Jack Dillon, Bill Taubin—and many of the bright young talents still turned out superior work. Yet new business wasn't coming, and old business was leaving.

And agencies that did consistently mediocre work often kept clients forever.

More than weeding creatives needed doing in Doyle Dane Bernbach's garden.

◆ ◆ ◆

12
The Basic Stump Speech

"The most freshly sculptured phrase will eventually become a cliche."
—Bill Bernbach

It became known as "The Speech." *New York Times* columnist Philip Dougherty, covering an industry conference with Bernbach on the program, would archly ask, "Is he giving Speech One or Speech Two today?"

Trade reporters eventually stopped calling for advance copies of Bernbach speeches. They learned that none was ever available. When they attended and took notes, they realized that the material was familiar; whole segments were repeats from earlier speeches.

To Bernbach's closest associates, his speeches became another puzzlement, another area of sensitivity, another source of discontent. Joe Daly remembered it as "always the same speech, and to this day I don't understand why he always read it. Because he knew it by heart. I always wondered why. I guess he didn't have enough confidence."

Daly never asked Bernbach why. Like so much else in the upper reaches of the agency, questions about The Speech were strictly off limits.

* * *

If the grid of The Speech never changed (being, after all, Bernbach's core philosophy on the art of persuasion), the embellishments did, constantly. Bernbach built the structure taller, broader, stronger. He tested new segments, tossed out old ones. By the time he summed up, he'd created "a stunning tour de force, a compelling presentation that should be required reading for anyone connected with creating advertising," in the words of the American Association of Advertising Agencies (the 4As), which published it as a booklet in 1980.

But to a biographer, it is the changing anecdotes, quotations, observations and comments over the years that offer glimpses into Bernbach's heart.

* * *

Early in the 1950s, before he'd ever spoken at an industry event, Bernbach was called to the podium at a Max Factor convention. He was handed an award for a Max Factor ad, and invited to say a few words. He shook his head and flushed, "I make ads," he said, "not speeches."

Before long, he was making speeches too.

He would never be comfortable in front of audiences. He would always clear his throat before he began. And even with the most familiar passages, he would peer through his glasses and read, as though seeing the words for the first time. His lack of ease would create tension in audiences, so used to the confident charm of more typical agency leaders. Audiences filled with admirers of the agency's work would be quick to laugh at the small jokes he told; they were on his side. A wind-up with a reel of agency commercials brought audiences to their feet in a standing ovation. Speaking did have its rewards.

* * *

A winning touch of self-deprecation, so rare after Bernbach's elevation to full-fledged legend, opened a speech in 1960.

"For some reason which is not altogether clear to me, I have been in some demand as a speaker these days. Perhaps because I know my limitations so much better than those who ask me to speak, I have turned down virtually all of these invitations. In this case, my great desire to spend some time in your wonderful San Francisco has overcome my natural discomfort at addressing large groups. . . ."

For the rest of his life, Bernbach turned down many more speaking invitations than he accepted—not surprisingly, given his discomfort before large groups, an aversion to travel, and an unwillingness to discard the basic stump speech and start from scratch.

* * *

The earliest version of The Speech, delivered at a 4As regional conference in 1956, quotes Albert Einstein on the supremacy of intuition over logic in arriving at cosmic laws. That quotation remained a fixed part of The Speech to the end.

In 1965, however, an additional Einstein reference appears, for no apparent reason.

"Someone once approached Einstein and said to him, 'Master, how do you keep all these things in your mind, all these equations, these things that you have to think about and work with?' Einstein turned to him and said, 'I have had to keep very few things in my mind. I've only had two ideas in my whole life.' Everything else to him was just a tool to work with."

The "two ideas" anecdote had a respectable run, repeated into the 1970s. Inasmuch as it seemed to connect with nothing else, one can't help wondering if this was Bernbach's preemptive justification for repeating his own ideas in The Speech.

* * *

The puzzling part, to those paying close attention, was trying to reconcile the points Bernbach made with the unvarying words in which he made them.

"In communications, familiarity breeds apathy."

"What is the use of saying all the right things in the world if nobody is going to read them? And, believe me, nobody is going to read them if they are not said with freshness, originality, and imagination."

"The truth isn't the truth until people believe you, and they can't believe you if they don't know what you're saying and they can't know what you're saying if they don't listen to you and they won't listen to you if you're not interesting. And you won't be interesting unless you say things freshly, originally, imaginatively."

"No matter how startling or provocative or effective a new idea may be, it is the nature of the human animal to soon tire of it. Was there ever anything more exciting than the first space trip? All of us took our little transistors to lunch so that we wouldn't miss a minute of it. Did we ever feel that way again? Didn't most of us say about the later trips, 'Well, we'll see it on tonight's news'? If our interest in such an historic adventure could diminish so rapidly, how do we expect lesser things not to grow stale? Only the new, only the fresh can continue to provoke interest and excitement."

But if our interest in space trips diminished so rapidly, how did Bernbach expect his use of that image, over and over, not to grow stale?

"Do it different," urged Bernbach. Otherwise, your message won't even be heard.

The industry press tuned out at moments like these:

♦ In 1964, speaking at the 4As annual convention at The Greenbrier, Bernbach tells the audience he is going to re-read what he said in San Francisco in 1960. And he does, six full pages.

♦ A week later, at the Copywriters Award dinner, he re-reads what he said at the Greenbrier, another re-reading of his 1960 talk.

♦ In 1965, at a regional 4As meeting in Pebble Beach, he says he'd "like to begin this talk by repeating some of the things I said at the Copywriters Award Dinner." And having done that, he introduces another portion with, "Let me read you what I said on this subject [the need for freshness and originality] nine years ago at a 4As meeting."

♦ In a 1970 speech to the Association of National Advertisers: "At the Greenbrier nine years ago I said. . . ."

♦ At the 1971 annual meeting of the 4As: "What I had to say at the last A.N.A. convention is perhaps relevant here. . . ."

♦ In a 1978 speech to the A.N.A.: "What are our responsibilities [to our clients]? I first talked of them to a group of writers and art directors in San Francisco some years ago. I would like to re-read them to you here." And he did.

And yet Bernbach would also say, "Even a truth must be told in a new, fresh, artful form or it will bore the beholder . . . Joyce Cary said it clearly, 'The prayers said every day tend to become a meaningless gabble, and the cathedral seen often tends to become a mere building. So churches invent new prayers to carry the old energy and architects invented Rheims to succeed Notre Dame.'"

Why, his colleagues wondered, if churches had to invent new prayers to carry the old energy, did Bernbach consider himself exempt from this imperative?

* * *

Frequently, Bernbach would include a quotation from Sir Kenneth Clark, "I believe in courtesy, the ritual by which we avoid hurting other people's feelings by satisfying our own egos." It always seemed a bit shoe-horned into The Speech, not quite merging with its surrounding components.

Now, one supposes it was a reflection of something he felt about the old scenes from his life with, and rejection by, his parents.

* * *

A segment of The Speech in the early '70s relates to the departure from the agency of a number of DDB creatives to join other agencies.

He tells of a Big Five agency head who hires, and soon fires, a "copy star." The agency head, a friend, tells Bernbach, "Those bright creative types sure need an editor, don't they? You just can't take them out of their environment and expect them to perform the same way. They're too volatile and sensitive and human not to be affected by the things and people that surround them."

Bernbach pauses to let the comment sink in. Then:

"This is one of the soundest lessons that management can learn. You can't transplant the flower from one soil to another and expect it to grow the same way."

Attention, DDB creative people! You are foolish to think you will go on creating great advertising anywhere else.

Attention, other agencies! You are foolish to lure my children with big money, because they need us to guide them to greatness.

"You're not going to do it by having a man without great creative skills himself as their editor. Unless the man doing the editing has a great creative record himself, two things will happen. He will 1) not be accepted by the writer or art director as their teacher, and 2) they will not learn and grow, because their editor is not one of them and therefore not sensitive to the problems of style and creative technique with which they are coping."

My children need *me.*

Of course, like children and parents everywhere, the more the father insists on his importance to the progress of his children, the more the latter need to prove they can cross the road themselves.

Moreover, like children everywhere, Bernbach's creatives knew that if they left him, Bernbach would always take them back, and celebrate their return.

* * *

Audiences around the country, and later around the world, flocked to Bernbach speeches, eager to learn how to make their own ads better. They hung on his words, for he was the man who was changing the face of advertising. But they didn't always get the connections he made between advertising and men such as Albert Einstein, Isaac Newton, Shakespeare, Artur Rubinstein, Thelonius Monk.

Intuition, not mathematics, led Einstein and Newton to the great theories named for them. Artistry, not the plots he stole, made Shakespeare the world's greatest playwright. Daring, not cautious perfection, put the brilliance into Rubinstein's unequalled performances. And a final word from jazz pianist Thelonius Monk: "The only cats worth anything are the cats who take chances. Sometimes I play things I never heard myself."

Facts are not enough. Information uncovered by research is not enough. It takes artistry and insight and intuitive leaps to clothe the facts in a message that people will pick out, and remember, and be moved by, and act upon.

"Even among the scientists, men who are regarded as worshippers of facts, the real giants have always been poets, men who jumped from facts into the realm of imagination and ideas."

First-time listeners were dazzled. Advertising was being elevated to an awesome plane. The words implied a parallel between the genius required for great advertising and the genius that produced great art and science. This was hardly the usual advertising conference stuff. The speech concluded in the obligatory way, with a reel of the agency's unmatchable commercials. Now the audience could see how Bernbach's philosophy bore fruit.

To copy and art people working for more prosaic agencies, a Bernbach speech could be incredibly inspiring. Managers of those same agencies, hoping for instruction on improving their product, instead left the auditorium a little miffed at all this talk about giants and geniuses, and the implication that only Doyle Dane Bernbach had the magic.

Over time, the speeches did nothing to dispel a growing industry perception that the Cinderella agency was becoming infected by the potentially fatal flaw of arrogance.

* * *

Fragments of The Speech appear in other chapters throughout this book, meshing with events and undercurrents in Bernbach's life, most affectingly with his illness and his own, unwritten book.

Although it always seemed to be the same speech to his colleagues, it was in fact a work in progress. And any future Bernbach biographer will have to sift through its stages, seeking clues to the life of an exceedingly private legend.

Account Gains and Losses in the key year of 1974

In:	Out:
Borg-Warner	Burlington
	Ralston Purina
	Terminix
	Tropicana
	Uniroyal

◆ ◆ ◆

13
The Guy from Ogilvy

"It is almost a definition of a gentleman to say that he is one who never inflicts pain."—John Henry Cardinal Newman

Attend now to the short, unhappy history of Jim Heekin's reign—from March to August 1974—as president of Doyle Dane Bernbach.

Its end was foreshadowed in a conversation between Joe Daly and his American Airlines client, Bob Crandall. "Joe, I want to give you some advice," Daly remembered Crandall telling him, "It's from Machiavelli. 'When you conquer a country, you cut off the leader's head, you don't give him a room in the castle.' I'm telling you what to do with Mr. Heekin."

And that's what Daly did. But in all fairness, that's what Heekin was trying to do to Daly.

* * *

It started as so many Doyle Dane Bernbach stories do, with an impetuous hiring. Heekin, looking for a new job, wrote to Bernbach, describing how he would handle the agency's vexed Uniroyal account. Bernbach, eager not to lose another account, took the bait. Soon after, Heekin "appeared out of the blue," in the words of then-personnel head Dick Kane. His arrival and his title, executive vice president, were announced in December, 1972.

Perhaps the idea of a personnel check on Heekin struck Bernbach as unseemly. Heekin, after all, had been president of Ogilvy & Mather from 1966 to 1970. And Ogilvy had a fine image of being well managed, by well-bred, well-schooled, well-mannered men. Nice. Heekin was one of them. Well-connected—from the Cincinnati family that owned the Drackett company—monied, stylish. His striped shirts with stiff white collars and cuffs became his signature at DDB; account men copied the style, until Heekin fell from grace, after which such shirts were never again seen at the agency.

"Bill was looking for a rabbit," Heekin said later. "He thought perhaps that I was a rabbit." A piece of magic to pull out of a hat and save the day. Heekin felt Bernbach always looked for a rabbit, rather than facing the hard problems.

Bernbach saw Ogilvy & Mather as an agency full of rabbits, and it was with pride that he initially referred to Heekin as "the new guy from Ogilvy." Daly hadn't turned out to be a rabbit. Clients kept on leaving. They were not, as in Doyle's day, rapidly replaced. Uniroyal was a deeply troubled account. American Airlines was halfway out the door. The agency looked bad to Wall Street after a series of rash acquisitions of so-called "under-marketed properties." That galled Bernbach more than anything. Possibly excepting Daly's lunchtime drinking.

"If you have to see Daly, do it before noon." Any description of Daly, whether by agency or client people, came to include that phrase. The words were often spoken with tolerance and amusement. Daly was a character, *our* character. DDBers adored Daly stories.

Account man Arie Kopelman recalled being in Daly's office, asking for help on a problem.

"Joe puts his hand to his forehead, looks up through his fingers, says 'Oh, shit,' and limps out of the office. Twenty minutes later, I ask Jeanette [Daly's secretary] where Joe is, assuming he's gone to the men's room. Says Jeanette, 'He left for lunch.'"

While Daly headed for lunch and Tanqueray gin martinis at Le Mistral or La Cote Basque, Heekin took his lunch with the plebes, in the 19th floor Eatery. He never pulled rank to cut into the queue. In his stiff and formal way, he would make jokes about how trying to "cut into the queue" had cost him his job at Ogilvy.

He used another image in explaining his end at Ogilvy to Bernbach and Daly. O&Mers were constantly encouraged to "grasp the nettle," said Heekin, "I thought that meant Go for It, and I did." He'd made an ill-timed run at the top job, and wound up on the street.

So that was it. Heekin played for power, hard and fast. King of the mountain. No sharing. Daly got the picture quickly, and warmed up for the game. Soon one heard reports of a call from an Ogilvy executive to DDB about Heekin—"Don't touch him with a 10-foot pole." Years later, I learned the origin of that report was Daly.

Here is Daly calling to let me know another account is leaving DDB.

"Jesus!" I gasp.

"Don't Jesus me. It wasn't *my* account," responds Daly, triumphantly. He's happy! The agency he's president of has just lost a big piece of business, and he's happy because it's a black eye for his challenger.

* * *

Through 1973 Heekin supervised a group of accounts, spending much of his time trying to identify the sources of the agency's problems. Daly heard from a couple of client contacts that Heekin had said to them, "We know you've had problems with the agency, but we're working to fix them." Daly's version was that these clients had assured Heekin they had no problems with the agency, and "What's with this guy, Joe?" they'd asked him.

Since Daly operated on an "everything is great" wavelength, these reports gave him more ammunition to undermine confidence in Heekin. He began to send up small balloons of doubt about Heekin's stability.

* * *

Bernbach heard reports about Daly's drunken behavior at an international meeting of Polaroid people in Paris. The last straw. Daly had to be fired. Or, if not that, Daly would have to agree to naming Heekin president of the agency. Doyle, back on the scene as a sounding board to the increasingly-worried Bernbach, prodded both Bernbach and Daly to take that route.

Daly stepped up his covert aspersions on Heekin. Heekin, growingly confident of Bernbach's support, stepped up his research on who did what at the agency, and how well or how badly. He soon identified the reason DDB was failing in its new business efforts.

"It's the 'asshole syndrome,'" said Heekin. "In the hallways, you constantly hear DDBers referring to other DDBers as assholes. That contempt for one another is palpable in our new business presentations. Why would an advertiser give his account to a place where everyone thinks everyone else is an asshole?

"We went through a period like that at Ogilvy. And we were getting no new business. We did some soul searching and changed our ways. When our presentations came alive with the fun of working together, of admiring and liking and respecting one another, advertisers wanted to share the magic. The new business rolled in."

Heekin hoped the syndrome would stop at Doyle Dane Bernbach. If anything, it accelerated.

* * *

Something about Heekin's immaculate Waspiness—the way his skin pulled tight over his fine-boned face, the tightness of his persona, the perfectly-rolled umbrella look—left many DDBers feeling far less comfortable than they did in Daly's rumpled presence. But he saw with fresh eyes, and he saw deadwood, and old-time department heads who hadn't grown with the agency, and downhill creative work, and he said so.

"What did you do that I didn't, Jim?" asked Bob Levenson, who had badly wanted the presidency of the agency, after Heekin got the appointment.

"I had the guts to say what was wrong," responded Heekin.

Just about everything was, in his opinion. Media, research, marketing— all needed new department heads. So did the creative department. So did international. The general manager should go. A strategy review board should be set up, to keep the advertising on track for every client.

He pushed for the chance to implement these changes. Bernbach and Doyle pushed Daly.

An agency lawyer remembered a meeting, in the second week of March, 1974, called to name Heekin president and to fire Daly. "To this day, I can't figure out what happened," said he, "but when it was over, Heekin was president, and Daly was chairman of the board."

Daly later reconstructed a piece of the meeting like this:

Bernbach: "I've got to talk to you, Joe."

Daly: "What's the problem? There ain't no problem around here."

Bernbach: "There is a problem."

Daly: "What is it?"

Bernbach: "You drink too much."

Daly: "What do you mean, I drink too much? You know how much I drink and how much I don't drink, and I've always done that, and it's never caused a problem."

Bernbach: "I understand you made a fool of yourself at the Polaroid party in Paris."

Daly: "Who told you that?"

Bernbach: "I'm not going to tell you."

Daly: "Well, I'm going to tell you something. I remember that night very distinctly and specifically. I never put on a better performance in my life."

Instead of a *mea culpa*, Daly defended himself so vigorously that Bernbach's resolve withered. "I just can't do that to Joe," said Bernbach, then, and on several other crucial occasions.

* * *

On March 15, a press release announced Heekin's ascension to President, Domestic Operations. Daly moved up to Chairman and CEO, Domestic Operations. Bernbach took the title of Chairman and CEO Worldwide.

Heekin came to rue the meeting as a "grave mistake." He'd had enough clout then, thanks to Bernbach's dissatisfaction with Daly, to insist that Daly be removed from power altogether. "It's very, very difficult when you have two men on top," said he.

Three days after Heekin's appointment as president, Uniroyal announced it was moving its account from Doyle Dane Bernbach to Ogilvy & Mather. Heekin lost credibility as a rabbit. Bernbach lost heart. Daly was jubilant.

Doyle wondered if it was time to have lunch with his old friend Mary Wells.

* * *

Heekin, meanwhile, demonstrated his ability to upgrade service departments by bringing the highly-regarded Mike Drexler from Ogilvy as media head.

Drexler was stunned by the differences between the two agencies. "When we did new business at Ogilvy, we all got together and worked for days on end," he recalled later. "We would each do our own part, then meet as a group, then we would discuss, and rehearse. We'd rehearse with scripts. There was never anything extemporaneous in a presentation because we had fixed timings and it was important to keep to them. We'd rehearse for hours. We listened to one another and made suggestions and corrections."

He'd been at DDB for a few months when Daly called him and said they'd be doing a new business presentation for Scott Paper.

"Great," said Drexler. "When is it?"

"Tomorrow," said Daly.

"Tomorrow? When do we rehearse?"

"We don't need to rehearse. Just get up there and tell them something about media."

Scott Paper didn't move its account to Doyle Dane Bernbach. Maybe it had to do with the unrehearsed presentation. Or with the asshole syndrome. Or with the growing impression in the industry that, as Ted Factor told Bernbach in June, 1974, DDB was "the worst managed agency in the business."

Management's inability or unwillingness to deal with hard problems was exemplified in a comment by Daly to Doyle, in the early '70s. "This place is going to go down the drain, but I'll be out of here before it does."

* * *

Machiavelli would have enjoyed the Daly-Heekin contest. Deadly serious stuff it was for the participants, and who knew what this would mean for the rest of us. Still, it had its funny moments. One of the funniest came in a musical we produced for the agency's 25th anniversary. The Joe Daly character is portrayed looking bewildered on entering the company cafeteria. He sings, to the music of "I've Never Been in Love Before":

"I've never been in here before
   On other days by noon
   I'm out the goddamn door,
I'll tell you, since you didn't ask
   I far prefer the food
   And drinks at La Cote Basque,
But since I learned that Heekin eats inside
   I got myself a guide
   To lead me to this floor,
So please forgive the puzzled state I'm in
   I've never really been
   In here before."

Everyone howled, including Daly and Heekin.

* * *

Heekin, aware that Bernbach had lost faith in him but determined to restore it, set to work on a plan, later known as "Heekin's book," to correct the agency's problems. Unknown to him, merger talks with Wells, Rich, Greene had opened just weeks after he became president of DDB. (see next chapter) He learned about the talks when the rest of us did, just before the story broke in the press.

"Now Bernbach thinks perhaps Mary is a rabbit," Heekin told me at the time. "He believes she's sensational with clients. But she isn't perfect either; she lost American Motors and Dr. Pepper. Nobody's perfect. There are no rabbits."

* * *

Heekin gave his "book" to Bernbach and Daly in July. Soon after, a staff memo from Daly announced "an extended leave of absence" for an executive vice-president who "has not been feeling at his best." The man, an old DDB hand, had been targeted in Heekin's book.

"Two more of our executives have 'gotten sick,'" Heekin told me a few weeks later, picking up, as the rest of the agency had, on the Orwellian term for getting sacked.

The next scalps belonged to the president of DDB International, and the head of DDB's research department. Both old-timers. Both targeted in Heekin's book. Bernbach left for Europe to avoid the ugliness of the international head's firing. "Wait 'til my plane takes off," he instructed Daly, who did the deed.

The fired research director stops in my office to tell me his story. Heekin had asked him to resign. Shocked and disbelieving, he had gone to Daly for a reprieve. Daly said he was sorry, but he'd given Heekin a free hand and thus could not reverse the decision.

Aware by this time of a Bernbach-Daly plan to oust Heekin, I profess sympathy and offer help in writing a press release. And I think, Daly, you S.O.B., making every last bit of use of Heekin before announcing that *he's* "gotten sick."

* * *

Heekin's book concluded with the point that "two men cannot run one company." "He was right about that," Daly said to me later that year. "And he was right about his other assessments of people. It's a good book; I've got it in my drawer now. The only thing is, he won't be implementing it—I will."

* * *

An on-the-scene observer, former DDB account man Bill Wardell, related the theater-of-the-absurd episode of Heekin's firing.

"When Bernbach and Daly decided to get rid of Heekin, they concocted an offer which essentially was to demote him from president to executive VP in charge of something. Jim was meant to be at a meeting at Stroh's with Daly and me on the very day this was happening, but he cancelled and went up to Williamstown.

"[Lawyer] Josh Levine, who is the carrier of all news both good and bad, was delegated to write the letter and send it to Heekin in Williamstown, telling him this is what the agency decided to do. Not only was he not going to get more responsibility blah blah blah but he was in fact going to get less responsibility and what do you think of that.

"Daly tells me all this in his usual mental state out in Detroit and says it's going to be really fun and I can't wait to see his reaction—he thinks he's going to get more power and we're firing him.

"What Daly didn't know was I'd just been on the phone for two hours with Jim from Williamstown, and Jim told me he was going to accept the job, totally overturning everybody's plans, and take another run later. Live to fight another day . . . and they think I'm going to walk out, but I'll trick them, I'm not going to do that.

"Well, I felt duty-bound to tell Joe this was happening. Joe gets outraged. This is clearly not the plan. And he gets on the horn to Josh to have him change the offer. He says before Heekin can write some statesmanlike letter, I want another letter, registered and all that stuff, telling him we changed our minds and that he's out of it.

"Meanwhile, we're running around telling Stroh Brewery he has the sniffles and can't make the meeting. It was one of those wonderful days."

* * *

One of Heekin's most gentlemanly urgings in his brief reign dealt with press relations. Too often in recent years, DDB's leaders had lashed out when a client left, defensively giving out proprietary information about market shares, etc., to prove the agency had done good work. No other large agency had such bad public manners about client departures.

Heekin's point, one I had tried without success to purvey, was that lashing out kept alive longer the news of another agency account loss. And no segment of the industry—advertisers or agencies—felt comfortable with the display of bad manners and with giving away client information. Better by far would be a simple and graceful, "We wish them well in their new relationship."

In that respect, Heekin was a man after my professional heart. So it was with incredulity that I picked up the *Advertising Age* issue of September 2, 1974, and read a front page headline, "Heekin quits as president with a blast at DDB's execs."

Nothing gentlemanly here. Heekin, defending himself, sounded like Daly and Bernbach on departing clients. Worse.

Among other comments, Heekin flew out at the "impetuous and unstable behavior that has characterized DDB over the past two years, and which I have been unable to prevent."

A careful statement on Heekin had been worked out with lawyer Josh Levine, while Bernbach champed at the bit, threatening to phone the trade press and reveal the "truth about Heekin's stability." Daly and Levine all but sat on Bernbach, extracting promises that he wouldn't. That night, from his home, Bernbach called reporters anyway. He never told Daly and Levine, and they never knew. That was press relations at DDB.

* * *

The agency's weekly employment report for the weeks ending 8/30/74 and 9/6/74 listed nine positions filled and 29 "resignations and terminations." Among the latter was James Heekin, Jr., President, Domestic Oper. Date released—8/31/74.

◆ ◆ ◆

14
William and Mary

"Historically, Americans have tried to solve their problems by leaving them behind."—Arthur T. Hadley, *The Straw Giant*

On April 22, 1974, Ned Doyle bought lunch in the Algonquin Hotel Rose Room for one of his favorite people, former Doyle Dane Bernbach creative star Mary Wells Lawrence. The following week, Mary took Bill Bernbach to lunch, and offered to buy his agency.

Bernbach went back to his office and called Neil Austrian's Wall Street office. Austrian was on a business trip to Seattle. Bernbach reached him there.

"Can you fly back tonight? I've just had an amazing offer from Mary Wells."

Austrian flew back, and one of the most remarkable chapters in the history of Doyle Dane Bernbach opened.

* * *

"None of it would have happened," a participant later recalled, "if Bernbach hadn't been such an insecure person."

This time his insecurity about his image was overwhelmed by his insecurity about money, about providing for his family's future. The obsessive drive "to take care of one's own" again came to the fore, crowding out worries about legends, and the company he had built, and the people who were part of it.

The loss of the important Uniroyal account, for which the agency had created the superb "Rain Tire" campaign, had shaken Bernbach badly. Worse, it felt like a pre-tremor to the Big One still to come. Bernbach's greatest fear was that American Airlines, after a year of threats, would finally pull its account out of DDB, and in the process bring about the collapse of the financially weakened agency.

Heekin, brought in to reverse the outflow, only brought dissension with Daly, turning every working day into aggravation and misery.

It seemed sometimes that everything was wrong. So many important clients had left in the last few years. Lever Brothers, Quaker Oats, Warner-Lambert, Whirlpool, Sara Lee, Cracker Jack—the first losing streak in the agency's history. Why? DDB's advertising had given Lever its first successful new product in years, Close-Up toothpaste. The agency had rebuilt the image and sales of Cracker Jack. Sara Lee still used DDB's campaign, "Nobody doesn't like Sara Lee," at its new agency. Yet they all left. They'd all had great advertising.

And now American Airlines was about to leave. Joe Daly assured him American would stay. But Daly always told Bernbach things were great. Daly didn't realize it, but Bernbach didn't feel much more confidence in Daly than he'd had in Heekin.

At the same time, the agency's investments were coming to grief, one after another. Ross MacLennan, Mac Dane's successor, had bombed. Bernbach and Daly had felt relief when Dane retired in 1971—"The Obstructionist" would be out of the way, the nay-sayer who threw cold water on every proposal to invest in outside opportunities. To be sure, Dane had proved right about KMS, a tiny company Bernbach and Daly had visited in Ann Arbor, Michigan. In their enthusiasm for the company's search for fusion energy, they'd proposed that the agency invest a million dollars in KMS. Dane had talked them down to a half-million. And Dane's was the only voice objecting to bringing in an Italian theatrical company's production that Dane, with foresight, called "Orlando Fiasco."

Still, the agency had money to invest and wanted someone with vision to invest it. MacLennan's first find was Trade Mart, the Oklahoma discount stores. Busy seeking more acquisitions, MacLennan had failed to keep an eye on Trade Mart or on Snark, a styrofoam sailboat company that once seemed DDB's most promising acquisition. By 1974, Trade Mart and Snark were rapidly and terrifyingly heading down the drain, hemorrhaging the agency's profits as they went.

Few people, in or out of the agency, realized the extent of the damage. Advertising agency stocks, a miniscule category, had sunk almost out of sight in the general Wall Street OPEC-induced slough of despair. Analyst reports on the category issued forth occasionally, usually from the newest kid on the brokerage house block. As for Madison Avenue, its practitioners at the time were still innocently and charmingly focused on advertising, not finance.

Maybe the agency shouldn't have trumpeted its policy of seeking "under-marketed properties" and building them up with its marketing skills. What might prospective clients deduce from the agency's inability to save its own properties from failure?

All this would be swallowed up, would threaten no longer, in a merger with Wells, Rich, Greene.

* * *

It's hard to imagine an event that would strike Madison Avenue as more unlikely, at that time, than a merger of Doyle Dane Bernbach and Wells, Rich, Greene. As for the step beyond, that the buyer would be Mary and the seller Bernbach, the concept was so outrageous that it had no credence whatsoever, not even after the deal fell through.

They regularly bad-mouthed each other. Privately, Mary would say that Bernbach was living on an inflated reputation and was lazy. What she had to say publicly made for humiliating copy in *Advertising Age*—"DDB is yesterday; Wells, Rich, Greene is today."

Bernbach had suffered other humiliations at Mary's hands. As copywriter on the agency's French Government Tourist account in the 1950s, she and the Bernbachs had traveled together through France, the standard agency indoctrination trip. Evelyn later recalled that at every hotel, Mary took the grandest suite and arranged an ordinary room for the boss and his wife. Bernbach seethed and Evelyn trembled, but they didn't complain to Mary. Neither could bear confrontation.

The fact that Mary had achieved greater success than any of Bernbach's alumni had not, previously, seemed a matter of pride to her former boss. In the privacy of his office Bernbach would speculate, in pre-Lib terms, on the means of Mary's rapid rise in the industry.

"She's a c—," added Daly, no mincer of words.

Who could credit their talking merger?

* * *

Daly: "Mary told him, 'Bill, I want to come home,' and Bill bought it."

Bernbach proudly repeated to me, at the time, something else Mary told him: that she knew she would never be what he was to advertising. That she had become fascinated by the business and financial side, and that was where she meant to be tops.

As the negotiations got under way, Mary took to sending large bouquets of flowers—daily, Evelyn recalled—to the Bernbach apartment in United Nations Plaza.

Mary wowed them. "She is so smart," everybody said.

* * *

Bernbach, who with his wife owned 266,780 shares of the agency, couldn't forget the brief period when Doyle Dane Bernbach stock rose above $50 a share, boosting the value of his holdings to a heady $13 million plus. Since then, the shares had tumbled to $9, and his total value to under $2.5

million. What was to prevent the price from dropping through the floor? Mary offered $17 per share in a leveraged buy-out. That would mean $4.5 million to the Bernbachs, far below the bird-in-the-bush old high, but at least firmly in hand. Secondly, and irresistibly, she offered Bernbach a 10-year contract that would continue to be paid to Evelyn in the event of his death. All the nagging worries about his family's security would end.

He told Doyle in confidence that "things were afoot" that he could not disclose, but that he ought not sell off any more of his agency shares. Doyle didn't tell Bernbach that Mary called him frequently, and that he had suggested that she insist on the title Chief Executive Officer of the merged agency.

Doyle: "I told her, that way nobody can ever touch you."

"Well, that will gum up the deal," said one of the negotiators, who knew Bernbach well. Bernbach would never accept an organization chart that put Mary over him. Even Mary had her doubts. Doyle remembered her asking him to call Bernbach and float the idea. But Doyle couldn't, without revealing his close contacts with Mary. He confidently asserted that a call from Mary herself would secure Bernbach's agreement.

And indeed, Bernbach soon after astonished his negotiators by informing them that Mary would be CEO and that was fine with him. Clearly, the only thing he wanted was Out.

* * *

Neil Austrian and Mike Herman, brainy young partners in a small Wall Street investment banking firm, looked at the numbers and shook their heads. They'd been retained by Doyle Dane Bernbach a year or so earlier, to screen acquisition proposals and prevent further disasters. They had recommended against every proposal since, either because the people were wrong, or because they "couldn't get comfortable with the agency's strategy—what the fit was and why," Austrian said later.

They had no ax to grind; they exuded financial brilliance and honesty, and Austrian was a nephew by marriage of Bernbach's brother. Bernbach trusted him profoundly. But he didn't want to believe Austrian's assessment of Mary's proposal. Austrian and Herman understood the intricacies of a leveraged buy-out as no one in the agency did, and they thought this one was "not financeable."

"Meaning," Austrian explained later, "Mary was going to try to do it with debt. Given all the problems Doyle Dane Bernbach was perceived to be having—in terms of losing business, a boat company losing millions of dollars a year, a discount store operation that was heading for bankruptcy—it would be a very, very tough deal to finance."

They did believe that the agency could survive the loss of American Airlines, "and that Bill himself could come out financially far better off than what Mary had offered at the time. And we recommended against it, on a pure financial basis, not understanding, quite honestly, then, all the emotional wrenching that you go through, in terms of your own ego, your own pride, and the public relations impact on an agency when you lose an account like that."

Bernbach listened to them, but they didn't say what he wanted to hear. Instead, the bankers and lawyers began the business of quietly working out terms for the takeover. Within the agency, only Daly and MacLennan were taken into Bernbach's confidence in the earliest stages of negotiations.

Jim Heekin remained in the dark. He went right on working on ways to regain Bernbach's faith in him. When the talks seemed at an end (though they were not), Heekin sent a note to Mary, expressing his regret that her plan hadn't worked. It had been "a bold stroke," and there were few enough bold strokes in this business. Mary responded by sending Heekin a small woven silver basket filled with candy kisses, and a handwritten card: "Dear Jim. Thank you for your lovely note. Mary."

"She is so smart," said Heekin.

Gentleman Jim. His exclusion from the talks should have told him he'd be the first to walk the plank in a merger. At that point, he was still hoping for a chance to fight another day.

* * *

As the talks progressed, some department heads, sworn to secrecy, began meetings with Mary and her people, working out details of the coming combination. The agency's international head brought two glasses and a bottle of Dom Perignon to his meeting with Mary. (He walked the plank when the deal failed and Heekin's "book" was implemented.)

On the highest level, the talks addressed the great account conflicts a combination would produce. Mary had TWA; DDB had, though shakily, American Airlines. Mary had Sun Oil; DDB had Mobil Oil, a strong relationship.

Mary hadn't yet succeeded in raising the money, financiers having grasped the magnitude of the Trade Mart and Snark fiascos, when the advertising news columnists for both the *New York Times* and the *Chicago Tribune*, Philip Dougherty and George Lazarus, called to say they knew about the talks and would publish what they had unless the agency could convince them that their sources were wrong.

How would American Airlines react to that piece of news? AA's executives had not, of course, been told of the talks. A major point of the exercise was Bernbach's wish to get out from under the sword the airline held over the agency's head. Given the tensions of the past year, AA might well surmise that DDB had been plotting to beat the airline to the kill.

If Mary couldn't raise the money, Doyle Dane Bernbach would be dead with AA—unless the agency could convince its client that reports of merger talks were greatly exaggerated, that the reality was far less than met the eye.

That afternoon, June 6, a legalistic statement was quickly issued, in a *genre* not yet familiar to the advertising trade press. The chairmen of the two agencies, Bernbach and Mary, "announced today that the agencies have been holding talks concerning a possible combination of the two advertising agencies. The talks have not been fruitful and have been discontinued."

Legally, technically, the statement was true. What remained under wraps (including from me, although I was now handling press relations on the story) was that Mary had until June 21 to raise the money.

Two very strange weeks followed.

* * *

Dougherty's June 7 column, headlined "Doyle-Wells Deal Is Reported Off," described the original rumor as "unbelievable," and noted that "even the discussion of 'the possibility of combining the two advertising agencies' will boggle most minds in the business."

That disbelief, inside and outside the agency, could be counted on to help stamp out the fires of the story. I spoke my part with complete conviction, sure in my heart that my agency would never merge, unaware then of the fears and insecurities that bred the episode, un-briefed on the depth and breadth of the talks, and uninformed of the fact that the two agencies might yet combine.

The latter point, at least, came clear when Bernbach asked me to add the words "for the moment" to a follow-up statement about the discontinuance of the talks. He quickly accepted my warning that such words would flag the press that "the melody lingered on." He saw at once that they had flagged me. He understood that I now understood. Something changed in our relationship—perhaps for the truer.

Most of the trade press took our word and let up on the story. Then we heard from *Advertising Age* reporter Bob Donath. He had a quote, he said, from a WRG client, who had been reassured that if there was a merger, his account would be kept and the conflicting one jettisoned.

"It has to be TWA," Bernbach and the agency lawyer agreed.

"Maybe it's Sun Oil," I offered.

"No, it's not Sun Oil," responded Bernbach. That clarified the plan on the second large client conflict.

If the TWA quote ran, American Airlines would surely leave his agency, said Bernbach. Fred Danzig, *Advertising Age's* editor, assured me there was no way the TWA comment would *not* run—"because uppermost in the story about the merger talks is the problem of client conflicts."

Through the difficult hours that followed—which included calls to Mary about whether she had in fact given such assurance to TWA (she said she hadn't), and whether she would call *Ad Age* to say she hadn't (she wouldn't, but she'd be happy to call Al Casey of American Airlines and tell him, an offer Bernbach quickly refused)—Bernbach reacted as Bernbach often did in crises. Quiet agitation, deep and rapid breathing, set jaw, flaring nostrils, and in his eyes, his incredibly blue eyes, a look of having been betrayed by life, by fate. He could stir in those around him profound feelings of protectiveness.

We went to work and hammered out a statement to the press that we hoped would pacify American Airlines:

"Since the discussions were terminated at an early stage, there was no reason to talk to or reassure any of our clients. The talks just had not advanced to the point where client conflicts were resolved."

* * *

Neil Austrian proved right; Mary's plan was not financeable. He urged Bernbach not to worry; if it was the 10-year contract he so badly wanted, he should ask Doyle Dane Bernbach for one. Surely they'd give it to him. (They did.) As for mergers, there were other prospects, Austrian advised. He'd talk to Needham, Harper in Chicago—that could be a good fit. Austrian was right about that, if prematurely. And Bernbach's stock, at a low, could in time prove far more valuable than Mary's four million dollar plus offer. Austrian was right about that, too.

A few days after the proposed deal broke up, Austrian had a visitor, who arrived without having called ahead, at his investment firm office at Fifth Avenue and 54th Street. A man named Ned Doyle, announced Austrian's secretary. The two men had never met.

Doyle entered, and stood studying Austrian, who stood a head taller than Doyle. Like Doyle, Austrian had been a football star in college, and like Doyle, he was a jock with a brain.

"So you're the guy who keeps saying no to all the deals we want to do," Doyle opened, dead-pan. Austrian knew he was going to love this guy.

"Well if you're so goddamn smart, why don't you come work for us?" pressed Doyle. Austrian replied that he'd rather stay in investment banking than move into advertising. But Bernbach was pressing him too, and before summer's end, the founders had convinced Austrian that the opportunity to turn Doyle Dane Bernbach around could bring him fortune, fame, and a helluva lot of fun.

* * *

American Airlines never did leave Doyle Dane Bernbach. In 1981, during another crisis on the account, an angry Bernbach demonstrated his still-powerful hold on the industry by signing up the Pan-American account and dumping American faster than the airline could say, "Bozell & Jacobs," the agency slated to compete with DDB in a creative shoot-out. But that's another story, with yet another unhappy ending. We'll get to that.

* * *

On Monday, June 3, 1974, Doyle Dane Bernbach celebrated the 25th anniversary of its founding with an exuberant party on a Hudson Dayliner. Its climax was a musical, written and performed by DDBers—a funny and touching and rousing tribute to the agency. The troops leapt to their feet at the end, cheering and singing along, in love with DDB and its founders and everything they represented, professionally and ethically. Ned Doyle, Mac Dane and Joe Daly laughed and cheered with the rest of the staff. Bernbach sat quietly, somewhere between grim and pensive. Why did the joyful songs have such an unexpected effect on Bernbach, and on no one else? Later, I would wonder if he had felt pain, hearing a thousand DDBers celebrating the agency he was in the process of trying to sell off.

♦ ♦ ♦

15
Once More, from the Top

"Pick yourself up, brush yourself off, and start all over again."
—Popular song

"I bequeath my liver to '21,'" intoned Tom Gallagher, settling down to draw up a new will, after a liquid lunch at that Mecca of achievers.

"Another in the line of drunken Irish presidents of DDB," sighed more than one agency staffer.

"Joe, your agency can afford only one drunk," said a client to Daly, "and you were there first."

Welcome to the post-Heekin era at Doyle Dane Bernbach.

* * *

It should have been wonderful, and for several years it was. Heekin had vanished, the awful merger story had dissolved, American Airlines had settled down with a new DDB campaign ("Doing what we do best"), and a new management team had been installed. Tom Gallagher, president, worldwide. Neil Austrian, executive vice president, chief financial officer, chief administrative officer. Marvin Honig, executive vice president, creative director.

Not that the powerful old managers had faded into the sunset, or had "gotten sick." Bernbach remained CEO worldwide. Daly kept his old title, chairman of the board. The press release said his domain had been expanded from domestic to cover worldwide responsibilities. Whatever that signified.

In truth, Gallagher was meant to be over Daly.

"When Daly left for England to tell Gallagher he had the job," Ned Doyle recounted, "I rehearsed him three times before he left. I said, 'Joe, I want you to repeat what you're going to say: This guy is the boss, and you are going to take orders from him.' Someone had to run the place, and Joe said he didn't want to. So we sought Gallagher out.

"Now I'll guarantee you that Joe never told that to Gallagher. Because when Gallagher came over, Daly did everything to cut his nuts out. He wouldn't let him in on Polaroid; he wouldn't let him in on Mobil; he tried to keep him away from Volkswagen. And even when we got Bayer Aspirin, Daly took that over rather than give it to Tom. He made the guy helpless. (Pause) Now then of course Gallagher liked the liquor."

The chicken-or-the-egg question around the agency became, did Daly keep the power accounts in his own grasp because Gallagher drank? Or did Gallagher drown his woes because Daly wouldn't give him a room in the castle?

Bob Levenson later commented that all the men who followed Daly as president, drinkers and non-drinkers alike, had in common that "they were presidents of Doyle Dane Bernbach except for American Airlines, Volkswagen, Polaroid and Mobil. And being president of Stroh beer and Scott fertilizers is not really the job that any of them thought they were going to get. The self-destruct seeds were there a long time ago. There was no way in the world, except for death and old age . . . *maybe* . . . that would allow for letting go of the power base."

* * *

Tom Gallagher was widely known in England, where he was an international rugby star. A large man of 45, with the sad/alert look of a champion basset hound, the soul of a poet, and the temper and strength of a bull. And his voice! Ah, his voice. Honey-gravel bass, enchantingly Irish. He was charismatic and contradictory; erudite, eloquent and witty, but also politically innocent, unpredictable and self-destructive. In a place where people with big titles too often manifested their littleness, Gallagher loomed refreshingly larger than life. He could have made the difference, said DDBers. If only. . . .

Here was a man who "lives and dies the business," in a key phrase from a confidential report on Gallagher. Ross MacLennan sent the report to Daly, Bernbach, Doyle and Ted Factor—the search team—on July 2, 1974. By then Mary Wells had failed to raise the money for the takeover. The next move, dumping Heekin, required a replacement president.

Several of the agency's account managers politicked for higher office, confident of their ability to be president. They felt, and said, that going outside to fill top positions demonstrated DDB's lack of management depth and preparation for succession. Alas, none of the politickers had stature or the support of the troops. Not a rabbit in the lot.

On the other hand, outsiders of presumed stature had brought only grief to the agency.

Someone floated Gallagher's name, and things fell into place for the search team, except for Factor, who objected to choosing "from a field of one."

Gallagher did have a double advantage. He would count as an insider, for he ran the agency's London office, having been acquired with the Gallagher/Smail agency three years earlier. Since then, he'd built a strong new business record. Good, very good. Yet, being overseas, he had the advantage of distance, the boon of underexposure. The deficiencies of the politicking account managers were known all too well. Not Gallagher's. Daly and Bernbach knew him chiefly from international meetings, where he reveled in the night life of the host city, but . . . everyone did, if less indefatigably. And throw in his fame as a jock. Quite irresistible.

Still, after the haste and burn of the Lubow, MacLennan and Heekin hirings, the search team needed a bit of independent reassurance. MacLennan attributed his confidential report, anonymously, to "a source." British? American? Insider? Outsider? Client? Journalist? Never mind, it supported the team's hopes.

The report ran five paragraphs. The first two recounted Gallagher's agency background, as a key account man and top new business getter for Norman, Craig & Kummel, and then for Gallagher/Smail. The final three paragraphs are worth perusing in light of the aftermath.

"Even in those days, when in his early 30s [working for NC&K-London), Tom tended to operate at the top level of client companies. He was well known as an international rugby player and, of course, did not hesitate to capitalize on this. However, his success was not at the 'old boy' network level but among the leading marketing managers. He was and is able to get to people high up in a company and to convince the prospect of his willingness to give a great deal of his agency's and his personal time and attention.

"He apparently lives and dies the business. He is meticulous about details yet willing to delegate a great deal of responsibility. Creative people like working with him because he gives them a clear sense of direction—what can meet the marketing need and can be sold to the client—and avoids directions which might prove to be a waste of time. He worked here in New York, for NCK, for a little less than a year, on the Colgate account.

"The negatives are he spends a great deal of time and money living with and entertaining his clients. While generous in this regard, the money is spent on clients and not necessarily on himself. Tom can be stiff-necked, stubborn, and quite rough on people at times, but most apologetic after one of his 'rows.'"

Nothing about excessive drinking.

"Nobody in New York knew," Neil Austrian said a dozen years later.

But perhaps it wasn't even so. Perhaps the situation exacerbated the condition? Austrian thought the question over.

"Bill Bernbach told me that he thought, in hindsight, Tom should have been a lot tougher coming in, and demanded all the accounts, and maybe the title CEO before he took the job. Not let the accounts stay with Joe. Maybe the board should have insisted on that. I didn't know from nothing. I was just the new kid coming in."

The board didn't insist. A participant remembers Bernbach saying at the time, "I couldn't do that to Joe."

* * *

Why not? Austrian responds that Bernbach was "an extraordinarily loyal person," and so he stuck with Daly, as he'd stuck with Doyle.

"Loyalty was really important to him," John Bernbach affirmed. "That's something he taught us, the importance of loyalty. If you're associated with something, you defend it, you protect it. Even if you know it's wrong, you deal with the problem privately, but as far as the outside world is concerned, it's a united front. That's the way he was, and he drummed that into us as kids growing up."

Ned Doyle was the risk taker who put Doyle Dane Bernbach together. Daly had helped to build it bigger than Doyle had ever envisioned. Bernbach bitched about each to the other, but somehow left each feeling that he remained in Bernbach's favor—at least most of the time.

"Ned was a cross to bear," Paul Bernbach remarked, years later.

And Daly? Well, here is what Bernbach once said, in respect to all his presidents: "Imagine what I could have done if I'd had Jock Elliott."

Elliott, the man most responsible for the superb management of Ogilvy—the ultimate rabbit of Bernbach's dreams.

* * *

Daly saw Bernbach's behavior to Doyle less as loyalty than as an inexplicable inability to "stand up" to the older man. Certainly it had nothing to do with fear of losing any business, for Doyle controlled none, and believed as a matter of principle that no individual should. Daly believed otherwise, as we have seen.

Gallagher arrived in New York in 1974, just a year after Bernbach's damaging encounter with Polaroid's Dr. Land. The memory still burned. This was hardly the moment to press Daly to relinquish his death grip on Polaroid.

Daly didn't then, or any time after, feel a single compunction about refusing to let other presidents near his accounts.

"When I did, they fucked 'em up," said he simply, when the tumult died.

And that's possible. But the problem, as Neil Austrian mused after the mega-merger, was that "the account group looked at Joe as their leader. And the senior level of account management believed that the way you succeed at DDB is you lock in your own account. Don't worry about the agency; worry about yourself. A terrible way to run a business.

"Maybe way back, the risk [of Daly walking] should have been taken. And you takes what you gets. Because to live under the gun like that forever was a terrible, terrible way to run a business. It permeates the agency. We tried for a long while to break that, to make it Our Client, One Agency, and it's very tough.

"Joe played games with Tom on that when Tom came in. This is mine, this is yours. It should have been ours."

* * *

The triumvirate of Gallagher, Austrian and Honig worked well initially. They liked and respected one another—no "asshole syndrome" in their relationship. And they tackled some of the most egregious problems fast.

Late work, for instance. It would be hard to measure how much client goodwill had been worn down by cliffhanger due dates. Young creatives thrilled to Helmut Krone's dictum, "I don't care about the air date, we're going to get this *right*," but clients got heartburn. Too often young creatives struck the attitude, without compensating with a great late ad. Honig made the creative trains run on time.

Another source of client aggravation was DDB's unique stand against back-up advertising—campaigns ready to replace running campaigns, just in case. The agency's point: Why use talent and time and money for such an exercise before a real need arose? Circumstances change. By the time a real need arose, the back-up campaign might not be the answer. Yes, but clients felt safer with that insurance. And Doyle Dane Bernbach was no longer the only game in town. Bright young agencies were happy to do back-ups. The mainstream agencies had always done them. And there was a recession going on, enabling clients to turn the screws of demands tighter. Under Gallagher-Austrian-Honig, DDB moved decisively into the world of back-up campaigns.

But Honig, like Gallagher, ruled over only part of Gaul. The old greats—Gage, Krone and Jack Dillon among them—had the clout to refuse to report to Honig, who, at 38, had only 10 years at the agency. His persona ranged somewhere between street smart and smart-ass—a cigarillo-smoking copywriter who looked and sounded like a skinny Dead End kid, convulsing the troops with his deadpan delivery of irreverent remarks.

Joe Daly lost no time worrying about the implications of the anarchic creative set-up. Ingeniously, he devised the term "floating stars," creating an image of a firmament afire with famous talents, available to any client. The striking concept served for a time as the centerpiece of his new business pitch.

The battle of egos had its nasty moments. At an Art Directors Awards luncheon in the Hilton Hotel, Old Greats sat at one table, Honig and his cohorts at another. The latter included Mike Mangano, Jack Mariucci, Jim Scalfone, John Caggiano. Helmut Krone paid a waiter to send over to Honig's table, with his compliments, a bottle of "dago red."

* * *

Bernbach came down to Honig's office a few months into the team's tenure and said, "You're doing a great job, Marvin. And I want you to know that I picked you." (Actually, Heekin had, in his "book.")

"So I knew he had to be happy with the job I was doing," Honig said later, "because if anybody knows Bill, that's the way he would say it."

Honig recalled his first two years in the job as "pretty clean. Then somewhere along the line . . . I think Bill was very disturbed through the early '70s. He'd had such great years, in the '50s and '60s. Something was going wrong, and he didn't really know what was going wrong. And it began going right again, in 1975, slowly but surely. And he was happy with that. Then he . . . I'm just guessing . . . wanted to get more involved in the agency, and I couldn't let him get that involved. It's very hard to put it that way. But he was a very intimidating man. It was his agency and he was Bill Bernbach.

"One of the problems the agency had in the early '70s and the reason they lost so many accounts is they didn't react to clients' requests, and the work was late. To get work out of there on time, I had to make decisions. And then to take it to Bill after . . . it wasn't just an ad, it was a TV campaign, maybe four or five storyboards. And if he saw it the week before it was supposed to go to the client, and said he didn't like it, that put us in a very difficult position. He'd say, 'It's up to you, though, Marvin.' And I would tell the account guy to take it over there. But the account guy felt very uncomfortable about it now. Bill Bernbach isn't one hundred percent behind it. So to have two people involved as creative director wasn't good, wasn't the solution to anything."

Times had changed. Bernbach "used to sit at his round desk and people would bring in mostly print," said Honig. "He'd change it, and make suggestions, and they'd come back in a couple of days with the new work. That's the way the agency ran for fifteen, twenty years. You can't do that with television. And Bill was never that comfortable with TV story-boards. After he saw the commercial, he was very accurate. He knew what was good about it and what was bad about it. But that's not helpful when it comes to TV commercials. You've got to know before you spend the hundred thousand dollars."

Ned Doyle's short version attributed Honig's undoing to his failure to spend a couple of hours with Bernbach each week, bringing him into the picture.

Bernbach in time began referring to Honig contemptuously as "the jokester," and quoting Daly on Honig as a "shit presenter."

"One of the problems at DDB," reflected Honig, "is that when you get in a high position, on the account side or the creative side, you're competing with the people who run the agency."

* * *

"I knew he drank, but I didn't think he was a drunk," Joe Daly maintained about the hiring of Gallagher.

Honig did not perceive Gallagher as a drunk when he arrived from London. "But he came into this complete surprise," said Honig, referring to Daly's refusal to let Gallagher near his "own" accounts. "After all, *they* called *him* and asked him to come. They went over to England to get him. He had no idea about the personalities. He was very surprised by what happened."

Another surprise awaited Gallagher—that the power of the purse, for raises and such, went to, and stayed with, Neil Austrian.

Drinking perhaps didn't seem such a bad alternative.

Still, Gallagher did what he could to help clients feel good about coming into, and staying at, Doyle Dane Bernbach.

"Not a team player," a Harris survey of advertising agencies reported in the early '70s as a strong opinion among advertisers about the agency. All such polls showed DDB tops in creativity, but only in creativity. Clients expected more.

Bernbach loved the creation of the advertising, and had no patience for the rest of it. There's a problem on an account? Do better advertising. "If your advertising goes unnoticed," he often said, "everything else is irrelevant."

Gallagher turned to "the rest of it," bringing media and research into strong focus for the first time. With Mike Drexler heading media and Ruth Ziff recruited by Gallagher to head research, the emphasis, in presentations and interviews, shifted to client services. It worked. Drexler and Ziff were heavyweights in their fields and helped alter the perception that DDB too often shot from the hip.

At the same time, Gallagher never took his eye off the creative ball. "Even the greatest marketing plan needs a great creative idea to bring it to life," Gallagher said, and intensely believed.

He worried about the agency's lack of organization and apparent lack of interest in organization. As account man Bill Wardell said about working there, "The fun was, that management didn't manage."

"That's what everyone cherished," said Mike Drexler. "You're given a job, and it's your job; nobody looks over your shoulder, it's really up to you. They give you the freedom to do it your way, and they support you. On the other hand, that can lead to things getting out of hand." And things did.

Gallagher tried to show the difference between "freedom to" and "freedom from." Every account group ran on its own rules and systems and history. Great for long-time and well-run accounts; devastatingly chaotic for others.

Gallagher codified, bringing into one huge book everything an account person needed to know to run an account at the agency. Honig, introducing the book to the account staff, each of whom would receive a copy, hefted it once or twice, and let it drop with a great thud on the speaker's table.

"This is the kind of book," he deadpanned, "that once you put it down, you can't pick it up."

* * *

An infallible indicator of power at the agency was who signed the letter to shareholders in the annual report. (I wrote it.) From the year he became president, in 1968, Daly signed along with Bernbach. Doyle and Dane signed, too, until their retirements. Since 1971, only Bernbach and Daly had signed.

Gallagher should have signed the 1975 report as president. But Daly said no, not yet. Surely, then, the 1976 report. After all, the agency's claim to "new strengths in the top management structure" lost credibility when the annual report kept featuring the same old management twosome. By the time of the '76 report, Daly had won the title of CEO, on Bernbach's reaching the age of 65. He promised Gallagher that he would sign that year.

But in mid-February of 1977, with the boards for the '76 annual report almost ready for the printer and Gallagher out of town, Daly called me into his office and asked me to strip out Gallagher's photograph and signature. I knew what that meant.

When Gallagher returned, he called and asked to see the boards. I brought them to his office with a heavy heart, sure that Daly had failed to inform him of the ominous change. Right. Gallagher's expression didn't alter as he studied the pages. Nor did the pitch of his voice as he asked why the change. I muttered lamely that Daly needed to be the sole signer of his first annual report as CEO. I felt sad for Gallagher and furious with Daly for ducking the first blow. Gallagher rose, and strode to Daly's office to argue for restoration of photo and signature. He was back in ten minutes, the wind quite out of him.

"I'll sign next year's," he said, in almost sheepish tones.

But before next year's report went to the printer's, a press release had announced that Gallagher would "step down" as president of the agency "for personal and family reasons." He would remain a member of the board.

By that time, the entire industry knew Gallagher as "a drunk." Daly cheerfully related stories about clients who unfavorably compared Gallagher's drinking habits with his own. ("They could talk business with me, but all Gallagher keeps saying is, 'Bring this man another drink.'")

Gallagher couldn't fight Daly. He withdrew, and sought solace elsewhere. His office was often empty. So was the desk of his secretary, a lovely young Englishwoman whom he later married. Bernbach's secretary, commenting on their frequent absence, said, "We ought to mail them their checks."

But it was too embarrassing to admit the agency had blown it with yet another president. Thus the face-saving gesture of keeping Gallagher on the board. Thus Daly's statement for official consumption: "Tom will be part of DDB for many years. He's done a great job in helping us build up this agency. We are deeply grateful to him."

And so Tom Gallagher didn't sign the next annual report. Neil Austrian did.

* * *

Austrian dazzled from the day of his arrival, at age 34, at Doyle Dane Bernbach. He was our St. George, slaying with one mighty stroke the dragon that was mysteriously sucking the life blood out of the agency.

Before Austrian, DDB's board was paralyzed by its inability to deal with the monster its "under-marketed properties" acquisition program had become. How, other than selling the whole kit and caboodle to Mary Wells, could the agency rid itself of Trade Mart and Snark, and keep secret the humiliating losses?

Fear not, said Austrian, fresh from Wall Street. Everybody makes mistakes. The sin is to keep holding on to those mistakes. Bite the bullet. Wall Street understands and respects that. And so he cleared the decks with one gigantic multi-million-dollar write-off, and once again, he proved to be right.

Out from under the "under-marketed properties," Austrian proceeded to strengthen DDB worldwide by acquiring foreign agencies. He initiated studies of entrepreneurial ways to make profitable use of agency capabilities. He wasn't an advertising man, but he was a quick study, and determined to learn. Shirt tail flying, one sleeve rolled up, tie askew, Austrian strode the agency halls, halloing everybody by name, from mailroom kids on up, learning in record time what everybody did.

He initiated five-year plans, ten-year plans, baseball teams, Friday night parties. He yanked the agency out of its dreary old offices at 11 West 43rd Street, raising morale by moving to spiffy space in a fabulous location—the block running from 49th to 50th streets on Madison Avenue. He let the money flow for a series of glamorous housewarming parties, for clients and media, on the marble-and-glass executive floor, an expanse that Marvin Honig referred to as "the egomaniac hall of fame."

Austrian loved his job, loved the agency, loved its people. Some saw in this athletic, energetic young leader a mix of the best of Doyle and Dane. A big heart, a joyous playfulness, empathy for the underdog, a willingness to risk, a deeply-rooted self confidence, and a gentle fearlessness. Moreover, he was immune from the Bernbach-Daly competitions. Neither could begin to understand his financial wizardry. The agency's stock would rise, split, split again. Why challenge him, when he made them richer and richer?

Some noted that he "wasn't an advertising man." But he propelled DDB onto a non-stop energy high. He handed out bonuses and established incentive plans to hold good people. He brought new technologies to every department.

Even the alcoholic downfall of Gallagher didn't cause much of a blip among the staff. Austrian absorbed Gallagher's job, too, and helped bring in important new clients whose language he spoke—IBM and Citibank. He won the Atari account by scoring three points in a computer game of "Tank" with founder Nolan Bushnell.

Billings surged. Morale surged. These were the great new days, Harvard Business School style.

Only later, when the place was a shambles, did the phrase return to haunt: "But he wasn't an advertising man."

Account Gains and Losses—1975-78

In:	Out:
Atari	Bank of the Commonwealth
CBS Broadcast Group	Hills Brothers coffee
Diamond-Sunsweet	Jamaica Tourist Board
Hershey Foods	Madison Laboratories
Intergold	Sony
Publishers Clearing House	Sterling Drug (Bayer aspirin)
Shaeffer Pen	
Standard Brands (Blue Bonnet)	
Sterling Drug (Bayer aspirin)	
Twentieth-Century Fox	
Wrangler jeans	

♦ ♦ ♦

16
Fathers and Sons

"You would not believe, my dear, how we long for parents, or their substitutes, to acknowledge our importance."
—Amanda Cross, *Sweet Death, Kind Death.*

Helmut Krone, one of the greatest art directors in the history of the agency, and perhaps of advertising, left DDB in 1969 to open his own shop, Case & Krone. Bernbach dealt with the blow his way, by insisting to his colleagues that he was "glad, because while Helmut was a great talent, he had dried up."

Three years later, Krone returned to the agency with the comment that Bernbach was the only person, other than himself, that he could work for. Bernbach was elated. Helmut, he told the same colleagues, "was still one of the great talents in advertising."

In the mid-'60s, co-copy chief Ron Rosenfeld left Doyle Dane Bernbach for a high-paying job at J. Walter Thompson. Bernbach took three agency copy stars to a festive lunch at the Algonquin. He expressed relief at the departure of someone who underwent as much psychoanalysis as did Rosenfeld. And Ron's leaving, added Bernbach, resolved the thorny problem of co-chiefs.

Almost as soon as he arrived at JWT, Rosenfeld rued his move. He called Bernbach. He'd made a terrible mistake—could he come back? Of course he could come back, replied an ecstatic Bernbach. Could he have his old title back? Of course he could have his old title back. And so he did. (He would later leave again, to open his own agency.)

People come and go in business—in the ad business, notoriously so. But the reactions of Bernbach to such comings and goings were out of the ordinary. As one listened to his colleagues remembering Bernbach, that emerged as a defining characteristic

Bernbach's son John put it this way:

"Very often when he was disturbed about certain things in the business, whether it was somebody leaving the agency, or a piece of business going, there was an element of . . . *outrage* is the wrong word, because he didn't express himself that way . . . *incomprehension* at the injustice of what was going on. Or the personal rejection that was taking place when somebody would leave."

Not just anybody, of course. His children—the creative talent he'd nurtured and brought to maturity. But children grow up and leave home, to find their own strengths. Sons are driven by an almost primeval need to show 'em, if not to beat 'em. To prove themselves worthy of the golden bough of succession.

"Every boss is a daddy," said Phyllis Robinson. "And you know how people feel about their daddies."

Bernbach knew, having tirelessly preached the importance of "insight into human nature [as] the key to the communicator's skill." Such insight led to the understanding that "your brain, your intellect, works for your genes and instincts, and never was there a more ruthless boss. . . . The basic instincts dominate." Motivations "lie deep in the realm of passions."

Bernbach understood in his head that every success achieved by his grown-and-gone children was a tribute to his teaching and nurturing. But in his gut he felt only personal rejection.

* * *

One last look now at the story of Bernbach and his parents. The rift remained in the years after Bill's request for help, despite occasional attempts by his siblings to bring them together.

On the morning after John's birth in 1944, Bill's older brother Harry went to his parents' apartment on the Grand Concourse.

"Come on, Pa," said Harry to Jacob, "I'm going to take you to see your grandson." Jacob, anxious and hopeful, got dressed to go with Harry.

Rebecca threw herself across the door. "If you go, I'll die," she told Jacob. He paused, and did what he'd always done to keep the peace. He gave way to Rebecca's demands. He shook his head sadly, and told Harry that he couldn't go. "What can I do?" he pleaded.

Harry and his wife Helen remained close to Bill and Evelyn. Sister Minna, who never married, made the trip to Bay Ridge often to visit Bill and Evelyn. Bill saw his brother Graham, though less often. But his parents, not at all, until his father's final illness.

In 1953, Jacob, a heavy smoker, lay dying of larynx cancer. Bill put aside his anger and went to the hospital for what would be a death-bed reconciliation. Evelyn accompanied Bill, trembling with the memory of her last meeting with Jacob—the awful night in 1938 when Harry and Helen invited them all to dinner, and Jacob wouldn't speak to her. But Evelyn's conciliatory mother had counseled her that a wife's place is by her husband's side at such times. That meant, even more terrifying, going to the Grand Concourse apartment after the funeral. Diffidently, Evelyn tried to help in the kitchen. Each time she did, Rebecca would grab whatever Evelyn had picked up and scream at her, presumably (Evelyn thought) something to do with the kosherness of her household. That ended their contact, until the mother's final years, when she was quite senile, and Evelyn arranged for her sons to see their grandmother for the first time.

Soon after Jacob died, Rebecca went into a nursing home on the Upper West Side of Manhattan. Bill and Harry paid the bills until she died.

John Bernbach remembered the story of his father's parents thus:

"I never met my grandfather. Never. I wasn't allowed to, basically. My father's mother I met, but by the time I met her she was senile. I'm sure that's the only reason I was allowed to meet her. So I have really no knowledge of that part of my family. I did get to know my cousins, and I know them now, and my aunt and uncles, all of whom have died as well. But the fact of the matter is, that was not part of my growing up. And I must tell you that any knowledge that I do have, any contact I had with them, was due to my mother, who forced that to happen. She didn't think it was right that my father should cut off his family."

He cut them off?

"Absolutely. Because of the difficulties they had. He just didn't want to have anything to do with his parents."

* * *

Perhaps his colleagues didn't know the origins of Bernbach's intense response to the departure of a "child," but they'd witnessed enough of his anger and depression to conclude that he wouldn't want any defectors at his 65th birthday celebration in August, 1976. Instead, he accepted at once a proposal to bring together his creative offspring, past and present, for the event. Presumably he realized that the gathering would be a widely-reported homage, a gala tribute to his influence in the world of advertising.

The timing was perfect. Of the good years in the '70s, none was happier than 1976. The triumvirate had mended many of the agency's broken fences through 1975. Only one client departed in the whole of that year—Madison Laboratories—and that because of a product conflict. The barren new business streak had ended with the arrival of CBS Broadcast Group, the Shaeffer Pen company, Diamond/Sunsweet and Intergold. Gallagher had reported to the Board that he was "extremely optimistic about prospects for new business in the immediate future." Importantly, the new willingness to listen to their requests, the on-time work, the back-up campaigns, the improved service departments, had altered client attitudes to the agency. They were now "extremely satisfied" with DDB's services.

The acquisition blunders of the past had been buried in 1975. Expenses had been cut in a significant staff reduction. ("Couldn't you put on somebody I don't know?" Bernbach had asked Marv Honig, in a jokingly-ethnic rising inflection, when he saw a list of creatives about to be axed.)

In March, 1976, the agency had moved to 437 Madison Avenue. Nothing pleased Bernbach more than the awe visitors expressed when they entered the marble-and-glass executive floor.

"Boy, this is an impressive place," enthused Paul Rand, the famed designer and one-time Bernbach mentor, invited up after years without contact. (Bernbach would ask him to put in a good word for DDB with IBM, a long-time Rand client. Rand did.)

"And Bernbach said to me," Rand later recalled, "'I designed it.' I mean, this is exactly what this guy said to me."

To paraphrase Honig, "If anyone knows Bill, that's the way he would say that he was happy with the offices."

* * *

The devastating uncertainties—about the agency, about his own financial security—had been put to rout. From the minutes of the September 12, 1975, Board minutes:

"The Chairman [Daly] said the Board should consider the fact that William Bernbach has reached the age of sixty-four and will come within the scope of the retirement policy of the Corporation next year. He stated that in his opinion, Mr. Bernbach's contribution to the Corporation is and has been and continues to be unique, and that his continued active participation is and will be extremely important to the Corporation.

"The Chairman went on to say that he was still very much in favor of the Corporation's retirement policy and would even go on to state that if he, the Chairman, requested a long-term contract when he was sixty-four or sixty-five years of age, the Board should not grant him one, However, he felt that Mr. Bernbach represented a very unusual and unique situation and that an exception should be made in his case."

Perhaps Daly's gratuitous comments on the retirement policy *vis-a-vis* his own future were meant to stroke Doyle and Dane, who continued as board members, and who may have felt some annoyance at the way the rules always applied to them, and always were bent for Bernbach.

Daly swore he meant what he said. Ironically, when events led to his being offered a five-year contract as he approached his 65th birthday, he grabbed it.

"I'd said, `When I'm 65 I want to get out of here,' he reflected later, "But now I'm 65 and I don't have a home life anymore. And what did I want? A five-year contract, and I'll give up the CEO. Bill gave up the CEO to me when he was 65, and he stayed on."

Bill and Joe. Competitive to the end.

* * *

Bernbach's 10-year contract was drawn up in October 1975 and was kept under wraps until August 1976, when it became the lead paragraph in a press release that only secondarily noted Daly's ascension to CEO. So Bernbach remained king. Officially, chairman of the executive committee. More importantly, as he laughingly pointed out, "owner."

What better time to show his "children," including the ones who'd left, how splendidly things had turned out for him? Gallagher's embarrassing fall hadn't yet happened, nor had Bernbach's disenchantment with Honig begun to fester. The perfect moment to invite the kids and take them through the marble-and-glass palace, let them see that the glories weren't all in the past. (But only the past would become legend. "The Australian aborigines have in their lore a kind of time called The Dream Time, when there was heaven on earth," Tony Morgan, executive VP of TBWA Advertising, remarked on a creative panel in 1989, "And their ancestors lived in it. I think for us in advertising, The Dream Time, whether we were there or not, is Doyle Dane Bernbach in the 1960s.")

* * *

Bernbach, as father, encouraged and developed the talents of his creatives, took credit for many of their accomplishments, felt devastated when they left him, and resented any implication of their outdoing him.

Ted Factor couldn't resist getting under Bernbach's skin by extravagantly praising Phyllis Robinson's copy. "I'd talk about how great Phyllis' work was on, say, Max Factor Pink lipsticks." Robinson wrote much of the body copy on the ads attributed to Bernbach. "Invariably, Bill would rejoin with, 'Do you know where Phyllis was when I found her?'" [In Grey's promotion department, that's where.] The impish Factor had "four or five statements with which I could pick away at Bill's ego, and I knew exactly what his response would be every time."

* * *

In proposing the celebration, I'd stumbled on one of the little secrets his colleagues kept close about Bernbach—his singular unforgivingness of those who'd left him. Once he agreed to the event, I stumbled on something that surprised me even more, his "children's" attitude towards him.

I wanted anecdotes for the occasion. Lively little stories from the creatives on lessons they'd learned from Bernbach. Collected, they'd provide a treasure for Bernbach, and wonderful material for publicity.

A memo asking creatives for such memories elicited one or two responses. Telephone follow-ups produced a fair return from former DDBers, nothing from working DDBers. What was going on? I walked into every occupied creative office and asked for anecdotes.

"Don't you know there *are* no anecdotes about Bill?" an old-hand copywriter stated.

"I don't wish to," said an art director, flatly.

"You wouldn't want what I have to say," said an associate creative director.

"Don't you know," a DDB veteran explained, "the creatives have always had a love/hate relationship with Bill." No, I didn't, at that stage, know.

My reaction was outrage. I turned scold, berating them for lack of gratitude to the man who taught the world the difference between advertising and great advertising. The man who'd made their best work possible. The man who'd elevated creatives to the top of the profession.

They began to come through.

* * *

All was forgiven in the love fest that was Bernbach's 65th birthday party. Embraces greeted the prodigals, eyes teared over, every trace of doubt and anger and resentment melted in the excitement of shared memories, sharing the historic celebration. And underlying every moment, the pride and wonder and gratitude for having lived in The Dream Time, when there was heaven on earth.

Bernbach stood glowing before them, and told what was in his heart: "I look around and I think, what a helluvan agency we could have."

* * *

On the block-long walls of the executive floor were pinned 22 anecdotes, blown up and mounted on large styrofoam boards. Bernbach flushed with pleasure as he read them. Some related funny inside jokes. Ken Duskin, former DDB art director, told a favorite agency tale of how he came a-cropper for his extravagant expense accounts:

"Everything I know about advertising (if I know anything at all) I learned from Bill. But the one thing I learned from him that stands out most in my mind is *never* to order Chateau Lafitte Rothschild wine when he was picking up the check."

Some were eye-witness accounts of well-known episodes, such as this from another former DDB art director, Len Sirowitz:

"Since this is a birthday party, I have a birthday anecdote to tell, the birthday of a DDB blue chip client.

"My memory takes me back to the middle '60s when I had the honor of attending the first orientation meeting with Bill at a brand new client, Mobil.

"A VP on the client side was speaking rather proudly about their newly proposed logo design commemorating the company's 100th birthday. He said, with starry-eyed pride, 'Just look at that. It will be displayed on gas stations all over America. Just look at that red O. Right in the center, it will say 1866-1966. Isn't that wonderful. Do you know what that means?'

"At that point, Bill stood up and, with cool aplomb, said to his newest client, 'IT MEANS YOU JUST DIED!'

"So what did I learn from all this? I learned, if you're Bill Bernbach, you can get away with anything."

Some illustrated how Bernbach connected the small things in life with the art of persuasion. When he suggested placing the tag in the middle as well as the end of a commercial, he told a surprised copywriter, Helen Miller, "Something that's almost like a mistake is what gets a person's attention.

"For instance, when my boys were little, they would come into the bathroom each morning to watch me shave. Now, I had one pair of shorts that had a tear in them, which my wife had mended. I wore those shorts maybe one day out of the seven in a week.

"One day when I was wearing them, my older boy said, 'Daddy, why do you *always* wear those shorts?' People remember the mend. The rough spot when everything else is smooth."

One anecdote illuminated how Bernbach's concern about "nice" affected the agency's advertising. It centered on a Sony campaign that showed Sonys turning up in news-making real-life situations, such as the '72 Democratic convention. About that time, *Life* magazine ran a photo of chess genius Bobby Fischer sprawled in his Reykjavik hotel room with a chess board and his Sony radio.

Copywriter Lore Parker described what happened.

"Bobby Fischer—the super-genius media star of the moment! In ten minutes, the picture became a Sony ad. Fischer's agency said yes. *Life* said yes. Bill Bernbach said no.

"*No!*

"'I think it's wrong,' said Bill, 'to work with someone so selfish and ill-mannered— a man [whose bad manners are] making this country look bad in the eyes of the world.'"

Parker "hated Bill for two whole days . . . and then I tried in vain to think of a single exploitative or morally questionable ad that had ever come out of DDB.

"How old-fashioned," she concluded. "How square. How wonderful."

All the anecdotal offerings had been set in type, save for one, the one that meant the most to Bernbach. Three one-sentence paragraphs, handwritten by Bob Gage:

"I brought my talent to Bill.

"He recognized it, educated it and inspired it.

"He put the feather in my cap."

Account Gains and Losses, 1979-81

In:	Out:
Allied Chemical	American Airlines
American Greetings Corp.	Avianca
Borden	Avis Rent-a-Car (second time)
Burpee seeds	Diamond-Sunsweet
C&C Cola	Levy's bread
Chanel	Ponderosa
Citibank	Publishers Clearing House
Diner's Club	Standard Brands (Blue Bonnet)
Gagliardi Brothers	Twentieth-Century Fox
IBM Corporate	Wrangler jeans
IBM Office Products	
Paine Webber	
Pan Am	
Sherwin-Williams stores	
Universal Pictures	
Weight Watchers	

◆ ◆ ◆

17
The Guy from Compton

"Nice guys finish last."—Leo Durocher

Inside and outside, the perception grew stronger through 1976 and 1977 that Doyle Dane Bernbach had got it back together. Early in 1977, the editors of *anny* gave their "1976 Hottest Shop award" in the above-$75 million category to DDB. Their reasons:

"Last year, DDB stayed busy on all fronts, not the least of which was in the billings area (up $78,929,000). Aided by prestigious new account gains, the shop also received further testimony of its abilities by multi-million-dollar added assignments from many existing clients. Additionally, its well-executed media purchases coupled with a direct mail agency acquisition proved to many that this granddaddy of creative shops had matured into a well-run business organization."

If "well-run business organization" seemed slightly extravagant to some sharp-eyed insiders, their observations were swamped in the prevailing excitement of new business, new products, new campaigns.

Neil Austrian's financial brilliance led the agency to record high income and earnings in 1976, 1977, 1978. Wall Street analysts couldn't issue enthusiastic "buy" reports fast enough. In 1978, the stock split 3-for-2. (And skipping just slightly ahead, to indicate how much Wall Street knows, Joe Daly won the *Wall Street Transcript* award in 1980 for "Best Chief Executive in the Advertising Industry," based on a poll of ad industry analysts. Daly won again in 1982, this time jointly with Austrian, making him the first ad executive to win the honor twice.)

With morale high and good news abounding, Tom Gallagher slid off the screen, and a new installment in the agency's tragi-comic presidential saga began.

* * *

In April, 1978, an outsider (again!) took high office at the agency, the usual politicking insiders having received the usual brush-off from their leaders.

Enter Paul Paulson, a man who'd just missed becoming president of Compton Advertising.

Compton?!?!

Procter & Gamble's favorite agency. The pits, to copywriters and art directors. The hatchery of slice-of-life commercials, with mothers and daughters sniffing laundry, lady plumbers bailing out distraught housewives, sink-scrubbing wives patronizing dumb husbands. A *Compton* man brought in as executive VP for client services, with a clear commitment to the presidency of Doyle Dane Bernbach?

Heresy! said the creatives.

Not so to Bernbach, who gave the Paulson hiring his blessing, for the very reason that Paulson ranked high at P&G's favorite agency. P&G, a DDB client since 1972, was a bone in the throat, a galling dilemma. Board discussions about P&G went like this one, from the May 15, 1976 meeting:

"The Chairman asked Mr. Austrian if he thought the Corporation would ever make up its investment on P&G. Mr. Austrian responded that certainly the Corporation would never make large profits on P&G but that it was still essential that the Corporation be involved with that client. Mr. Daly added that in his opinion the Corporation would not have been able to get the Bayer business if it had not previously shown its ability to handle P&G business. Mr. Kopelman stated that he had just returned from Greenbrier and that the P&G involvement with the Corporation was viewed by many people as a clear indication of the Corporation's ability to handle package goods."

By 1978, Bayer had departed, bringing back into currency the Madison Avenue chestnut that "Doyle Dane Bernbach can't keep package goods clients." For all the renewed admiration of the agency, all the internal fixing, all the world-wide growth, DDB still hadn't shaken off that perception.

P&G, meanwhile, kept assigning the agency financially-draining new products and barely-breathing old products. The expected payoff of a major brand hadn't materialized. Would it ever? DDBers recalled how the agency resigned General Foods in the 1960s under similar circumstances—money-losing assignments and no major brand payoff. Not now. For image reasons, DDB needed the P&G name on its client list. So the financial drain continued. As did the emotional drain. DDB creatives, watching their concepts tested into oblivion, equated working on P&G with a sentence in the gulag. More than once, Ned Doyle suggested setting up a separate agency to handle P&G, so it wouldn't "contaminate" the rest of the agency.

Ridiculous, in Bernbach's opinion. Spoiled children. Bernbach's competitors for immortality in advertising—David Ogilvy and Leo Burnett—had great success with their giant package goods accounts, and the industry continued to admire their creative work.

Oh, for a Jock Elliott.

Austrian, named president when Gallagher left, couldn't be expected to solve every problem in the place. He'd shoveled out the deepest patches of the agency's Augean stables.

"But there was a real nervousness among the executive committee," Austrian recalled later, "that we didn't have, in me or anyone else at the time, a senior package goods marketer in the account group who could keep clients like P&G, and go after clients like General Foods. That my reputation and skills were not in the marketing area, and that I ought to go out and get someone" to fill the bill. The search, this time thorough and professional, turned up Paulson.

Bernbach never doubted that attitudes inside and outside the agency would change if P&G gave DDB a Tide, an Ivory, a Crisco, a Duncan Hines, a Crest.

Paulson might be the rabbit to make that happen.

* * *

"If I can put Doyle Dane Bernbach on the right track," mused Paulson, after sizing up the way things worked at the agency, "I'll go down in advertising history."

But what was the right track?

To Paulson, instantly tagged "Mr. Procter & Gamble from Slice-of-Life City" by DDB creatives, the right track put the account group at the center of the agency universe. Media, research—and creative—would orbit around the account people.

Bernbach's philosophy and the history of the agency put the creatives at the center. The advertising was what counted. Whatever the upgrading of agency services, the creatives were the magic, and were treated accordingly. They weren't about to relinqush a wisp of their privileged status.

Paulson's approach, the creatives believed, would turn DDB into "just another package goods agency, another Compton," where strong account people and endless copy testing would drain the life blood out of the creative process.

Unless DDB adapted to the package goods world, Paulson countered, it would not be able to attract or hold the large clients needed for growth—General Foods, General Mills, Quaker Oats (all three were former DDB clients), and P&G. The agency would dwindle into a creative boutique.

And where stood Bernbach and Austrian in the ensuing mayhem? They, after all, hired him.

Paulson, before taking the job, had "spent a lot of time with Bernbach to find out whether he was interested in my coming aboard to try to do something to improve the professional reputation of the agency." Not surprisingly for a Compton man, Paulson saw DDB as a place where the account people were "bag carriers," sent off to the client to sell ads the creatives thought were right.

"Bill was, at the beginning, a very strong advocate of what I was trying to do," added Paulson. He'd made it clear before signing on that "I was going to run the agency, or I wouldn't come. Not just account management."

But he agreed to start with account management, to rebuild that department with stronger, more sophisticated marketing types, who would give clients confidence that their needs, in a constantly changing world, were understood.

"Because if you have weak account people, clients don't respect them, and then what happens is the creative guy rises or falls every day. If they love the ad, it's a good day. If they hate it, it's a bad day. And that's no way to manage a relationship over the long run. Nobody produces great stuff every day."

Bernbach seemed to support Paulson for a long time. They lunched together at least once a week, most compatibly, for both were total advertising men, dedicated to the business of selling the client's product. Neither doubted that the differences in their approaches could be reconciled.

Certainly Bernbach appreciated Paulson's view of who had done what, historically, to make Doyle Dane Bernbach great.

"In my experience," said Paulson, "Doyle did the posturing. 'If they don't like it, to hell with them.' But Bernbach was the guy who'd go in and listen to the client and if the client didn't like something he would suggest other ways. Most of the clients felt Bernbach was on their side. That what he was trying to do was in their best interest. And he solidified the relationships with clients, and provided the leadership within the agency, and gave a clear-cut direction to what the agency produced."

Bernbach appreciated Paulson, too, for the exemplary way he fit the oft-preached (and alas, oft-breached) qualifications for becoming a DDBer—nice, and also talented. In fact, every description of Paulson, then and later, by admirers and detractors, opened with the words, "He's a nice man." And Bernbach, as we have seen, needed "nice." (Once, having approved a piece of work brought him by an art director widely loathed as a sadistic swine, Bernbach said to his secretary, "He really is a nice man.")

Paulson had a gentle manner, and twinkling eyes, and didn't tower over Bernbach. He wasn't a loud-mouth, or a drinker, or a womanizer. Solid, stable, reassuring. A truly nice man.

And Austrian's position on Paulson? Who can say? Not until much later did agency people figure out that Austrian's decisions and support were based on whatever he'd heard from the last person he talked to.

* * *

"The day I arrived, Marvin [Honig] said he was going to quit," Paulson remembered, "because, he said, 'The account guy from Compton is going to be president. . . . '" Honig didn't make good his promise for a year and a half. Until then, he did everything possible to undermine Paulson. He succeeded. But in doing so, he brought down a great deal more, including his own position at Doyle Dane Bernbach.

* * *

That Paulson strengthened the agency's account staff was generally conceded. In fact, his recruits would later be wooed by the Ogilvys and Young & Rubicams—a reversal of historical proportions in adland. "He seduced a lot of good account people," noted one observer, "and the bait he held out was a better DDB." Which meant, a DDB with account people at the center.

They were known as "the new breed," and "Paul's team."

"A lot of veteran DDB account people who genuinely liked Paulson as a person, and liked his manner of running things, felt at the same time, 'There's nothing I can do to get on this man's team because I don't have an MBA, or I've been around here for fifteen years, and he's only interested in younger hotshots with MBAs,'" recalled Dick Kane.

Call them "the old breed." Some had considerable clout, and all of them drifted into Marvin Honig's camp.

Honig never missed an opportunity to crack snide jokes about MBAs and about research, in small meetings, or at gatherings of the entire staff. Drip, drip, drip. It worked like anti-Semitism. Soon, any irritant within the agency was attributed by the brain-washed troops to the rising tide of MBAs. Top management, including MBA Neil Austrian, laughed somewhat uncomfortably at Honig's unrelenting MBA jokes, and did nothing.

True to DDB management style, Paulson had won the job and then received no support to do what he'd been hired to do.

In April, 1979, he was named president of the agency, as had been promised. That in the teeth of a threat by Honig and Roy Grace to leave if it happened. So, didn't Paulson's promotion tell the creative department that "this is the way it's going to be?"

"Yeah, but you've got to back it up," Paulson said later. "What was happening was that Marvin wouldn't put good people on most of the package goods accounts—a lot of subversion and a lot of Mickey Mouse stuff going on. Maybe Bill said, 'We're going to do it,' but they didn't enforce it. What you really had to do was say to Marvin and Roy or anybody else, 'Look, this is the way it's going to be, and if you're uncomfortable with it, you've got to go somewhere else.'

"We were our own worst enemy. I'd talk to people I knew—such as General Foods, which we were pitching—and I'd say, 'It's a new operation, we really are interested in building a business and in professionalism.' And then at cocktail parties guys like Marvin and Roy and others were saying, 'That's all bullshit. Paulson is off doing his thing, but we're still a creative shop, and screw those guys.'

"So the General Foods, etc., people would say to me, 'Maybe *you* think it's a different operation, but we're hearing it's really the same old operation, even worse. The inmates run the asylum over there.'

"We had junior copy people who, after hearing client comments on their work, would say, 'I'm not changing this; I'm not changing that.' It was total anarchy. The worst was the arrogance from people who had nothing to be arrogant about. Because they worked at Doyle Dane Bernbach, they thought they were blessed with a talent that could do no wrong."

The Stroh client complained to Paulson that the creatives brought in ideas that seemed all wrong for their beer drinkers, and they'd never come to focus groups to listen to their customers talk about beer. "What the hell does he [the client] know?" the creatives responded when Paulson told them of the complaint.

Stroh left.

American Tourister's new management agreed that DDB's gorilla campaign was right for selling the durability of their luggage. But would the agency please try a fashion approach? Roy Grace did a storyboard.

"A gorilla coming down a runway with sneakers and velvet. You wonder, what the hell is that all about? We lost credibility, and we lost the account."

So it went.

"I was naive," Paulson reflected, later. "I remember a call from a friend who asked what I was going to do with those insiders who did not get the presidency of DDB. I told him I meant to work with them. My friend said, 'You should fire them at once, or they'll undercut you, they'll politic against you, they'll be lying in wait for you to fail.'"

He was the political innocent who didn't have the stomach that Daly had for the Machiavellian game.

To his more accomplished antagonists, he was the easy target in a vigorous game of "Kill the stranger."

* * *

Marvin and Roy would leave—that was the constant threat. One heard it (as I'd heard it from a worried Bernbach) expressed as though they'd merged into one person, MarvinandRoy. They'll leave if we make Paulson president. But what can we do? We promised him the presidency.

When Paulson hung in despite the laughter at the MBA jokes, despite the "subversion and Mickey Mouse stuff," Honig walked—in September 1979, five months after Paulson's ascension to the presidency.

The surprise was: Roy Grace did not leave with Honig. Instead, he took possession of Honig's job and title, Executive Creative Director, plus 30,000 shares of agency stock, acquired with financial help from DDB.

It's unlikely that anyone was more surprised than Honig.

Three months later, Honig returned to DDB, having found no better agency job in the meanwhile. Austrian asked him back to work on IBM, "the second biggest mistake I ever made," Austrian later rued.

In bringing Honig back, he put into play a deadly new rivalry, between Marvin and Roy, those good close friends, now cloven forever.

* * *

Grace hadn't become executive CD to preside over the dissolution of the creatives' empire. Honig's walk, and Grace's rise, changed nothing in the imbalance of power. The original promise to Paulson that he would run the whole agency dissolved in the agency's increasingly murky vapors.

Through 1980 and 1981, the situation deteriorated. The agency polarized into pro- and anti-Paulsonites. Under those two umbrellas, factions and fiefdoms spawned. Creatives grouped generally under the anti-Paulson umbrella, but there was no unity in the department. Grace, Honig, Levenson bad-mouthed and undercut one another. Account managers split into Paulson's camp and Austrian's camp.

"The place became like a bunch of separate agencies," recalled Dick Kane. "Groups didn't care much about the progress being made by other groups, as opposed to pulling together as one agency. They weren't cooperating with one another. They were interested in the contribution their own group was making versus any other group. Hoping the other groups would do less well to make them look better."

Procter & Gamble people got the drift. Any hope of a Tide, a Crest, a major brand, evaporated. Nor did Paulson manage to land any other large piece of new business. Another non-rabbit.

Austrian stepped up his search for a merger partner.

Account Gains and Losses, 1982 (the year of Bernbach's death)

In:	Out:
Cigna	American Tourister
Litton Industries	Lehman Brothers
Murjani	Paine Webber
Philip Morris (Parliament cigarets)	Pan Am
	Procter & Gamble
	Sherwin-Williams
	Stroh Beer

♦ ♦ ♦

18
What's in a Name?

It is with literature as with law or empire—an established name is an estate in tenure, or a throne in possession."
—Edgar Allan Poe

Bill Bernbach reached his arm up and over the shoulder of tall, New England-handsome John O"Toole, as they walked out of the Sky Club, the elegantly traditional, exclusive dining club on the 56th floor of Manhattan's Pan Am building.

"John, we have to make this happen," said Bernbach.

"Bill, you're damned right," replied O'Toole.

They'd talked through lunch about the planned merger of their two advertising agencies, Doyle Dane Bernbach and Foote, Cone & Belding. O'Toole felt a sense almost of awe. "Talking to Bill about it . . . he was a man that I'd idolized from the time I'd been a copywriter in Chicago."

Bernbach had never admired the creative work of Foote, Cone & Belding, an agency that produced vast quantities of competent but unmemorable advertising for a long string of clients, only one of whom came quickly to mind: P. Lorillard. Maker of cigarets.

Cigarets!

Yet Bernbach profoundly longed for the consummation of the merger. Visibly wasting from the effects of leukemia, he was, more impatiently than ever, in the grip of the "obsessive desire to . . . take care of one's own." This merger, Neil Austrian had convinced him, would ensure the financial future of Doyle Dane Bernbach. And that meant Bernbach's children and grandchildren.

They, not cigarets, were on Bernbach's mind when he sincerely told O'Toole that "we have to make this happen."

* * *

Austrian and his FCB opposite, Norman Brown, chief architects, looked at their plan and felt pride. Unlike so many marriages arranged on Madison Avenue, this would be a merger from strength, a merger of equals. The consummation date was set for the first week of May 1982.

Each agency billed about $1.150 billion. Combined, their billings would make them the second largest U.S.-based agency worldwide. Geographically, they were a near-perfect fit. Doyle Dane Bernbach had never made it in Chicago, FCB's most important turf. And FCB needed a boost on DDB's home ground, New York. Internationally, their offices complemented one another's.

The stickiest wicket was Los Angeles, where FCB handled the Mazda account, a blatant conflict with Volkswagen. In deepest secrecy, FCB prepared blueprints for the sale of its L.A. office to the management. (Two years later, the idea would be revived when Needham Harper sold its L.A. office, agency for Honda, to clear the decks for its own merger with Doyle Dane Bernbach.)

Other account conflicts existed, but both agencies were prepared for fallout. On Doyle Dane Bernbach's side, several of the conflicting accounts were shaky anyway, and one, Procter & Gamble, was everybody's favorite "let's-dump-'em" candidate.

Austrian would be chief executive officer of the merged operation. But ambition wasn't the strongest propellant in Austrian's forceful promotion of the plan. What Austrian sought was no less than total invulnerability to threats, or actualities, of client departures. Almost from the day of his move from Wall Street to Madison Avenue, Austrian perceived a vast inequality in the comparative power of clients and agencies. Brilliant financial strategist that he was, he looked for ways to regain the agency's control over its destiny.

Once, such control had derived from DDB's reputation as the only game in town for great advertising. Now its disciples were in practices of their own, all over the world. In any case, the creative product wasn't Austrian's area. He looked for other solutions.

Having rescued the agency from its disastrous non-advertising acquisitions, he restlessly explored the possibilities of selling various agency services to small agencies around the country. That, and other arcane concepts, were meant to provide sufficient income to stiffen backbones and reinvigorate a spirit of independence.

Austrian soon saw that the best protection of all was a client base broad enough to withstand a series of departures. But the process of winning new business was too slow, and the need too great, to go it alone. A merger with a big, successful agency—preferably headquartered in the Midwest—seemed the answer to Austrian. He looked at prospects, and talked to many, including Leo Burnett and Needham Harper, in the years that followed.

* * *

Bob Levenson watched for Bernbach's arrival on the marble-and-glass executive floor one Monday morning in April, 1982.

"And I attacked. Because I couldn't believe it," he recalled later.

"I want to hear it from your lips," he told Bernbach, "say it in your own words, what you feel about the cigaret business."

Bernbach calmly replied with almost the exact words that Austrian had quoted to Levenson on Friday: "I've turned the agency over to a new group of people, and they are responsible for its destiny, its well-being. They can't be slaves to a decision I made nearly 20 years before this." So there it was.

Levenson: "And with that obstacle out of the way, Neil and Norm Brown were pushing pretty hard to make it happen. And I think the only thing that Marvin [Honig] and Roy [Grace] and I ever agreed on was that we weren't really happy with the thought of working for John O'Toole."

* * *

It would have been hard to find an agency leader more decent, thoughtful and intelligent than John O'Toole. (He would go on to become chairman of the American Association of Advertising Agencies.) O'Toole wrote charming and instructive staff memos, often reprinted in the press. He took positions—such as promoting a minimum five-minute length for political commercials—that gave the profession an air of statesmanship. He spoke often and engagingly at industry gatherings. And he accomplished one thing that so far had eluded Bernbach—he had just published a book on advertising.

But he hadn't the passion that Bernbach had, the ability to set creative hearts on fire, to coax and cajole and nurture until his people brought him work that surprised themselves, ads that touched, and moved, and persuaded. Great advertising.

O'Toole had no pretensions on that score.

"I always felt that Doyle Dane Bernbach was doing superb work," he told me later."That kind of work was not incompatible with what we were trying to do. They were better at it than we were. And I was all for having that spread throughout our organization."

* * *

O'Toole sensed, from the Saturday in March that he'd driven over to Austrian's house in Old Greenwich for lunch, that things were right for the merger. "The numbers and everything else don't mean as much as whether it feels right," he said, "and it was feeling right to me. It felt good. And then, talking to Bill..."

It felt quite something else after an evening with Doyle Dane Bernbach's top three creative guns—Roy Grace, Marvin Honig and Bob Levenson. A trio whose attitudes toward one another led a later CEO to describe them as "three nuts with hand grenades."

They gathered, O'Toole and the three DDBers, in Levenson's Park Avenue penthouse apartment, after work on Wednesday, April 28, the night before the board meetings scheduled to vote on, and presumably finalize, the deal.

O"Toole later reconstructed the meeting like this:

"They seemed very concerned that I would be the judge of their creative work. And I tried to assure them that this is not what I had in mind. I had other things to do. But that seemed to bother them. So I said, 'Whoever is passing creative judgment on your work now will continue to. I assume Bill Bernbach does some of that.' They kind of smiled and said, 'Oh no, Bill doesn't.' So I said, 'Okay, in that case continue to operate the same way you are now operating, and continue to report to Neil.' At which point they told me that they didn't report to Neil.

"At this point, I wasn't smiling. A company has to operate in some sort of fashion that approximates a business. 'Whom do you report to?' "Nobody.'"

O'Toole was incredulous. They surely would have to report to somebody in a merged operation. Perhaps the head of the New York office. Perhaps the CEO. *Somebody.* "I was not going to face the shareholders or the financial community with some sort of bizarre commune. So that was not resolved when I left."

Bizarre commune? These were Bernbach's children—talented, egotistical, competitive, able to live and work under the same roof only because they were still working for Bernbach's approval, whether or not they reported to him.

Roy Grace guilefully asked O'Toole a question that was "really sticking it to Levenson.

"John, when you go around and make your speeches, do you show commercials?"

"Sure, I show the best of Foote, Cone."

"Then you would show some of our commercials, right? Take some of Doyle Dane Bernbach's classic commercials and put them on your reel?"

Grace watched Levenson squirm. Levenson was DDB's designated hitter as creative spokesman—the person who took the agency's treasures and represented them. He did it well, but not very often.

"The thought of John O'Toole doing that with DDB's work," Grace chuckled, "I mean, you have to understand the sensitivity. It was more than salt in the wounds. It was very painful to deal with."

"If that's what Levenson did," mused O'Toole years later, astonished that the creative spokesman role had underlain any of the hostility at the meeting, "it was a well-kept secret."

The trio, allegedly testing for philosophical compatibility, went through a list of FCB's accounts, often disparaging the work. "I didn't take umbrage," said O'Toole. "I just said, 'Terrific, you can help us.'"

To Levenson, corned beef sandwiches became the metaphor for the encounter. The talk went on longer than they'd expected, and so Levenson's wife Kathe called Kaplan's Deli for sandwiches and beer.

Levenson: "The stuff came. And we were sitting around this brass table, and we unwrapped these foil packages. And I swear O'Toole looked at it like he'd never seen a corned beef sandwich before. And he started looking around for the silverware . . . He's looking for tools, and we didn't have any tools. Then he started looking at his watch a lot, and mumbled something about his driver had been waiting too long, and went out the door and disappeared into the night.

"Marvin and Roy and I sat around for a little while longer, finished the sandwiches, and all agreed that even without the corned beef sandwich episode, O'Toole was operating in a universe that we didn't know anything about, and really didn't *want* to know anything about . . . And I think we agreed we would get back to Neil the next day and tell him what our impressions of O'Toole were."

O'Toole: "I think they had made their minds up to that [the corned beef metaphor] before I arrived. I frequently have sandwiches, corned beef and otherwise, at my desk. They were not buying, from the moment I walked in. And if one of them had decided to buy the merger, the other two probably wouldn't have."

Honig had walked O'Toole out to Levenson's elevator before returning to the sandwiches. O'Toole, non-plussed, had asked Honig, "What just went on in there?"

He'd just attended a rather typical late-life Doyle Dane Bernbach meeting.

* * *

The rest of the story was a shambles. Austrian worked through the following day to soothe fears, allay doubts, give assurances, explain again why bigger was necessary in an economy increasingly multi-national. Bernbach could have convinced any of the doubters, but he'd recently come home from the hospital, where a quart of fluid had been removed from his lungs. His lawyer son, Paul, would represent him at the board meeting, and express his pro-merger position.

The board met late in the afternoon, and proceeded to argue until 3 a.m. without coming to a vote.

They could not agree on a name for the combined agency.

Roy Grace: "That was the illusion. You tell me that you have two billion-dollar companies who think they have good reason to get together who are not able to decide on the name?"

Six names in the hopper. Ned Doyle, Maxwell Dane, Bill Bernbach all still alive and on the board. Fairfax Cone dead but important in agency lore. Don Belding dead and less important. Emerson Foote a vestigial remain. O'Toole had proposed Bernbach & Cone, or Cone & Bernbach—"either way, the only two names that mattered." Or, FCB, for Foote, Cone & Bernbach. Or any combination of initials. As long as it didn't end up with six full names: Foote Cone Belding Doyle Dane & Bernbach. Or Doyle Dane Bernbach Foote Cone & Belding.

"Sounds like an insurance company," said Roy Grace when the names rolled off that way. "So what's wrong with an insurance company?" retorted Austrian, a response that lost him points with the creatives.

Every combination led to dissension. Initials? Bernbach's name must not disappear. What about Doyle's and Dane's? Um, well. Foote Cone first? Then the world would think Doyle Dane Bernbach had been taken over. But Austrian would be CEO; FCB needed something to show it wasn't being swallowed up. DDB/Foote Cone? Why should they get the names and we the initials? Who the hell is Foote anyway? Etc.

Paul Bernbach: "I walked out into the anteroom and called my father at home. He was home sick; he and my mother were both there. And I said, people are basically in favor of it, but the name has become a sticking point. And he said—he and my mother were both on the phone—'Why don't you call it FCDDB?' I went back into the meeting and said he suggested that and was met with hoots and catcalls, because it sounds like Fuck DDB—which never would have occurred to my father or mother in a million years. But he didn't even care if Foote Cone came first or if it was all initials. He cared about the health of the business, and frankly at that stage about the financial well-being of the family, and he thought if that would help secure his children and grandchildren, that was fine."

At 3 a.m. they adjourned, exhausted, prepared to resume next day. But there wasn't another meeting. For the next morning, the financial and advertising press began to call with questions about why Doyle Dane Bernbach's stock had risen two points, a gain of 14.5 percent, in a single day after months as flat as a Long Island potato field. Were reports of merger talks with FCB accurate?

Security and Exchange Commission regulations force a response. Either "Yes, we're going ahead with merger discussions" or "No we aren't." Austrian and FCB heads quickly opted for "No we aren't," recognizing that the many potential client conflicts could not be dealt with before a "Yes we are" would hit the press.

A mandatory 90-day cooling-off period followed. But it was all over.

Much later, Austrian and others rued the outcome. In retrospect, the two agencies were "a perfect fit." The time was right, the numbers were right, the geography was right.

And the lack of enthusiasm by the creatives?

"They were opposed because they felt FCB's product was so inferior to ours," said board member Bob Pfundstein. "But a lot of these people were still living in the '50s and '60s. The quality of the work was still good, but nowhere near as sparkling as back then."

♦ ♦ ♦

19
Out in the Wash

"The time has come, the walrus said, to talk of many things."
—Lewis Carroll

The failure of the Foote Cone merger brought about a flurry of "whither DDB" meetings, one of which sealed Paulson's fate. It was an "off-campus" meeting on Friday, July 30, 1982, of the New York board. "The cheese board," in the nomenclature of Gecova Doyal, the agency's maitre d', to distinguish what he served with drinks from "the shrimp board," the international board.

Summer Fridays had a holiday air. The agency closed at 1 p.m., so the absence of top guns wouldn't be noticed by any lagging troops.

The shrimp board, also known as "the geriatric board" to its few youngish members, had long since narrowed its focus to earnings. Whatever the subject, the context most often was its impact on earnings.

The cheese board, made up of key creatives, top account managers and department heads, dealt with the philosophical questions. They gathered at the Rye Hilton on this day, with this agenda:

1. What should the agency's positioning be?

2. What should be the goals for our creative work?

3. Should we have a policy regarding the kinds of accounts we accept?

4. What should be our position regarding research as related to our creative product?

5. Why are we losing accounts?

* * *

Most of the members lived in Westchester or Connecticut, and came directly from home in relaxed weekend wear. None of the usual office distractions broke the flow of talk.

"What was most notable about the meeting," recalled Bill Wardell, who set it up, "was how out of it Paulson was. Nobody ever talked to him. It's like he wasn't there. And I don't think it was an out-to-get Paulson meeting, but it was one time when so much of what was said started making so much sense to so many people that a consensus evolved, and Paul was odd man out."

The consensus on the agency positioning: "Creative work should be dominant; everything else should be support."

On the goal for creative work: "The goal should be Great Advertising."

On the kinds of accounts we should accept: "Those accounts that appreciate great advertising. We should exclude people like Procter & Gamble and other big package goods accounts that do that kind of advertising."

On research as relates to our creative product: "The less research the better, and we should never volunteer it unless the client demands it."

On why we are losing accounts: "The major reasons identified were: 1) personal political situations, 2) the passing of the guard in client offices, 3) failure to open another office, 4) creative work that was not well received by clients. It was agreed that many account losses could have been avoided by good ties at the top between agency and client, which would have enabled us to recognize imminent problems and take corrective action."

* * *

Creative executive Mike Mangano remembered the meeting as "the same old bullshit. I just wanted the agency to be the Doyle Dane Bernbach of the '60s."

Account manager Marty Kreston remembered it as a day when "nobody was leveling with anyone else."

Wardell thought everyone had "called a spade a spade and left feeling very good."

Arie Kopelman recalled its being "out of control."

Bob Gage couldn't remember "what it was about."

Neil Austrian said his only memory of the day was a phone call from an associate in a drilling investment reporting that they'd struck oil.

Roy Grace believed the meeting was "a public hanging of Paulson staged by Neil."

Even consensus has its Rashomon aspects.

* * *

Paulson was flabbergasted by the meeting and its outcome. "Discussions, discussions, discussions about what do we want DDB to be. When I was hired, I thought they'd already decided what they wanted to be. Bill and Joe and Neil said they wanted to retain the kinds of sophisticated companies they'd lost in the past. It was that simple.

"Bernbach realized, whether just from a financial standpoint or otherwise, unless DDB could compete and retain those kinds of clients, the agency couldn't grow with the other big agencies, the Ogilvys and the Young & Rubicams. Bill told me he no longer wanted the agency to have only a creative reputation. He wanted to maintain that reputation and importance, but he recognized that you have to have more than that.

"What happened was, I'd say to Joe Daly and Neil, 'I'm going to replace this person; we're going to get account people who know what the hell they're talking about. Do you support that?' 'Yes we do.' Then came the politicking, and the account guys who felt threatened began to say, 'This isn't the right thing for DDB. These new guys don't know advertising—they're MBAs.' And all of a sudden Neil started talking about too much emphasis on MBAs. And the creative people complaining that the creative product would be destroyed, and the unwillingness to work on package goods accounts.

"So here the organization says they want to do this, and meanwhile you've got one department that says, 'We're not going to do it,' and raising hell and sabotaging the operation.

"How can somebody let that happen? You hire somebody to do something and then it starts to go to hell. The guy with the title of CEO is the guy who has to put that to rest. And that was Joe Daly at the time."

Daly. He'd grown more bleary-eyed and titular with the years, keeping late night hours with a young stewardess who'd become his constant companion. Austrian made the decisions, though it wasn't clear how long he'd hold them. Neither of the two leaders, in all likelihood, could have worked out an amicable solution to this War of the Roses.

"What Paulson hated was irresponsible creative, and that's what he labeled Marvin," observed Bill Wardell. "What Marvin hated was personality-less rules that hampered the creative process, and that was labeled Paulson.

"Creative people *like* information, *like* good briefings," Wardell continued. "They're sitting there with their reputations on the line. Rather than make up ads out of whole cloth, they'd much rather have something real. None of that is incompatible with creative brilliance. It's supportive of it. But we didn't have anyone who could sell the agency on the proper value of research. It was served up in a goddamn box called Procter & Gamble/Paul Paulson, the antithesis of DDB, and it never got off the ground.

"So those two people, Honig and Paulson, became labels, and then with their personality problems came to stand for the black-and-white issue. So petty. A non-issue, lying on the table, that everybody has labeled and caused to become a conflict."

* * *

"Everybody says they want creative," sighed Paulson. "The question is, what's your idea of creativity? We said, we know what creativity is, and that's what we're going to deliver.

"The client says, I want creativity, but nobody asks him what he means by that. An IBM thinks one thing, P&G another. The Japanese think that if it's funny it's creative. You go to P&G or General Foods or General Mills, they take their checklist out. They say, does it have the right selling idea? does it demonstrate the product? will it break through the clutter? That's their idea of creative. Polaroid's idea is a celebrity. Stroh's is: understanding the beer drinker's psyche, does our advertising look like what the beer drinker likes to identify with.

"DDB commercials had clever ideas, well-produced, from an artistic point of view well done, clever, cast right, visually interesting, well-written. From a dramatic standpoint, terrific. From a selling point, they could be terrific, they could be disastrous.

"The old-timers who started with Bill knew what a selling idea was. That's how they built the agency. They really knew how to sell. The generation that followed were caught up with clever and different as their criteria for great advertising, and that was the world of difference."

* * *

The off-campus meeting wasn't quite "the same old bullshit." The P&G decision made it different. Roy Grace made clear how much he didn't want P&G in the agency. Austrian "had some issues about whether we should continue to invest against P&G," recalled Paulson. And, he added, financial chief Bob Pfundstein "had pretty well concluded that we were not going to make money on P&G and maybe those kinds of accounts weren't right for us anyway. So we were starting to make decisions about what kinds of clients we wanted. And at that board meeting we were cutting off a major portion of our market potential by that attitude towards the P&G kind of accounts.

"And if that was the attitude of the agency, then the agency sure as hell didn't need me," concluded Paulson, "because that's the kind of business I was going after, and the kinds of people I was bringing in."

Three weeks after the meeting, Paulson resigned, leaving behind a sadly-fragmented Doyle Dane Bernbach.

♦ ♦ ♦

20
Passages

"Everybody has got to die, but I have always believed an exception would be made in my case." – William Saroyan

It never was easy for Bernbach's associates to watch their words, monitor their expressions, feign belief where they felt doubt. Deference to the sensitivities of leaders exists in every sphere—business, government, the arts, academia. But that expectation seemed uniquely hard at Doyle Dane Bernbach. For it went entirely against the grain of philosophy and corporate culture espoused by Bernbach himself.

Doyle Dane Bernbach radiated the joy of creating advertising that was open, honest, never boastful, with a winning touch of self-deprecation, as in "It's ugly, but it gets you there."

Truth was an article of faith, a cornerstone of the agency philosophy. One often saw reprints of the house ad that the agency created from the words of its first client: "I got a great gimmick. Let's tell the truth."—N. M. Ohrbach.

Clients who wanted advertising that, figuratively, put their products on pedestals were teased with literal interpretations. Viz. the ad headlined "For six years now, the Chairman of Chivas Regal has been pleading for this ad," and illustrated by a Chivas bottle atop a massive Ionic *pedestal.*

Advertisers who balked at poking fun at themselves were chided by Bernbach. What if Volkswagen had rejected the "Lemon" ad, or Avis "We're only number 2"? In advertising, as in life, Bernbach would tell them, "Nobody's perfect, and nobody's going to believe you if you claim to be."

A loose and open environment—an adult Summerhill, a copywriter called DDB in the '60s, after the unrestrained British public school—encouraged the wonderfully fresh concepts and the confidence needed to sell them. People were who they were, and said what they felt, without self-censorship or fear.

And so it was, everywhere but at the very top, where pretense became a way of life, in the need to protect the self-image of the agency's greatest asset.

* * *

The most difficult, and most poignant, pretense came in Bernbach's final years. Then the script called for acting as if the ravages of a terminal disease were invisible.

A regular checkup in 1977 had turned up an abnormal blood count. Perhaps the laboratory had erred. The test was repeated. The lab had not erred. Bernbach's doctor put the news in a positive light. Although the diagnosis was chronic lymphatic leukemia, there was no present danger. People lived for ten, twenty, twenty-five years with chronic leukemia, and died of other causes.

Nonetheless, it was cancer. And Bernbach had an almost preternatural fear of cancer. His father, his sister, a brother had died of cancer. It seemed a family curse. He'd given up smoking after his father's death from throat cancer. He'd spoke up against advertising cigarets after the Surgeon General had pronounced the link between smoking and cancer—a costly business move (but "a principle isn't a principle until it costs you something"). Now the dread disease had caught up with him.

"It's true," an ashen-faced Bernbach told his secretary, Nancy Underwood, on coming back to the office. She was the one person in the agency he trusted with certain kinds of information. About his health, for she made his doctors' appointments and filled out his medical forms. About his finances, for she kept the records and even selected bonds to purchase for his portfolio.

Her immediate response reveals her insight into Bernbach's way of suppressing bad news, by pretending it hadn't happened.

"Are you going to tell Mrs. Bernbach?"

A pause, and then, "I don't know."

Perhaps he wouldn't have, at that time, but for Underwood's prodding. She was scheduled to leave for a vacation in Portugal the following day.

"If you don't tell her, I won't go," she insisted. She would call the next morning; if by then he hadn't told his wife, she would cancel Portugal and return to the office. When she called, Bernbach assured her he'd told Evelyn. Underwood went off, "feeling horrible."

Both women were sworn to secrecy, and kept their word.

* * *

The disease progressed somewhat faster than expected, and Bernbach's doctor urged him to let his sons know what was happening. Bernbach asked John and Paul to lunch at "21," and at an upstairs corner table, gave them his news, downplaying it as far as possible.

They ought to know that he had leukemia. But it was not the kind of leukemia that killed you. It could go on for a very, very long time. Drugs were available now, and were constantly being improved. Under the circumstances, they ought not to worry. And above all, they must tell no one. Only they, their mother, Nancy and the doctors knew. He wanted no one else to know. No one at all.

They understood why. They had absorbed his philosophy through their growing years. They knew the quote he often cited from Romain Rolland's massive work, *Jean Christophe,* a novel close to Bernbach's heart for its proposal that art should express moral truth and thus combat the disintegration of values.

"A sick, passive man's words may go completely unheeded, but a healthy, vital, energetic man uttering the same words may rock the world."

Paul: "He believed so much in the strength of the voice for effective communication. If people know you're sick, it changes the way they look at you, the way they listen to you. . . . He said, don't tell anybody, and we didn't."

Never again, not even in the final week of his life, when he lay in the hospital with a high fever, did Bernbach mention his leukemia to his sons.

* * *

In 1978, Bernbach added a new passage to his basic stump speech on the art of persuasion and the power of insight into the compulsions that drive a man, instincts that dominate his actions.

"We want, more than anything else, to stay alive."

* * *

John remembered the moment when he fully realized his father would die:

"He had come to Europe on a business trip. We were in Paris, alone, which was unusual; my mother wasn't there. I suspect she was in London with Jane. We got to the airport, the Charles de Gaulle airport, where they have moving stairways between various parts of the main terminal building. There's one series that's on quite a steep angle, because they cross inside of a circle with futuristic plastic tubing.

"We were halfway up when he stumbled and fell backwards, and rolled down this lengthy thing. And it was obvious to me that he was so weak that he couldn't stop himself. When I raced back down against the treadmill, he couldn't stand up. And he was terribly, terribly upset. And as a result of course

I was upset, and what he was so upset about was he was so embarrassed. Not for me, but for himself in front of the public, so to speak. You know how fastidious he was. His coat had got wrinkled, and his shoes had got scuffed, and he was terribly, terribly upset.

"I guess there's always a time, except in the case of sudden death, when you become aware of just how mortal a particular loved one is. And that was the moment."

* * *

The disease took a leap from stage one to stage three without pausing at stage two. Attacking the immune system, the disease left Bernbach vulnerable to opportunistic llnesses.

"People think leukemia is a relatively painless disease, but it's far from that," Evelyn would recall.

From 1980, Bernbach was ill much of the time with, among other afflictions, a painful case of shingles. "And for all the time he looked terrible," Paul related. "People kept on asking 'How's your father?' John and I dutifully said, 'He's okay, he has a cold, or he has a sore throat, an infection, or something.' But obviously we were not going to violate our trust."

John: "He was in terrible discomfort. It was a very difficult time. He could have stayed home in bed; he was tired, he would have liked to. But on the other hand he realized the importance of the effort of getting up, getting dressed, going to the office, sitting at his table, and writing, or doing something useful every day.

"It was a time when maybe he felt that people weren't appreciating him. He felt it incumbent upon himself to prove to the organization that he was still needed, necessary."

Who didn't appreciate him? we asked.

John pulled back a touch. "I don't know. I think he just generally felt that way. Rightly or wrongly."

* * *

Needed or necessary wasn't the issue for the inhabitants of the other offices along the marble-and-glass executive floor. What preoccupied them was the agony of being in thrall to a dying king who showed no sign of passing the mantle of his creative authority. They clustered, and whispered, and worried, and when Bernbach approached, they broke into death-denying smiles, supporting his pretense that all was well.

"In that last year, anybody looking at him would know that this man was on the way," recalled Joe Daly, long after.

Nancy Underwood kept track of his medicines, handing him cards telling him what to take and when. He asked no questions about what he was taking. Hearing the medicines named would give substance to the unthinkable.

Eventually, John and Paul took Neil Austrian into their confidence, knowing that their father believed that, in Paul's words, "of the people who were around, Neil was the only one he thought capable of running the company."

Now Austrian was sworn to secrecy—and also pledged to conceal his knowing from Bernbach. To go on acting, in effect. Moreover, as chief operating officer of the agency, he couldn't even discuss the truth with Daly, the chief executive officer.

But Daly knew, "through a third party." In typical Doyle Dane Bernbach management style, Daly was sure that only he knew, and he didn't tell Austrian what he knew; Austrian was sure *he* alone in top management knew. So that left Austrian discussing a "game plan"—who would do what when Bernbach died—not with the CEO, but with Bernbach's secretary.

* * *

One day, late in the summer of 1982, Bernbach sat down in Austrian's office and began to talk about Daly and the job of running the agency.

"Remember, I knew he was dying, and he didn't know I knew," Austrian related. "He said he wanted to make a change; he wanted me to be CEO. We chatted about it, and I said, 'I'm more than willing to let Joe remain CEO until he's 65.' [Daly would turn 65 the following year.] Bill got very upset and said, 'No! We're going to do it right now, at the September meeting. I don't want to wait any longer. I want to make sure this company is in good hands.' And knowing about Bill's health, it was very clear that he wanted to make sure this took place while he was still alive and had control over the situation, that he didn't want the CEO issue unresolved."

Bernbach got that wish at the next board meeting, two weeks before he died.

"Running the company" had no emotional connection for Bernbach with the creative leadership of the agency. Through a string of creative directors, Bernbach held the throne, ignoring the contenders, sitting tight, clutching to his bosom the golden bough.

Austrian and the others waited, unable to ask Bernbach the fateful, necessary question: Who is your creative heir?

* * *

Moments remembered:

Ned Doyle, frail with emphysema, and Bernbach, late in his illness, heading for lunch at the nearby Four Seasons.

"I have to walk slowly, Bill," says Doyle.

Bernbach: "Ned, so do I."

—

Winter of 1979-80. Long-time art director Lester Feldman returns to the agency after recovering from a heart attack. Bernbach slips down to Feldman's office, closes the door and asks, "How are you, Lester?"

Feldman: "Fine, Bill, how are you?"

Bernbach: "Everybody has something."

———

Spring of 1982. Executive VP Arie Kopelman, in earlier years a frequent dinner guest at the Bernbachs and something of a surrogate son, is in Bernbach's office, telling him about a vacation trip with his wife. Bernbach asks how everything is going. Kopelman responds, "We have a wonderful marriage, the kids are great, and everything is going great in our lives at this point."

Kopelman: "And his eyes welled up, a couple of tears came out. I'd never seen him cry before. And he said, 'Arie, that's what it's all about. Nothing else counts. That's what it's all about.' Those are the last words I remember him saying, 'That's what it's all about.'"

———

Roy Grace, Marvin Honig and Bernbach lunching at the Four Seasons, late in 1981, regaling one another with anecdotes. "We were talking about advertising, the way it was," remembered Grace. "And we didn't know he was talking about Everything. We were talking about the fun we used to have, we didn't have headaches. At that point we had Atari headaches, Polaroid headaches, Pan Am—they were all headaches, nobody wanted what we were doing. And Bernbach said, 'It sure was wonderful, wasn't it?'"

* * *

Once he'd engineered the change in CEO, Bernbach's full attention moved to a proposed Volkswagen ad. Excitedly, he showed the ad to everyone who came into his office. Under a large photograph of dummies being shaken up in safety test procedures, the headline read: "Volkswagen is at the mercy of a bunch of German dummies."

"Isn't that great?" he'd ask. "That's old Volkswagen." But when the account people brought it to the factory, the ad was rejected.

"Germans no longer don't know what 'Lemon' is," said account manager John Leonard, one of Bernbach's frequent lunch companions. "They know what German dummies are. So they turn it down, and you can understand that. So you look at it and you say, you can fix it, just take out the 'German.' But at the same time, the factory was saying 'We have to go back to our German heritage; we don't want to say we're made in Pennsylvania.' The feeling they wanted is, We're made in the Black Forest by gnomes. So German is important. But then the factory won't buy it."

Like a *deus ex machina*, Bernbach's old friend and admirer, client Arthur Stanton of Volkswagen of America, stepped in. He would sponsor the ad if Germany would not.

John Leonard: "And then Bill shows it to you in proof form, with 'German' in it, and says, 'Arthur Stanton is running it, isn't that great? That's the way clients should be.'"

The ad was scheduled for the *New York Times* on Monday, October 4, 1982. Bernbach forgot his pain in the joy of imagining the stir the ad would cause, certain it would convince the industry that Doyle Dane Bernbach still had the stuff to turn out classics.

* * *

Bernbach and his wife planned to fly to London after the mid-September board meeting. They had next-day tickets when Bernbach developed another fever and his doctor insisted he check into the hospital.

Evelyn Bernbach vividly remembered the look on her husband's face when they checked him in. "It was a look of 'I know I'll never come out of here alive.'"

For a week he ran a temperature of over 105. When the fever broke, visitors came to his room in New York Hospital. He told them about the upcoming Volkswagen ad, asked questions about the agency, and spoke not at all about his illness.

* * *

On Monday morning, October 4, the ad ran, with the headline: "Volkswagen is at the mercy of a bunch of dummies."

At the last moment, a *New York Times* person called the agency to say the paper couldn't run the ad as it stood. The switchboard found a mid-level VW account executive, who made an impromptu decision.

"Take out 'German.'"

* * *

Bernbach never saw the ad as it ran. He died at 3 a.m. on Saturday, October 2, without having passed his creative crown to an heir.

◆ ◆ ◆

21
Now What?

"The Future comes like an unwelcome guest."—Edmund Gosse, *May-Day*

"He couldn't pass on his prestige," mourned Ned Doyle, after a 1986 mega-merger had dropped the founders' names into the trashcan of advertising history. Later, many of the agency's top executives would come to feel that things might have worked out differently if Bernbach had anointed a creative successor.

But . . . who?

In the late 1970s, the *Wall Street Journal* began a print campaign featuring interviews with advertising's creative leaders. The architect of that campaign, Jim Johnston, later wrote:

"The program began with three obvious choices: William Bernbach, Leo Burnett, David Ogilvy. Once ads featuring Bernbach, Burnett and Ogilvy had been completed, the issue was whence to proceed.

"The advertising director of the *Journal* put the question to Bill Bernbach. Bernbach drew himself up to his full 5 foot 7 and said, ever so softly, 'You've done Leo, David and me. There aren't any other giants in our business.'"

* * *

Bernbach had never accepted another creative person into topmost management ranks. As far back as 1967 he'd demonstrated that disinclination. A phalanx of his creative stars, learning that Joe Daly was about to be named president of the agency, surged into Bernbach's office and urged him to reconsider. Bob Gage was the man for the job—Bernbach's creative partner, the greatest of all art directors, the man who broke new ground with every campaign. Daly's appointment would "send the wrong signal" about the agency's commitment to its creative heritage.

Bernbach's blue eyes turned steely, his jaw tightened, his breath came fast. His children, questioning a decision about matters they simply didn't understand. They saw his reaction and sheepishly turned tail. Daly remained the designee. (The agency's history bristles with warnings of "sending the wrong signal"—warnings usually disregarded, and afterwards rued.)

Bernbach did, when Daly became president, give the title of Creative Director to Gage; the volume of work produced by the booming agency could no longer all be seen and edited by Bernbach. Gage hated the job and gave it back in a year or two. Next up was Bob Levenson, from 1969 to 1974. Marvin Honig followed Levenson, his term running from 1974 to 1979. Then, Roy Grace, who held the job at the time of Bernbach's death.

So why wasn't Grace the heir by virtue of being in the chair at the right time? Because this was Doyle Dane Bernbach, and nothing was ever as clear-cut as that. Each creative director had been found wanting by Bernbach. Each began with his apparent enthusiastic support. Sooner or later, that cooled. Then Bernbach would confide, to the men who ran the agency, his perceptions of the creative directors' flaws. He sat at his round table, ready to override creative judgment calls.

Moreover, he undermined their authority by backing the agency's unique "floating stars" system, whereby the great old creatives operated outside the organization chart, with Bernbach as final judge of their work. As long as Bernbach lived, there was only one creative head of Doyle Dane Bernbach.

And when he gave up the supposedly-ultimate power title of CEO, he topped that (as we have seen) with the truly-ultimate power title of "owner."

* * *

Bernbach must have sensed the irritation and impatience stirred by the passive-aggressive way he dug in his heels and pretended, and thus forced others to pretend, that succession had no pressing relevance.

Well, let them be angry. They'd all let him down in one way or another. Drinking, womanizing, mismanaging, misjudging, not measuring up, not even appreciating his importance in the history of advertising. They'd begun almost to patronize him. They kept him away from presentations to whiz-kid companies, as though he was old hat.

Perhaps one day they would learn that he was, in fact, irreplaceable.

Certainly he wouldn't assuage their vexation by declaring Grace or Honig or Levenson worthy of stepping into his shoes. Grace didn't care about nurturing creative people; he bruised too many egos. Honig, The Jokester, didn't seem sufficiently serious. Neither Grace nor Honig could be counted on as effective spokesmen for the agency. They were the Peck's bad boys of Doyle Dane Bernbach, enjoying the discomfort their utterances created. (As PR director, I became adept at steering the press out of their range.)

Levenson, on the other hand, expressed the agency's philosophy more eloquently, more warmly and winningly, than Bernbach himself. To many staffers, Levenson was Bernbach's only possible creative heir. But not to Bernbach, who remained highly critical (out of Levenson's earshot) of the lax and indecisive and ultimately detrimental way he had run the creative operation a decade earlier.

Bernbach had worked too hard, come too far, shaped the image he'd wanted. He'd buried his past, swallowed the bitter anger of ostracism by his parents, risen to world fame. The legend must remain his—pure, undiluted by the imperfections he would sanctify by choosing Grace, Honig or Levenson as his heir.

There was another factor. When you hand over your role, you die before you're dead. We want, more than anything else, to stay alive. Not giving up could make a difference in the progress of a life-threatening disease. The mysteries of spontaneous remission gave hope. And any day, a miracle drug might come out of a research lab somewhere in the world.

It wasn't handing on the golden bough to support a merger with Foote, Cone and Belding, or to force Joe Daly to relinquish the CEO title to Neil Austrian. Those acts had to do with protecting the Bernbach family wealth, not with passing on one's legend.

To be sure, anointing another might have changed the course of Doyle Dane Bernbach's history, protecting the Bernbach family wealth along with the future of the agency itself. But how much did the future of the agency itself figure in his thoughts?

After the Wells, Rich, Greene episode, it was easy for Bernbach's colleagues to feel skepticism on that score.

* * *

Bernbach's death left each of his three non-heirs watchful for opportunities to outlast the other two. It wasn't a situation that made for collegiality. Rather than the orderly transition one might expect when a leader has had time to contemplate his demise, another destructive contest was about to begin.

* * *

CEO Neil Austrian and post-Paulson president Barry Loughrane pondered Bernbach's death, and tried to assess how best to deal with it—by enshrining his memory, or by blanking it out.

Almost from the beginning of the agency's fame, and strongly from the time it went public, the question had been asked: "What would Doyle Dane Bernbach be without Bill Bernbach?"

In his presence, the question would be phrased, "What happens if you're hit by a truck?" The remoteness of such a possibility cloaked the certainty of eventual death, and in this euphemistic framework Bernbach (and the rest of us) would confidently respond, "It won't change things. The idea is too strong here." The idea being Bernbach's creative philosophy and the nurturing of talent that gave it life.

To that workable response, an addendum was now added: After all, Bernbach wasn't involved in day-to-day operations for many months before his death, and things hadn't changed. So why should they now? It was a comforting thought to everyone who worked for, or cared about the future of, Doyle Dane Bernbach.

Even Helmut Krone, who so often had said there were only two people he would work for, Bernbach and himself, professed a calm assurance, pointing with a frown to the massive press coverage of Bernbach's death and asking, "What's all the fuss about Bernbach's death, when he hasn't been active in the affairs of the agency for so long?"

The clients, chief among them Seagram's, who had continued to ask, "Has Bill seen this ad?" and been told "yes" at times when he hadn't, did not, in their sorrow over Bernbach's death, stop to cross-examine their account people on the accuracy of their earlier assurances. And they remained clients of the agency through the stormy months ahead.

The "fuss" about Bernbach's death, of course, was a measure of the impact of the man and his philosophy on advertising everywhere. The man who launched the creative revolution; who changed the face of advertising; who brought pride and joy to the business, who altered the power structure of the industry; who elevated advertising to an art.

But once the tumult and the shouting died, what then, Austrian and Loughrane mulled, should the agency do with Bernbach's memory? Loughrane had learned, when he'd taken over the agency's West Coast operations several years earlier, that his toughest problem was the perception that Doyle Dane Bernbach wasn't as good as it used to be. And that every reference to its great past reinforced the thought that it wasn't as good as it used to be. Mary Wells' old line, "DDB is yesterday," still reverberated. The sentimentality of Bernbach fans notwithstanding, new business could not be won with old quotes and classic ads. And old clients might find reminders of Bernbach's absence perturbing. Doyle Dane Bernbach would have to stand young and tall and proud in the present, not on the glories of its past.

They elected to bring up Bernbach's name as seldom as possible.

* * *

The decision wasn't announced, but it was felt.

"It was almost as if people were afraid to mention Bernbach's name in the hallways," recalled an account group head. He sensed "an understanding" not to talk about Bernbach. "Instead of honoring and revering him, saying he left us with something important, there was fear at the very mention of his name."

Perhaps some words that Bernbach's friend Brendan Gill wrote in another context have relevance here:

"With some diffidence, I suggest that when distinguished figures in any field of endeavor come to belong to us through an earned fame—a fame bearing not the least taint of mere celebrity—we begin to count on them never to die, since our lives will be irreparably narrowed and lessened by their deaths . . . They have had imposed upon them without their knowledge a family relationship and by dying have committed the fault, inexcusable in any family, of abandoning us. May not this be the reason that, as so often happens, we ignore the great dead for a time and seem to forget them, and then, when the fault of their abandoning us has been forgiven, bring them back eagerly into our lives? . . ."

* * *

Early thoughts of turning Bernbach's office into a kind of museum, a hallowed ground, with great ads on the walls, a place to go and perhaps meditate on Bernbach and what he stood for, drifted out of the corner windows overlooking the spires of New York's glorious St. Patrick's Cathedral.

Instead, Austrian contemplated the power symbols of office space. The marble-and-glass executive corridor (called by the troops, depending on the news of the moment, either "the 'A' deck on the Ship of Fools" or "the 'A' deck on the Titanic") stretched a full block, from 49th to 50th street, on the Madison Avenue side of the building. Bernbach's office covered a large corner on the 50th street side. Joe Daly's spread over the 49th street corner.

By now Austrian had succeeded Daly as CEO. But Daly had a 5-year contract and dibs on his corner office. Austrian's office lay in the dull center of the stretch, between Bob Pfundstein's and a small kitchen. Loose as Austrian looked about appearances, with his shirt tail out and one sleeve rolled up, he couldn't long ignore the implications of having a lesser office than Daly. Especially given Daly's remarkable record of holding onto power while presidents crashed around him.

Austrian waited for a respectable period, then commandeered Bernbach's office as his own. He even expanded it, absorbing the space occupied by the small kitchen. Everyone agreed that the aesthetics of the "A" deck were improved by eliminating the view, en route to the CEO's office, of a sink full of dirty coffee cups.

Nobody ever after mentioned the Bernbach "museum."

* * *

Bernbach's memory wouldn't stay down. Austrian himself soon found need to call it up, trying to muster enthusiasm for a cigaret account. (See chapter "Tobacco Road") But at the May 1983 annual shareholder meeting, neither Austrian nor Loughrane spoke of Bernbach in their addresses.

"There wasn't a word about Bill until finally, at the end of Bob Levenson's talk, he nervously brought Bill's name in," recalled Evelyn Bernbach, still angry three years after the episode. She added, "I waited outside and when Neil came out I collared him and berated him, and he responded with 'That was planned.'"

Yes, of course, as part of the "we can't live in the past" strategy. Mrs. Bernbach didn't buy that. "What they should have said was, 'He was ours, and what he stood for is what we will continue to stand for.'"

Eventually, too late, they did.

* * *

The slighting of Bernbach's memory at the 1983 shareholder meeting ripped it for the Bernbach family. Evelyn and her sons, John and Paul, sat down and discussed their feelings about the matter.

They concluded that Bernbach's "reputation, his standing in the industry," said John, "were not inextricably linked to the agency. That his reputation surpassed the agency."

Such psychological distancing of the Bernbachs from the agency was dangerous business, given that the family owned 914,910 shares (after two stock splits) of Doyle Dane Bernbach, about 16 percent of the company.

There would be plenty of heartburn over that in the months ahead.

♦ ♦ ♦

22
Tobacco Road

"If you stand for something, you will always find some people for you and some against you. If you stand for nothing, you will find nobody against you, and nobody for you." Bill Bernbach

Looking back, many DDBers set as the moment that their agency died, the Christmas party of 1982, when CEO Neil Austrian buoyantly announced that Doyle Dane Bernbach had won the Philip Morris Parliament cigaret account.

A stunned and deadly silence fell over the celebrants in the Waldorf-Astoria Grand Ballroom. Austrian sensed the thud at once and moved quickly on to the next piece of business. The gloom persisted. Within minutes, Austrian knew that his vision of an agency re-charged by the voltage of a Philip Morris account had been a massive and irreversible misjudgment.

The then-unspoken response to his news was: Bernbach died, and we grieved, but we'd known for months that he was dying; we didn't expect the agency's moral fiber to die with him. Afterwards, people said: this wouldn't have happened if Bernbach were alive.

But Austrian had good reason to believe that Bernbach's presence would not, in the cigaret caper, have made a difference.

* * *

No single point about Doyle Dane Bernbach had made its people prouder than the agency's refusal to handle cigaret advertising. The entire profession stood taller for this principled stand on a product harmful to health.

In academia, business professors, constantly sifting for examples of companies that choose ethics over greed, often cited Doyle Dane Bernbach as proof that business and morality were not incompatible. Cynical college students were impressed. After all, tobacco companies spent dazzling sums of money. And DDB wouldn't even consider accepting a pipe tobacco account, lest the purity of its viewpoint on cigarets be tainted.

One often heard the phrase played back: Doyle Dane Bernbach—that's the place that refuses to do advertising for cigarets. It spilled over from the advertising trade press to the general business press, into books and magazines of all stripes.

The anti-cigaret stand had become as integral to the agency's image as was its creativity.

Maddeningly, cigaret companies were increasingly buying up the kinds of businesses that Doyle Dane Bernbach wanted and needed to grow: beer and soft drinks especially. And the owners wouldn't listen to any agencies that treated their primary business as a menace to the health of Americans.

* * *

Doyle Dane Bernbach's historic stand dated from the report of the U.S. Surgeon General, on January 11, 1964, which stated unambiguously that the "health hazards" of cigaret smoking "far outweigh all other factors" in causing lung cancer.

Ex-smoker Bill Bernbach, three-packs-a-day smoker Ned Doyle, and non-smoker Maxwell Dane, lunching at their regular table in the northeast corner of the Algonquin Hotel's Rose Room, talked about their reactions to the report. Bernbach, whose father had died of throat cancer, felt most intensely and personally rancorous toward purveyors of tobacco. Doyle kept right on smoking. But he agreed with his partners that they should never again accept cigaret business.

They'd taken some Philip Morris business back in 1958, introducing Alpine Cigarets with a pool of warm, funny commercials. Like many introductory brands, Alpine didn't survive. Nor did the agency-client relationship, which foundered on the rocks of creative interference by the client.

"They'd insist on seeing the logo in six different sizes," recalled Doyle. "We couldn't work that way."

The agency hadn't had a cigaret account in the United States since Philip Morris left in 1961. But its young Dusseldorf office was, at the time of the Surgeon General's report, in the midst of an introduction of a new German cigaret, Bremen. Nobody in the home office informed Dusseldorf of the founders' discussion and intentions. The wounds of World War II were far from healed, and both Bernbach and Doyle made quips that revealed a lack of concern about safeguarding the health of Germans.

The founders didn't plan to announce a policy on cigaret accounts; it came spilling out at a press conference in Los Angeles.

Bernbach, in the West on Ohrbach business, met with the press on February 6, expecting the usual questions about the agency's great campaigns. And because there would be a public stock offering later in the year, publicity in this affluent part of the country could help build a market for the equities.

What the agency didn't expect was a news story that would go clear around the world. The wire services disseminated the version in the *Los Angeles Times*, with its catchy lead: "'I don't believe you should advertise cigarets. They're bad for your health. You're just selling sickness, and I don't want to be responsible for it.'

"The man who voiced the opinion doesn't represent the surgeon general's office; nor does he occupy a lofty ivory tower, removed from the daily grit of business and commerce. He's William Bernbach, president of Doyle Dane Bernbach Inc., advertising agency. He was recently selected by his fellows as 'The man who contributed most to advertising in 1963. . . .'"

The German client read the story and fired the agency before Doyle could fly over to resign the account personally—the only part of the affair that he rued.

Doyle Dane Bernbach had never since, to the knowledge of its people or the industry, entertained the idea of advertising cigarets anywhere in the world. (Somehow, a Kool cigaret – Snark sailboat promotion created by a DDB subsidiary fell through the cracks of perception.) And now, nearly 19 years later, when not only lung cancer but every respiratory illness, every circulatory problem had been linked to smoking, when emphysema had ruined Ned Doyle's health, when tobacco companies diversified to survive because of a growing abhorrence of their product, when legislation threatened every kind of cigaret advertising and promotion, Neil Austrian unwrapped, as a Christmas gift to the agency, the Parliament cigaret account.

* * *

In his role as elder statesman, Ned Doyle often warned that "an account too easy to win is just as easy to lose."

The Parliament account was Austrian's for the plucking.

It was held out to him by his Old Greenwich friend and neighbor, James J. Morgan, executive vice president for marketing, Philip Morris U.S.A. Accepting the prickly prize would be the equivalent of crossing the first barrier to the heroic challenges ahead, the quest for Philip Morris' two great and troubled beverages, Miller Beer and Seven-Up. With his boundless self-confidence, Austrian set out to build support in the upper reaches of the agency.

The Miller/Seven Up prospect would form half of his platform. The other half would focus on Bernbach's attitude toward cigaret advertising in the last year of his life. There was irony in that. Just weeks after Bernbach's death and the decision to move out from under his giant shadow, to mention his name as seldom as possible, Austrian found himself invoking Bernbach constantly. After all, he could truthfully say that Bernbach had accepted the concept of cigaret advertising by backing the proposed merger, several months before his death, with Foote, Cone & Belding.

* * *

That had been another time of strange silences, of hushed conversations, of protective feelings based on assumptions about what Bernbach's responses would be. One participant recalled that "everybody at DDB who was involved in the negotiations knew that cigarets were in FCB, but nobody ever came out and said it, until, finally, at the end, they said to Bernbach, 'Bill, do you realize if we go through with the merger, FCB has Lorillard business?'"

Bernbach's consistent response had been: "At the time I said we would not handle cigarets, I fully expected that the entire industry would follow me, that advertising for cigarets would finally become outlawed, but that has not been the case. I no longer run this company; the company is being run for the shareholders by new management, and I think it's new management's decision on whether or not this company handles cigarets."

The biggest shareholder, by far, was Bernbach.

New management, meaning Austrian as CEO, took Bernbach's meaning, and said that if the merger went through, FCB's $100 million in Lorillard business would not be resigned. A few old-timers shook their heads, but so much about the proposed merger perplexed them that they didn't stop to sort out the implications of the tobacco decision.

Had the board looked at the Lorillard account as a barrier or conflict? Mac Dane was asked, a few years later. "Not when it's that size," he drolly replied.

The merger failed to go through, and Bernbach died, but the board's shift on cigaret policy held. It had happened while Bernbach lived. That was the reality. Few wanted to believe it, and in time that fact vanished from the legend.

* * *

The real debating point, when Austrian asked for support of his managers, was, "Is it too soon after Bernbach's death?" Even if Bernbach himself had accepted the change, oughtn't more time pass before the agency sprang this on the industry?

The press will kill us, predicted the agency's public relations manager, Cary Bayer, a hard-digging and deadly-accurate former trade press reporter. Wait a little, he advised.

It's now or never, responded Austrian.

Then in my opinion, don't take it, said Bayer.

Dick Kane, who as the agency's personnel director knew best how potential recruits and staffers viewed DDB, argued long and passionately against accepting any cigaret at any time in the future. The agency would be "getting in on the tail end of something that is going to go away—the advertising of tobacco." And in doing so, it would be tossing out an asset that distinguished it from all other agencies—the perception of Doyle Dane Bernbach as the one agency with real values.

"I don't think you folks realize the impact this is going to have on people in the agency," Kane added. "The overwhelming percentage of people will look at this as just another step in the deterioration of Doyle Dane Bernbach."

"Take the business," said the majority of the shrimp board, the cheese board, and the operating committee.

"Take the business," said Ned Doyle.

On the international, or shrimp, board, Mac Dane, Paul Bernbach and Bob Pfundstein abstained. Only one member voted against it—vice chairman Ted Factor. On the New York, or cheese, board, the strongest voices against were those of Bob Gage and Helmut Krone, both unreformed smokers.

Ironically, Parliament would soon be the only account that Gage could get himself assigned to at the agency his talent made famous. His would be the last in a long string of ads and campaigns presented to, and rejected by, the Philip Morris people.

"First they loved it, then they fired the agency," recalled Gage. "I never ran across people as tough as these people. They don't smile; they don't do anything."

Jack Dillon, Gage's copywriter: "You'd think we'd gone there to ask for a loan."

Parliament, heralded as a $10 million account, left the agency two-and-a-half years after arriving, without a single ad ever having reached the engraving stage.

So that, as Mac Dane later commented, "We lost stature in switching our policy, but we never got any real revenue out of it. The wages of sin were not that good."

And Austrian could look back after leaving the agency and describe the reaction to his announcement in the Waldorf Grand Ballroom as, "Oops! There goes the agency!"

As for the real prize, the opportunity to compete for other Philip Morris products—well, that was a fresh, new, astonishing disaster of its own.

◆ ◆ ◆

23
Return of the Native

"Events are in the saddle and tend to ride mankind."
—Ralph Waldo Emerson

Barry Loughrane—at 49 showing the wear of a man long-divorced and generally at home away-from-home in bistros and restaurants—had taken over the presidency of Doyle Dane Bernbach in December 1982, destined to be the last of the "great white hopes" in the fabled agency's final precipitous decline.

Joe Daly thought Loughrane walked on water, said high insiders. From the time Daly first hired him in 1959, he'd introduced Loughrane as "my kid brother." The Irish connection didn't hurt.

Loughrane ran his accounts well, and was supervising fourteen of them by 1972. Then, disappointed that Daly didn't respond to a long memo he wrote on agency problems that needed fixing, Loughrane left to manage Mary Wells' newly-acquired Gardner Advertising in St. Louis. Loughrane's departure had jeopardized the Uniroyal account and opened the door to Jim Heekin's ill-fated arrival.

Daly and Austrian had lured Loughrane back in 1978, to run DDB's West Coast operations. In his just-under-five years there, DDB-West grew from one office billing $30 million, to four offices billing $70 million.

Somewhere along in the Paul Paulson years, Austrian began talking with Loughrane about returning to New York. The agency would divide its accounts into package goods and the rest. Paulson would continue running the former, with MBA-type people, and Loughrane would head up the rest. Loughrane rejected the concept as ruinous. But Daly and Austrian continued to see him as their back-up card in the event that Paulson self-destructed. Which he did.

So, enter Loughrane, to the great relief of Austrian, now CEO, who would give fuller attention to what he did better than anyone—financial and acquisitions.

"An account man who can work with Roy Grace," the word went out about Loughrane's return. Good news to the weary troops.

Roy Grace retrospectively viewed Loughrane's appointment in a different light: "He was crossing the street and got hit by a Brink's truck." Meaning, the money he got at the end.

Austrian, bruised in later battles over personal gains, would look back in anger and confide to friends that Loughrane's appointment was "the biggest mistake of my life."

* * *

Loughrane had in fact taken the job reluctantly, aware the agency was "in deep shit."

"I thought, there was no soul, no spine, no togetherness. We didn't really have a point of view. We had a bunch of all-stars who weren't playing on the same team. In creative, Grace and Honig and Levenson wouldn't even talk to one another. And they tended to say not particularly appetizing things about one another, not just within the hallowed halls, but to anyone who would listen in the public media. And they would relish the opportunity to do so."

Each of the three had "his own little band of warriors who wouldn't work for the other guys, so you had a lot of down time, and you couldn't really run departments properly." Same on the account side, with three top account group heads jockeying for power and undercutting one another.

"Each had high visibility. Nor was it like you could come in and fire somebody that was a nincompoop and give the rightful job to where it belonged and be heralded as 'Somebody finally did that.' It wasn't that. It was one guy was wearing blue and one guy was wearing grey and one guy was wearing brown. That didn't make one good, bad, or indifferent."

At the end of 1981, Pan-Am had done to DDB what it had done a year earlier to its prior agency, dumped it to go with an old friend. Bernbach's old friend, William Seawell, had retired as chairman of Pan-Am and been succeeded by C. Edward Acker. To DDB's surprise, Acker turned out to be an old friend of Mary Wells and her husband, Harding Lawrence. And so, irony of ironies, DDB's triumphant replacement account for American Airlines, the original spur for merger talks with Mary Wells, wound up with . . . Mary Wells.

The important Stroh account had left in 1982, as had the award-winning American Tourister account. Shortly before Loughrane arrived, the agency had finally resigned Procter & Gamble, not because of the consensus in the off-campus meeting, but rather because of clashes between P&G's restrictive conflicts policy and DDB's growing international package goods business.

So there was less business in the New York office. "But they'd hired all these package goods whizzes, and Neil said, 'We'll keep them all around and we'll get business for them.' But that never happened. And so the good ones were leaving and the lesser ones were hanging on for dear life, and of course when things start snowballing like that, it's very difficult," said Loughrane, looking back.

Departments weren't working well together. "Marvin Honig would kick [research head] Ruth Ziff right out of his office," grumbled Loughrane. "Everyone saw things from his own point of view—like the *New Yorker* magazine cover, there's New York and there's the rest of the country. Marvin's point of view towards American Greetings was 'What do we need all these account people for? I go out there; all they want is three commercials a year; they don't want all that other stuff.'

"Then you talk to the account people, who say, 'The people in Cleveland are really ticked off, because Marvin goes out and sits with the chairman and sells three television commercials, but Marvin doesn't want to do anything else. We haven't done any trade advertising, because Marvin is above that, and the trade is terribly mad, and Hallmark is killing us with their controlled distribution. But DDB is very lordly and snooty and won't do any grunt work.'

"I started to hear all these stories first hand from all these people and from client after client, about how fractionated Doyle Dane Bernbach was. DDB was not DDB, it was four or five disparate voices, clamoring for their own perspective. A lot of business was lost that way, because we were *not* an agency."

Another enormous problem: DDB was producing no advertising campaigns that people were talking about. The last one had been the James Garner-Mariette Hartley campaign for Polaroid. The agency's free-wheeling creatives didn't especially relish campaign work in any case. They preferred doing one-off ads, one at a time, custom-made. The one-off might *become* a campaign, as the gorilla had for American Tourister. Bernbach had taught, "We shouldn't be a slave to a campaign. If an ad is better than a campaign, or the strategy, let's run it because it's a terrific ad." You could, of course, do terrific ads within terrific campaigns, as for Volkswagen and Polaroid and Chivas Regal, or (gone but not forgotten) Jamaica Tourist Board and Sony. But few campaigns were that kind of great. Mostly, these days, "campaign" meant a big theme song and quick cuts of happy people.

Paulson, a son of Compton, thought strictly in terms of campaigns. If you have a campaign and the last commercial is a bummer, it's a bummer and you throw it away and do another one, because the campaign is still okay. But if you're only as good as your last ad, and your last ad is a one-off, you're heading for trouble, because nobody bats 1000.

The creatives disparaged Paulson's views on advertising. But here was Barry Loughrane expressing similar opinions about the agency's concentration on one-shot ads. Even when one-offs were wonderful, he said, they didn't help the situation. "We could go into an art directors show and win 50 awards. But nobody would ever see that advertising. Totally invisible. People remember campaigns, and we weren't doing campaigns."

On top of all that fundamental trouble, there were small but telling irritants. Neil Austrian's comments, in press round-ups of agency heads, tended to read like they'd come from the accounting office rather than from the leader of a great creative agency.

"We have met the enemy," Loughrane wrote at the time, quoting Pogo, "and they is us."

* * *

Was the situation savable? Ask any advertising industry buff, and you'll hear tales of expiring agencies that came back. Interpublic, from the brink of financial disaster. Young & Rubicam, from a moribund state.

"This is a very fickle business," said Loughrane. "You're cold in March, you can be the hottest agency in town in April. You need a couple of 'Where's the Beefs,' and $30 million goes to DDB. You're agency of the year. It's malarkey, but that can happen. I think it was pull-outable. If people were willing to put the company ahead of themselves."

Very iffy, considering what they'd learned about selflessness through the years of observing the actions of their two maximum leaders, Bernbach and Daly.

* * *

Loughrane left few footprints in the first year of his presidency, 1983. He became a frequent flier, checking in with offices and clients around the country, but chiefly flying to the Coast to wrap up unfinished DDB business, arrange for his move, and look out for the restaurants he owned there.

Restaurants?! Several in Los Angeles, and one to come in Manhattan, on East 49th street, three short blocks from DDB headquarters. Having no family obligations, Loughrane had room in his life for this long-held passion. But the *idea*, that the great white hope put *any* energy into this diversion when the agency had such severe problems, bugged many. "Barry's restaurants" would become a metaphor for "who's minding the store?"

Loughrane had no apologies for his sideline. Asked if the restaurants weren't taking too much of his time and attention, he responded in his deepest baritone: "Joe Daly has his horses, and I have my restaurants."

* * *

With Loughrane often out of town, the "deep shit" in the New York office deepened through 1983. Polaroid, a client since 1954, a company built on inventiveness and DDB advertising, assigned some pieces of its business elsewhere, and said it wanted no more of Joe Daly, or the team that had created its best campaigns—Bob Gage and Jack Dillon. Clearly, the entire account was in jeopardy. What signal would Polaroid's departure send to the advertising community? What defection could be more painful? Not even Volkswagen's.

Volkswagen's account head, who locked in the business after the agency moved him and it to Detroit, constantly threatened to steer it out of DDB unless his increasing demands were met. Another hostage situation, and on DDB's most famous account!

The bonanza of Atari Videogames began to dry up, along with the category.

Victor Technologies, a San Francisco client, filed for Chapter 11, leaving the agency stuck for $3.3 million.

Scratching for monies to pad earnings, the agency terminated the staff-wide pension plan. Meanwhile it was coughing up huge sums to fund incentive programs for "key" people, many of whom would stay only until the plans matured, then take the money and run. In ways, so unlike Mac Dane's DDB, that the agency nibbled at benefits for the low-paid help and couldn't do enough for the highly-paid in the '80s, it perfectly fit the Reagan years.

Signs of creative deterioration appeared. A full-page DDB house ad in the 1983 Agency Yearbook consisted of just one word, apart from the obligatory identification. One single, large-type, insipid word: "Hi!" (Perhaps anticipating the Quayle years?)

The line outside of Neil Austrian's office, of bleeders and pleaders, sycophants and jesters, all pushing to get in on the goodies, got longer. And everyone with a modicum of power was threatening to leave the agency unless
. . . .

Austrian's penchant for making promises led him, in the summer of 1983, to appoint Marvin Honig as Vice Chairman and Creative Director, DDB-U.S. "As a result of the re-structuring," explained an official release, "Roy Grace, Chairman and Executive Creative Director of DDB-U.S., will share the 'final word' responsibility for the agency's creative product with Mr. Honig."

Invitation to disaster! But no one could have foreseen the form the disaster would take.

Grace, a physical double for Egypt's Anwar Sadat and as unpredictable as any Middle Eastern ruler, took revenge into his own hands. Angry at Honig's

Lazarus-like return to power, and eager to let the world know that he, Grace, remained more equal, he invited *New York Times* ad columnist Phil Dougherty to his office for an interview. He told no one in advance. Not Austrian, not Loughrane, not public relations.

He made his points with Dougherty. Then Dougherty stood up to leave. As a by-the-way, he asked Grace whether DDB had really resigned, or been fired by, Procter & Gamble ten months earlier. Grace spoke his mind. Dougherty, a reporter with little tolerance for inflicting damage, held out a safety net.

"I assume this is off the record."

"Oh, no. I said it," responded Grace.

"You're sure it's okay if I print it?" Dougherty asked, offering one last chance.

"Yes, I said what I said."

So Dougherty printed it. And the Grace blast at P&G in the *New York Times* became another instrument in the wounding of the agency, the single most damaging episode of 1983.

* * *

Dougherty's September 7 column quoted Grace's remark that he had been "pushing very, very strongly for us to resign the business." That P&G wants creative work, but doesn't let its agencies do it. "They'll tell you you can do anything you want to do. So you submit a campaign, and three months later you wouldn't recognize it." That DDB lost money on the account every year because P&G insists on so much additional work. Etc.

Madison Avenue's Code of Silence prohibits the trashing of clients. Roy Grace had done it to the largest national advertiser, and in the *New York Times!* The agency's clients might well wonder what would one day be printed about them. As for prospective clients—well, the potential damage was incalculable.

How the event played out reveals much about the state of the agency at that time.

All eyes focused on Neil Austrian—no trace of Barry Loughrane in this tale, he being elsewhere. Austrian's phone kept ringing; horrified account managers stopped by his office with advice. "Fire Grace at once. Call a press conference to announce it. Let our clients and the advertising community know that we won't tolerate such out-of-control actions." Grace's camp followers stopped by *his* office to compliment him for "telling the truth, at last." But Grace knew he'd hit the fan. And a regular international board meeting was on the calendar for the following day.

He did what high-level DDBers with tough problems often did. He called Ned Doyle. "What should I do, Ned?" pleaded Grace. "Did you say it?" asked Doyle in his lawyerly fashion, first getting the facts.

"Yes, but I thought it was off the record," Grace told Doyle, who accepted that version. (The version I accepted was told me, at the time, by Dougherty, and later conceded by Grace.)

Doyle: "On or off the record, Roy, it was the wrong thing to do. But now, you can do one of two things. You can either do a big *mea culpa*, or you can stonewall it—don't apologize for a goddamn thing, and don't even bring it up."

Grace opted for the latter.

Meanwhile, Austrian telephoned and wrote to P&G's advertising head, Robert V. Goldstein, to apologize for the article and assure him the viewpoint was Grace's alone, not the agency's. (Four years later, Goldstein would be one of five advertising executives to die in an accident during a white-water rafting party organized by DDB-Needham Worldwide.)

The day passed without a press conference or a firing. Next day, the shrimp board met. Doyle continues the story:

"Neil got hold of me before the meeting and said, 'What do you think about it?' I said, 'I don't know what to say, Neil.' He said, 'I feel like firing him.' 'That happens to be your privilege; I'm not going to confirm or deny whether you should or should not.'"

Austrian didn't.

No one on the board brought the subject up. So Grace sat quietly, volunteering nothing. "They were afraid to do it," Grace believed.

Austrian finally said something, not at the board meeting, but directly to Grace. "The only person who ever mentioned it was Neil," Grace recalled. "He said he got a call from [client] Bruce Gelb saying, and I remember the quote exactly, 'You've got a loose cannon on board.'"

Grace stood his ground. Why should DDB "get kicked around by a client they never made a nickel on?" Finally they'd "had the balls to stand up to them, to do something that had some principles." What's so horrible about resigning a client?

And nothing else happened.

Except a kind of hopelessness began to settle over the agency that once had been cock of the walk.

* * *

"We are not altogether sorry to have 1983 behind us," opened the letter to shareholders in Doyle Dane Bernbach's annual report of that year.

The letter was signed by Neil Austrian as CEO, and Joe Daly, still Chairman of the Board.

The more things changed, the more they stayed the same.

◆ ◆ ◆

24
Monkey Business

"The great mistakes are made when we feel we are beyond questioning."
—Bill Bernbach

A memorable episode, one that vividly illustrates the chaos of the post-Bernbach era, was the agency's 1984 pitch for the $50 million Miller High Life account. Here at last was the opportunity that justified taking on cigarets. How many years the agency had longed for a shot at great beverage account—the colas, the un-colas, the major beer brands. Most of the work on such products was interchangeable, DDBers often said. Catchy music, quick cuts of happy people doing adorable things. You could (and someone at the agency did) switch their sound-tracks; viewers of the scrambled reel didn't know the difference.

Doyle Dane Bernbach could find a new direction. Zig when everybody else is zagging. That's what made the agency great. And surely they knew beer advertising. Their early '60s classic print campaign for Utica Club ("I sometimes wonder if it pays to make beer this way"), along with TV commercials featuring animated Schultz and Dooley beer mugs, brought fame and riches to an obscure upstate New York brand. The line "We must be doing something right," for New York City's Rheingold beer, went into the English language. And sales of Detroit's Stroh brewery soared to third place nationally—from twelfth place—while Doyle Dane Bernbach did its advertising. (So why did Stroh leave in 1982? Same old DDB story: superior advertising, neglected relationships,, fences un-mended, entropy. Still, past is past. On with the future.)

Miller High Life needed help. The brand had slipped onto a steep decline in 1981. Competitor Budweiser's macho commercials, set in friendly saloons, played to the masculine ego of the heavy beer consumers, blue-collar types. Same guys didn't identify with the Ivy Leaguers who shared a campfire and High Life when "Miller Time" rolled around. Hey!

A straightforward advertising problem. A brand in trouble not because of the quality of the product, but because of its image. Perfect for Doyle Dane Bernbaach.

* * *

It is a belief universally held in the industry, that a $50 million piece of new business will solve all of an agency's problems. Doyle Dane Bernbach needed a save as badly as Miller High Life needed help

Barry Loughrane and Roy Grace, heading up the Miller crusade, called some 40 staffers together in the sanctified, premiere 12th floor boardroom—a place designed to display without ostentation a deep richness in taste and resources, a place that attested to the solidity of past success and the assurance of a long future. As Loughrane spoke, a few literary minds drifted to King Henry V's charge to his outnumbered men before the battle of Agincourt:

"We few, we happy few, we band of brothers;

For he to-day that sheds his blood with me

Shall be my brother, be he ne'er so vile,

This day shall gentle his condition;

And gentlemen in England now abed

Shall think themselves accursed they were not here,

And hold their manhoods cheap whiles any speaks

That fought with us upon Saint Crispin's day."

So too the chosen band that would bring victory in this "biggest, most important, new business assignment that Doyle Dane Bernbach has ever gone after," in Loughrane's words. "All of you who are part of this will remember it as one of the great moments in this agency's history, and one of the great personal opportunities in your careers."

The uplifting rhetoric in no way struck the troops as overkill. For word on the street had Doyle Dane Bernbach the clear favorite to win Miller High Life.

As a good general, Loughrane gave a thorough briefing—what was known, what needed to be known, what needed doing, and by when.

Afterwards, Neil Austrian tossed in a word of caution: "Just don't do a bunch of smart-ass New York campaigns."

To the agency creative bulls, his admonition was a big, bright red flag. It meant, "Let's give 'em what they want." The line Bernbach had taught them contempt for.

* * *

Roy Grace still shuddered at the mention of the Miller pitch. "Its foundation was hysteria. Its undercurrent was, 'Let's not do DDB work, because that is not going to get us a beer. Let's do the kind of pap they do in the Midwest—*that* will get us a beer.' That's like having a band of the finest Sioux warriors, and asking them to drive a tank.

"The screws were tightened on everyone—but you don't change your way of working because you want to win. We were not good at working that way."

Instead of Agincourt, it would be Waterloo.

As recounted by a number of veterans of that memorable defeat, the *coup de grace* was delivered, eponymously enough, by Grace himself.

* * *

A momentary pause to remind the reader that among Doyle Dane Bernbach's most admired attributes was its refusal to do speculative campaigns. An agency had to have a strong backbone to say no to advertisers who insisted on spec work in new business pitches. A strong balance sheet helped, too.

DDB management held that, because agencies put their most talented people onto spec work in trying for new business, paying clients get shortchanged. Moreover spec campaigns are a waste of time, because the advertiser doesn't reveal sufficient information until an agency becomes his true partner. Then a "real" campaign is produced. So why play time-consuming games? An agency's past work should be a reliable enough indicator of its future performance.

The industry applauded. Alas, few agencies could afford to adopt a similar stance. Lost in history, and in the image projected by its leaders, was the fact that Doyle Dane Bernbach had done spec work once upon a time.

"When you're young and poor, you have to do spec to get accounts, and we did," conceded Ned Doyle, after Bernbach's death.

Now old and rich did spec too, as economic pressures worked to make advertisers more wary, more demanding, more frightened. Damned if they would hand over a $50 million budget to an agency without, at the very least, a theme, a concept, and often a piece of music, that brought them to their feet, then and there. The theme might change after the agency's full indoctrination into the advertiser's business, but the winning spec campaign provided fail-safe "parameters."

You have to change with the times, said Austrian.

Spec presentations, un-affectionately termed "gang-bangs," became a consuming part of work life in the agency's post-Bernbach years.

"And since we'd never done them before," said Grace, "we didn't know how to do them at all. Other agencies knew how. For us it was like re-inventing the wheel."

* * *

Bill Wardell, then head of new business for the agency, also shuddered at the memory of Miller. "It should have been like throwing red meat to the lions—to do a bang-up execution on an assignment with absolutely watertight strategic guidelines. It was like the yellow brick road, laid out very specifically for us, like 'fill in the blanks.'

"The assignment fundamentally was: Miller Time had a few great years. Bud's good campaign had pre-empted it, they were out-Millering Miller. So freshen up and contemporize, or replace, Miller Time. There was no guessing. Whether you believed in the strategy or not, that's what they wanted. So everyone went charging off to find better ways."

Including Roy Grace, who with his copy partner John Noble, quickly came up with a concept featuring monkeys. Monkeys!?!?

"Truthfully, I really love gorillas," said Grace in an agency Christmas party film, featuring monkeys, produced under his aegis. Indeed, his gorilla-banging-suitcase commercial for American Tourister luggage was a classic. That gorilla symbolized "clumsy bellboys, brutal cab drivers, careless doormen, ruthless porters, and all the butterfingered luggage handlers all over the world." To them, American Tourister said, "Have we got a suitcase for you!" Funny, memorable, effective.

The Miller monkeys would symbolize people who drank the other beer. Hmmmm.

"The way that concept came over was, if you're drinking the other beer you're a monkey," recalled research VP Wally Lepkin, who gathered data on responses to concepts for the Miller pitch. "And I thought, 1) why knock the competitor's product, 2) why alienate a prospective customer, and 3) a lot of Miller customers were black."

Copy-testing in markets with heavy black populations showed strong negatives to Grace's campaign. "I knew it was bad, I just wanted some reassurance," Grace told Lepkin, who thereupon assumed the monkeys were dead. To Lepkin's astonishment, they were not. Such surprises became less surprising in the months ahead.

Lepkin: "One example. We were going after Minoxidil, a hair restorer, which was waiting for approval by the Food & Drug Administration. We did so much research. I read literature this high. And learned if you're bald, it won't work. It doesn't restore hair. If your hair is thinning, it will thicken it. If you're starting to lose it, this will help you keep it. But you have to be of a certain age and have a certain kind of hair for this to work. We went through the clinicals, the research, etc. Then creative came up with a storyboard showing a tree with leaves, the leaves fall off the tree, and then in reverse motion, the leaves go back up onto the tree and grow again. Very dramatic, but totally fallacious, totally meaningless. It was as if the creative people didn't read the material.

"I've seen some terrible stuff go through here in new business. So bad you wonder if the creatives are working for another agency."

* * *

Roy Grace used words like "fanatic" and "neurotic" about his need to be the best. Where Bernbach nurtured the agency's creative people, Grace competed with them. Asked to select the year's five best agency ads for a special issue of *Advertising Age,* Grace chose five he himself art directed. DDB's public relations manager thereupon suggested that "it might be wise to pick a Polaroid ad, given the trouble we're having on the account." Grace retorted "You asked for the five best, and I gave them to you." Subject closed.

"Nobody has a bigger ego than I do," conceded Grace. "I'm serious."

Few creatives measured up to his standards. Bob Gage and Helmut Krone, he granted, were "major, major talents." But the frequent reaction by Grace to concepts submitted by other creatives was, "Why are you bringing me this piece of shit?"

The Miller work that began to cross his desk didn't improve his opinion of others' talents. He grew fonder of his monkeys. During a Mobil shoot in Los Angeles, Grace and John Noble shoehorned in the filming of a spot depicting little construction monkeys drinking another beer.

Every other campaign presented to Miller would be in the form of storyboards or animatics.

Bill Wardell: "So Grace and Noble come back from L.A. with the monkeys. And half of us are saying it's insulting, it's awful, and half of us are thinking, Well we don't have anything else yet."

As a knockout idea failed to turn up, panic increased. The chosen band became less exclusive. "Anybody with a job in the creative department got to play ball," said Wardell. "Even the babies. Hey, that creep who does radio. Anybody!"

"It got out of hand," remembered Mike Mangano, a 21-year veteran of the agency and one of its top three creative heads at the time. "Too many people were working on it. I'll bet 75 percent of the creative department, and it was eating them up. Other work was neglected."

Fifty-one (count 'em, fifty one!) campaigns came up for judgment by Grace, Noble and Mangano, who simultaneously were working on their own Miller submissions ("I hated that," said Mangano), and by Wardell and Loughrane.

"Instead of a tour de force," said Wardell, "it was a tour de weakness. But we were nearing pencils-down time because we had to finish up slides and make music, etc. We sat there and went over probably 22 campaigns, creative teams walking in back to back. And we had to pick three or four things."

They picked three: two with music, one without. All featured working people—construction workers, truck drivers, people who do unglamorous jobs but do them well. Only one campaign was "old DDB," the one without music. Visually, the working hands of Miller Men would complement an audio of short, compelling dialogues. Of the two with music, one followed the rhythms of the working day through to a rewarding finish at the saloon. The other took off from the Tom Wolfe book and film, "The Right Stuff." Agency bets were on this campaign. "Be the one who has the right stuff/ They're a very special few," urged the theme song. Alas, the film, released late in 1983, had done only middling-well at the box-office, although Wolfe's phrase had entered the language.

Mangano created "The Right Stuff" campaign, but he didn't even *like* it. He preferred the off-beat Miller Men campaign. Everything about the episode bothered Mangano: the "let's do conventional beer advertising" atmosphere; the courtroom proceedings where the judges were competing with those they judged; and, finally, the agency's "chicken-heartedness" in the presentations.

"We were afraid to take a stand. 'What if they like *that* one?' In the old days, when we were principled, we'd do something we believed in and we'd say, 'Hey, we think this is great.' I guess that went away."

The monkey commercial would be taken to the presentation under somebody's armpit, just in case.

* * *

"Oh, Jesus, we're in trouble," moaned Clay Timon, head of international, when he and Neil Austrian reviewed the finished slides and music for the Miller presentation. Timon had no ax to grind. Candid and cheerful, he was perhaps the only person on the management floor universally liked and trusted.

"We were the odds-on favorite to win Miller," recounted Timon. "The presentation was in a day or two. We didn't expect they'd buy it, but we did expect they'd give us another shot, because we knew they liked us."

If so, they didn't show it.

Wardell: "We must have gone through two solid hours of wall-to-wall creative, really whoop-de-doo. Music, song and dance, campaign A, B and C. And not one eyelash twitched among the eight jurors sitting there."

So Roy Grace pulled out the monkey commercial, with an "Oh, by the way" introduction. Chairs shifted ever so slightly. An eyelash or two twitched, almost imperceptibly. Nothing was said. But the final message was "Don't call us, we'll call you."

* * *

Miller instantly cut Doyle Dane Bernbach out of the running for High Life. Given the turmoil and hysteria and bruising that the agency went through in preparing its pitch, Barry Loughrane tried to put a hopeful spin on the news in a staff memo:

"What they told me is that they had not elected to test any of our recommendations at this time. That could mean we are out forever or that we will be considered if they aren't satisfied with the tests of the other agencies' work."

They were, of course, out forever.

Word that the monkeys put the lid on DDB kept filtering back to the agency. Its law firm heard it from another of its clients. A former DDBer who pitched a Miller product a year later reported that the brewery people were still shaking their heads in disbelief.

"The sense was, 'Why would any advertiser give its business to an agency that portrayed its potential customers as monkeys?"

* * *

The monkey story didn't reach the press, and wasn't known to many staffers within the agency. But the sudden-death end to the staggering effort on Miller sent the agency into a new depression. This was what a terminal illness must be like.

DDBers in record numbers turned their minds to the possibility of working elsewhere. Including the CEO.

Account Gains and Losses—1983-84

In: Out:

Brown & Williamson   Atari
Excedrin   Bankers Trust
Hyatt Legal Services   Bulova
Magnavox   El Al
Michelin tires   Israel Tourist
Western Airlines   Philip Morris (Parliament)
                                Polaroid
                                Porsche
                                Schaeffer pens

♦ ♦ ♦

25
Things Fall Apart

"It's hard to ruin a good agency, and God knows, a lot of good men have tried."—Tom Dillon, BBDO

Every profession has its Golden Age; advertising had Doyle Dane Bernbach in the '50s and '60s. The winds of fortune began to change in 1970, though the outside world didn't perceive that. Inside, the pride and joy of working for the mythic agency were palpable into the '80s. Waves of downsizing over the years depressed the troops temporarily; the survivors quickly regained their high spirits. They still worked at the best place, where the standards were highest, the reins the loosest, the fun most constant.

"Ah, but it's not like it was when I got here," one heard frequently. The speaker might have got there in the '50s, the '60s, the '70s, or even early '80s. Yet the comment was the same. For getting there, in whatever year, was adland's equivalent of dying and going to heaven. Being there, inevitably, brought awareness of trouble in paradise.

In the Orwellian year of 1984, the sounds of crumbling illusions echoed through the once raucous halls of Doyle Dane Bernbach.

* * *

Neil Austrian had led the agency through a renaissance in the mid-'70s, picking up when Tom Gallagher dropped the baton, and, with Marvin Honig, continuing what the triumvirate had started. Stemming the outflow of clients. Reinvigorating the creative work. Going after and winning significant new business. And, most clearly the work of Austrian, the great expansion of the agency's international network.

"We were back on a roll," said Clay Timon, recalling the period with a warm nostalgia.

Then came the Paulson presidency, the death of Bernbach, the lethal creative rivalries. Austrian confided to Timon that he "woke up one day and realized that the wheels were beginning to fall off, and he didn't know how to fix it." His natural exuberance had led him to believe he could fix just about anything, and in the past, he had. But having rebuilt a collapsing Doyle Dane Bernbach in the mid '70s, he couldn't (and wouldn't, being honest to his core) shift the blame for decisions that threatened its collapse anew: bringing Paulson aboard and bringing Honig back. Doubts were spreading now about Loughrane. Who could bear going through it all again?

And so Austrian listened when an executive recruiting firm, Heidrich & Struggles, approached him about the CEO position at Showtime/The Movie Channel.

On the morning of May 15, 1984, Doyle Dane Bernbach announced that Austrian had resigned to join Showtime.

Throughout the agency, through the morning and early afternoon, one heard and saw expressions of incredulity, bewilderment, anxiety, hurt, sadness. Doyle Dane Bernbach had lost its leader—a leader who had won the admiration and affection of . . . well, not all, but many employees. Austrian hadn't always ruled wisely, but he alone represented the whole of the agency, not one creative faction, or one account group fiefdom, or one department. His warmth and energy had fueled Doyle Dane Bernbach worldwide.

Groups huddled in halls, exchanging concerns, and then stories. Tales were told about promises made and never kept. One former executive who worked closely with him spoke of "his incredible capacity to say yes to everybody, no matter what their point of view. But who knew? I didn't know until the end of it, and then these stories started coming out and I thought, Holy shit!"

Said another, "You've never seen anybody dissolve from the history books of DDB faster than the 30 seconds it took for Neil."

By day's end, misery had metamorphosed into relief. It was time for Austrian to go. Now a real advertising man could get things moving again.

* * *

On March 8, 1984, Ned Doyle told me that the top guns of the agency had "lost faith" in Austrian. On the day of Austrian's resignation, two months later, Doyle asked me, in tones of dismay and surprise, if I knew "why Neil did it." The board hadn't expected Austrian's move. For all their growing dissatisfaction with his leadership, they weren't ready with an alternate plan. With some reluctance, they gave Austrian's titles to Barry Loughrane.

"Who were they going to make CEO, the president of Afghanistan?" growled Loughrane, looking back to the day of his promotion.

In fact, they talked about giving the CEO title to John Bernbach, whom

Austrian was bringing back from Europe as president of DDB-International, perhaps with the hope of grooming him for succession to CEO worldwide. Austrian had made clear, when he joined the agency ten years earlier, that he couldn't commit to advertising as a lifetime career.

"If you give it to John, I'll leave," threatened Daly. ("Threatening to leave" ranked with "sending the wrong signal" and "love-hate relationship" as common threads weaving through the agency management saga.) Other board members allowed as how John needed time to prove himself to the New York people. Very few knew him. Those who did gave him mixed reviews. The troops picked up the phrase, "Basically, all John wants is a pocketful of tickets on the Concorde and a limo to meet him when he gets off the plane."

Some thought that all Loughrane wanted was to be back in California, spending his days in the far more tractable DDB-West offices, and nights at his restaurants. His tenure in New York had, so far, impressed few. His bearing impressed fewer. A pot belly protruded between his red suspenders. Darting eyes set in a fleshy face, and atop his head, whitish-yellow hair that looked like it had been left out all night in the rain. Could this man inspire and lead the weary troops to renewed glory?

At least one board member completely lost heart at that point. And since he was Paul Bernbach, executor of his father's estate, the potential consequences were staggering.

Even before Austrian was off the premises, an explosion detonated that ruptured friendships forever.

* * *

Paul Bernbach had dutifully uttered the proper words to the press, after Bernbach's death, about his father's satisfaction with the management in place at the agency. In truth, Paul had some doubts then. Now he had none. It was time to shelter the Bernbach fortune from the vagaries of the company. He had a fiduciary, not to mention family, responsibility to his mother, his brother, their wives and ten children.

Bill Bernbach had never sold off agency stock to diversify, as had his partners. The Bernbach family held 16 percent of the company stock. A company that couldn't seem to get itself straightened out. A company that could conceivably go straight down the pipes.

Paul had sat on the shrimp board now for a year-and-a-half. A lawyer by training, he constantly weighed the risks of hanging in, and worried about possible detrimental effects to the agency his father founded, of pulling out. Austrian's resignation tipped the scale. Paul decided to sell the family's holdings. He had a buyer. Saatchi & Saatchi.

* * *

"The Saatchis had been courting us for a long time," Paul related, "even when my father was alive. They had come and talked to him, generally, but also with a view to doing some kind of combination."

Saatchi executive Tim Bell was a close friend of John Bernbach's, "and every time Dad came to London, I made sure that we either had a lunch or a meal or spent some time together, because Tim is a great talker and Dad was a great talker . . . they were very turned on by each other. At the same time, there were other conversations [with other DDB and S&S executives] going on. . . ."

Did Bill Bernbach have any interest in a deal with S&S?

John: "I think it's fair to say he recognized the fact that they were very interesting. I certainly had a lot of respect for their success. His attitude about that and a lot of other things was always, 'If you want to talk, I'm always willing to listen.'"

Paul: "Nothing happened then, but they never stopped being interested. After my father died, and I was left in control of close to a million shares, they saw the opportunity to get a foot in the door. They started talking right away, and they kept on pressing. They made many offers for the family stock."

Paul "talked a lot" with Maurice and Charles Saatchi. Here, there, all over. In Europe, where Paul went often on business. In New York. "I met with Maurice here; he was always the one who came here. A lot of meetings with him. He was always pushing the idea of a merger as a natural. And remember, in England S&S is a terrific agency that does wonderful creative work. And that's what mattered to them most, they always said. It was only after they bought Compton and Ted Bates that people started to say, 'Right, tell me about it.'"

Paul understood the Saatchis wanted the family stock as leverage in talking to management about a deal. He didn't want the family stock used as a crowbar, but he didn't want to keep holding the shares either. "There was an incredible amount of bad stuff, disruptive stuff, happening at that time," recalled Paul. Like his father a decade earlier, he wanted out.

One morning, before Neil Austrian had finished packing up at DDB, Paul called and said the Saatchis were going to be in his office in an hour; would Austrian come and meet with them? "Which I did," said Austrian. After all, he'd "been talking with the Saatchis forever."

Those talks included Morgan Stanley representatives for the Saatchis.

"During the time in Paul's office, the Morgan Stanley representatives were trying to find out, Could they buy Paul's block, and if so at what price, and what would it take to do a deal to buy Doyle Dane Bernbach? They were asking me questions personally, as someone who knew where the blocks of stock were and what the price would have to be. I certainly was not negotiating the deal. At least, I believed I wasn't."

Did that include opinions on which people the Saatchis ought to lock in?

"You bet," responded Austrian. "Who were the key people, who do you have to keep and what do you have to pay them, and what options do they have, what long-term incentive awards they have, etc. etc."

The storm broke two days into Loughrane's CEOship, when he learned that Maurice Saatchi thought he had a deal. In addition to the howling rage of Loughrane and his financial chief, Bob Pfundstein, at this apparent attempt to sell the agency just as they took power, there were many legal problems. The agency's lawyers weighed in at once, drafting a letter to all board members, informing them that only the CEO was empowered to discuss offers for the company; that the others had no legal right to negotiate the disposition of Doyle Dane Bernbach.

New waves of hurt, anger and disbelief had been set off by Austrian— this time among the directors rather than the staff. How *could* he, after a decade of trust and respect, *do* this to the agency as a final, lame duck act. (They forgot they'd lost faith in him months earlier.) For money, insisted Pfundstein. "He owned a nice block of the stock that had been given to him. [The April 1984 proxy showed Austrian owning 85,000 shares.] The Saatchis were offering something in the area of $30 a share when the price of the stock was $20, so he would have increased the value of his holdings by 50 percent."

Maybe, but while Austrian reveled in the sport of deal-structuring, and delighted in the rewards of success, personal greed wasn't part of his make-up. More likely, he couldn't resist one last grand opportunity to fix what was breaking in the way he understood best. And, at the same time, to discharge a responsibility he felt to the Bernbach family, who saw their fortune imperiled.

The new leaders, Loughrane and Pfundstein, campaigned hard amongst board members against a Saatchi takeover, their basic theme being that "you can forever forget Doyle Dane Bernbach and what we stood for if you do a deal with the Saatchis."

Charting the fever of hostility, the Saatchis pulled back, never putting their offer into writing.

Bitterness followed disbelief. Loughrane and Pfundstein stopped speaking to Austrian. Ned Doyle, a frequent Saturday visitor to the Austrian home in Old Greenwich, cut his ties to the Austrian family. Mac Dane felt a sad disillusionment.

"Even though Paul Bernbach may have talked with him about it," Mac Dane said later, "Neil should have been smart enough to stay away from any deal. Here he is, just resigned from the company, and he is handling negotiations with somebody who wants to purchase the stock. Most of us were surprised that he would not withdraw from any discussions whatsoever."

Dane and Doyle were dead against selling the agency, to the Saatchis or anyone. They talked privately with Loughrane and Pfundstein. "We said to them in effect," Dane related, "'Look, have you guys confidence in your ability to run the place and that it's in good shape? If so, we're willing to support you.' They in effect both expressed confidence that whatever the problems were, they could handle them. They agreed with us that we ought to forge our own destiny."

Could the agency afford to buy the Bernbach family shares? Dane and Doyle asked the two men. "Because if the Bernbach estate couldn't sell to the Saatchis, there had to be another purchaser, and the only way we could maintain control would be for us to buy the stock."

The corporation did, taking on a brutal debt to pay the Bernbachs $22.35 per share for their 914,910 shares—some $20 million.

Paul Bernbach said later that selling back to the company rather than to the Saatchis "cost the family an amount in the seven figures." The family "went out of its way to be loyal to the management, and not put them in a difficult position."

Pfundstein, still smarting, recalled recommending the buy-back to the board "to stop these kids from running around, constantly worrying about how much the money they inherited would be worth a year from now." He had been, he believed, "extraordinarily fair to the family—I could have let Paul sit there and stew with that stock for a long, long time. The Saatchis in no way would have bought the stock unless they knew they could get control of the company on a friendly basis."

Austrian disputed this, citing the premium value of a controlled block of stock.

Not that the fine points of the controversy matter now, only that they long remained contentious among the principals.

* * *

For all the *Sturm und Drang*, the board didn't ask Austrian to resign as a director. "I think," said Dane, "the feeling was, why upset things? There are enough changes that are going on right now, and if Neil is willing to stay on, let's keep him on."

Keeping him on worked. The press didn't get wind of the episode. But the bitterness lingered, long after the melodramatic ending of the meteoric—upward and downward—Austrian decade.

Account Gains and Losses, 1985 to the date of the mega-merger announcement, April 4, 1986

In:

Out:

Nabisco

Brown & Williamson (resigned)
Celanese
O.M. Scott
Sylvania

♦ ♦ ♦

26
Dead in the Water

"An advertising company is made up of a lot of creative prima donnas."
David L. Yunick, director, The JWT Group

Now Bill Bernbach's old corner office belonged to Barry Loughrane. Often, looking out on the spires of St. Patrick's Cathedral, Loughrane pondered the Gothic complexities within Doyle Dane Bernbach's hallowed walls. What had Bernbach thought as he sat here, aware of approaching death, yet attending not at all to the matter of a creative successor?

Loughrane remembered times past, when he'd talked to Joe Daly about planning for his succession. "'Joe,' you say, 'what happens if you get hit by a truck?' And Joe says, 'No truck is going to hit me.' There is no answer to that," shrugged Loughrane.

But when a truck roared down the narrow alleyway, straight at Bernbach, he still would not call out a name to the managers of his multi-national, billion-dollar-plus agency.

"Maybe," mused Loughrane, "Bernbach should have said, 'This is what I want, and this is how I see the future of the agency, and I see Bob Levenson doing it' . . . or whoever. It wouldn't have mattered what he said. The point is there would have been *something*. This place was rudderless. Neil came up out of Chief Financial Officer. He put a lot of points on the map, which was wonderful, but he created a much bigger monster. Because the core wasn't put back in order. And now all of a sudden, several years later, instead of having a five-hundred-million-dollar large boutique, you have a billion-and-a-half-dollar monster."

The core, at Doyle Dane Bernbach, had always meant its creative leadership. Loughrane was now stuck with the problem that Bernbach had willfully ignored.

* * *

Loughrane hadn't even warmed up the CEO seat when he was hit with the loss of Polaroid's U.S. consumer advertising—the client's 30th anniversary present to its agency partner. The blow, long expected, nonetheless hardened the sense of hopelessness induced by the Miller Beer affair.

DDBers had never doubted that, given a shot at a major beer or soft-drink account, they could out-create anything on the air. When the opportunity finally came, all the talent in the place had fallen short.

Miller shook their faith in the future. Polaroid was Doyle Dane Bernbach's history. The agency's growth, its power structure and its psyche were interwoven with Polaroid. To lose the biggest piece of Polaroid diminished the proud past.

Both companies had been the darlings of Wall Street, Main Street and Madison Avenue for their innovative work and high principles. In the '70s, both lost the aura of infallibility they'd acquired in the exuberant years of creative and technological discovery. Polaroid shares had tumbled from $149 to $14; DDB's from $51 to $9.

Polaroid's troubles began in 1972, when the company brought out its SX-70 camera. Analysts criticized the camera as too expensive and difficult to operate. In turn, Polaroid criticized DDB's introductory commercials. The campaign made news—the great Lawrence Olivier in his first role as a product spokesman. Impressive, dignified—and unaffecting. Olivier demonstrated the camera with photographs of inanimate objects such as flowers. Nothing for the heart here.

"These people are tired," Polaroid's inventor, Dr. Land, said to Ted Voss, head of advertising. Pressure built on Voss to "get rid of DDB." Instead, Voss released steam by adding a second agency, Needham, Harper Worldwide, for high-end cameras. Needham's creative star, Keith Reinhard, did such brilliant work that Voss urged DDB, for its own sake, to hire Reinhard as "a second creative director" on Polaroid. How differently the scenario might have played out had DDB heeded the suggestion.

But the second half of the decade were good years for Doyle Dane Bernbach and Polaroid. Under Neil Austrian's leadership, DDB acquired an admirable roster of agencies, in countries where Polaroid wanted servicing, gaining stature and vitality for itself in the process. "We felt we were financing that expansion," said Voss, "but we did not mind, because it gave us access to the best."

Meanwhile, Polaroid met Kodak's challenge in the instant photography market with a new generation of easy-to-use cameras. And DDB's Mariette

Hartley-James Garner OneStep campaign, by Bob Gage and Jack Dillon, captivated audiences, swept the awards shows, and won grand prize for the most sales-effective campaign of the period.

The '80s brought new troubles to both companies. At DDB, the divisiveness of the Paulson period and the death of Bernbach. At Polaroid, the erosion of the instant photography market by easy-to-operate 35mm cameras and one-hour film development stores. Polaroid cut staff and offered generous packages for voluntary departures. Some of its best people took the money and went to new jobs elsewhere. The marketing people who'd worked with DDB left in 1982. Sales people moved into marketing. A package goods man from Colgate-Palmolive came in. The free-wheeling, intuitive judgments of the high-flying years were gone. Now Polaroid tested commercials until their juices ran out, and *still* couldn't make decisions.

Package goods mentality—the agency's nemesis—on its paradigm account!

The people who'd moved from sales to marketing said they didn't want to see any more of Joe Daly. "That's the end," Ned Doyle told Neil Austrian at the time, in 1983. "Beat 'em to the punch by resigning." Instead, Austrian determined to save the account, and flew almost weekly to Cambridge, Mass. But Doyle proved right.

"Joe Daly abused the lower level of Polaroid for years," Doyle said later. "When they rose, Daly—and the agency—had it." The sales people "had never liked Joe," Voss confirmed. "They never understood what he could do, and they disliked what they saw of him at meetings."

They didn't like his unrestrained drinking and blonde-chasing at their sales meetings and conferences. They didn't enjoy hearing him crow about winning thousands of dollars at the track, betting on and racing his horses. Jim Heekin used to caution Daly about the insensitivity of bragging about big winnings to lower-level, low-paid client people. Daly did not alter his ways.

Dazzlingly free of self-doubt, Daly never stopped believing that the Polaroid loss was entirely due to Austrian's "talking me, and everyone else, into taking me off the account. I'll never forgive the guy for that," said Daly, soon after the denouement, the mega-merger of 1986.

But by then, Daly, in his late '60s, could look back on 30 years of power secured by his control of the Polaroid account. He had much to look forward to, as well. He would serve as a director of the new corporate parent, Omnicom. And, in the spreading CEO fashion, he would garner a trophy wife, marrying a beautiful young airline stewardess. No wonder he titled his memoirs, published by a vanity house, "Luck Is My Lady."

Ned Doyle would die believing Daly's luck was Doyle Dane Bernbach's misfortune.

* * *

Two postscripts to the saga:

♦ Ted Voss praised Daly for having had "the power to get what Polaroid wanted" from the agency. But, he added, he and Peter Wensberg, the company's brilliant VP-marketing in the glory days, "give more credit to Bob Gage than to Joe for the great work the agency did for Polaroid."

♦ Polaroid pulled the rest of its billings out of the agency worldwide (16 of DDB's foreign offices handled the account) in summer of 1985, further depressing earnings, and adding to an agency-wide sense of resignation that the end was near.

* * *

The agency's New York office workforce shrank by 198 jobs in 1984, down to eight hundred plus, from more than a thousand at the end of 1983. Downsizing on that scale hadn't happened since Austrian and Tom Gallagher mopped up after the disasters of the early '70s. The troops had long since regained their old faith that Madison Avenue's well-known revolving door didn't operate at DDB, that the agency kept people on through hard times, that those who had served it well were secure.

Austrian reinforced that faith by keeping people on after major account losses in the early '80s. Loughrane and his chief financial man, Bob Pfundstein, inherited the draining expenses of Austrian's corporate good-heartedness. They mandated cuts, needing to improve the balance sheets—and, they argued, to improve morale among a workforce with insufficient work to fill each day. Idleness bred fear. Busy people were less likely to feel vulnerable.

Instead, morale sank to lower plateaus with each wave of the year's blood baths. The human tendency to find justification for the firing of other people could not be sustained, given the loyalty and abilities of so many who bit the dust. Older staffers shuddered at the number of long-tenured and hard-working hands, such as media and research vice-presidents in their late 40s and 50s, who unhappily accepted non-refusable offers of early retirement packages. The beat of the agency's legendary heart slowed, and stilled.

At most advertising agencies, the link between account losses and payroll cuts is clearly understood and accepted. But most advertising agencies neither get nor deserve the committed love that DDBers gave their company.

Now, whether fired or fed up or plain old scared about the future, DDBers began to overwhelm headhunting offices. Barry Loughrane received a call from an industry friend who wanted to alert him to a possible exodus in the making.

"Most of the people who are leaving we don't want anyway," responded Loughrane.

* * *

Roy Grace had no twinges of compassion whatsoever for the many departing people in the creative department. On the contrary, he later looked back with pride on his sweeping achievements.

"I cleaned out the agency," he puffed.

Some creatives he fired; more were "encouraged to leave." He boasted of having found ways to "make it not attractive to stay" for a number of art directors and copywriters. His targets gave up and quit, which, noted Grace loftily, saved the agency severance pay.

"Here's an anecdote for you," he related. "Ned Doyle calls me up and says, 'Why the hell did you fire ————?' I said, 'She's not talented, Ned. I would rather have somebody in that job who has talent.' Ned said, 'So? She hasn't been talented for twenty years!'"

Grace's judgments of other creatives' talents were far from universally shared. (In fact, the agency would eventually rehire a number of those alienated or discarded by Grace.) Moreover, his "why are you bringing me this piece of shit?" approach continued to demoralize the very people whose egos he should have been nurturing.

Loughrane and Pfundstein, while encouraging departmental cuts agency-wide, eyed Grace's actions with growing unease. They began to question him about the departures of veteran creatives esteemed for the work they'd produced over the years.

Grace, unflappable when quizzed about those who'd gone, invariably countered with, "They never really were any good."

There seemed no more will to deal with Grace's handling of the creatives than with his lethal misjudgments on the Procter & Gamble story and the Miller monkeys. He remained untouchable. Why?

Because, one was told, "He's the only game in town."

* * *

Marvin Honig had gone on the heels of Neil Austrian's departure. "Neil left me unprotected," he said later. "He left me vulnerable to the people who knew I didn't think much of them. Like Barry Loughrane."

That eliminated one of the three contenders for Bernbach's mantle. It also offered an easy answer to why Polaroid pulled out. The Ned Doyle – Ted Voss theory about the inevitability of the agency-client split after "DDB's guys" left Polaroid was not heard in 1984. Then, one kept hearing the fault was Honig's, for failing to come up with a winning campaign after taking over creative responsibility on the account.

Honig's departure left his creative partisans as easy targets in Grace's moves to "clean out the agency."

Once, staffers had worked for Doyle Dane Bernbach. Now, they chose up sides, and lost their jobs when their leaders fell.

* * *

Bob Levenson had his own small "merry band" of creatives, with whom he worked on international campaigns, out of Grace's reach. He harbored the hope that "after Roy, Barry, Neil, and all the New York guys blew themselves out of the water, John [Bernbach] and I would be in a position to take control of the New York agency." Levenson and John had formed a close bond during Levenson's many business trips to DDB's foreign offices.

"We thought the campaigns done by those offices were the last best remaining example of what Doyle Dane Bernbach was supposed to do. Not uniformly true in every office in the world, but closer to the real thing than anything going on in New York."

Despite Bill Bernbach's silence on a creative heir, many DDBers still rooted for Levenson, preferring his decency and articulateness to Grace's apparent delight in shattering psyches and egos.

The Bernbach family showed their feelings by asking Levenson to deliver the eulogy at Bernbach's funeral. And then, when Michael Gill dropped out of the Bernbach book project, the family asked Levenson to "finish" Bill Bernbach's unwritten book. (The relationship soured somewhat when Levenson realized the family expected him to do the book "out of love of Bill," i.e. without payment. Levenson signed a contract splitting royalties with Evelyn Bernbach.)

Levenson's fantasy of eventually taking over gave way to the reality of events. "More and more I felt that it was all over, that it was a lost cause," he related. So did industry observers, on reading Phil Dougherty's *New York Times* column of January 22, 1985.

"In an unusual display," Dougherty led off, "Doyle Dane Bernbach yesterday revealed its 1984 woes to security analysts, relieving the drab litany with the news that earnings for the year should come to about $1.50 a share, up from $1.05 in 1983." The "woes" included "lost accounts, lost top executives, too much personnel, real estate that was too expensive, one third of the flagship New York office's accounts unprofitable, more than $13 million in accounts receivable, and employee morale sagging to new depths." The steps taken by the agency "to regain a pretty profit picture included cutting the New York work force by 198 people."

So much for the Camelot of the advertising industry.

The Saatchis, sensing the time was right, set out to win Levenson, seeing him as the true spirit of Bernbach, and just what they needed to lift the creative reputation of their U.S. acquisition, Compton Advertising. (Yes, Virginia, Compton. Paul Paulson's old home. Slice-of-life City.) The Saatchis' courtship succeeded. On April 10, 1985, Levenson announced he was leaving, after 26 years with DDB.

"How can you leave us, Bob?" pleaded Joe Daly. "You're part of the woodwork." Responded Levenson, "You just answered your own question."

To the many old hands who'd never lost hope that Levenson would outlast Roy Grace, his leaving marked The End of Doyle Dane Bernbach as they had known and loved it. And they said it, to him and his "merry band," all of whom he had arranged, as part of his deal with the Saatchis, to take with him to Compton.

"The End came long ago," argued copywriter David Herzbrun. "This is just the period that completes the sentence."

Throughout that day, financial chief Bob Pfundstein placed calls to Wall Street analysts, triumphantly announcing the departure of Levenson and his crew, and how the move would improve the company's balance sheet by one million dollars per year.

* * *

Well then, that resolved the problem of who, among the three contenders, would inherit, for good and all, Bernbach's golden bough. Didn't it?

Alas, the resolution-by-departures only exacerbated matters. With no back-up candidate on the premises, Grace showed ever-more contempt for ever-increasing numbers of DDBers. In truth, he had produced many more great campaigns than ever Bernbach had, but he had not acquired an iota of Bernbach's magical aura as a creative leader. The insiders who had shielded the Bernbach legend, while having some doubts themselves, came to a far greater appreciation of what had been lost. Bitterly did they swallow Grace's arrogant demand for a $60,000 raise on the day after he'd trimmed his staff to save on his departmental budget. Ruefully, some recalled Bernbach's oft-spoken words, that to work at Doyle Dane Bernbach, people must be nice as well as talented.

* * *

Grace—chairman and executive creative director U.S., and vice chairman of Doyle Dane Bernbach International, winner by survival, the only game in town—had no intention of hanging around much longer. He hadn't believed in Barry Loughrane since 1972, when he, Loughrane and Marvin Honig tried, and failed, to launch an agency of their own. The story was known only vaguely. Conventional wisdom had it as proof of a long and close friendship among the three men. On the contrary, Grace and Honig had blamed the failure on Loughrane, and came to unflattering conclusions about his business abilities.

Nothing in the first year of Loughrane's regime altered Grace's opinion. No excitement followed his installation as CEO. A sense of pulling together under a terrific new management didn't happen. So Grace started a series of secret meetings to plan a new agency with two other DDBers—a top copywriter and an account man.

At the same time, Loughrane was secretly interviewing "every creative star in the business, from Mal[colm] Macdougall to Jay Chiat to Burt Manning." He recalled weekends in Connecticut, sneaking into hotel rooms in Los Angeles." He "had to have a few alternate plans," had to protect himself, "because supposing Roy . . ." He didn't complete the sentence, as he looked back, in September of 1986, on his reign as CEO.

It was indeed a bizarre situation. A company desperately in need of inspiring, reviving leadership, whose two top executives, instead of working together to provide it, were secretly plotting moves to cut the ground out from under one another.

Others in high managerial positions looked in vain for the teamwork they hoped would bind the agency together at long last, under a "real" advertising man. Loughrane ran the place, some said, as a one-man band. Board members, who'd voted to buy back the Bernbach family stock on the assurance that the agency could make its own way, were given no more hint of Loughrane's maneuvers than he gave his colleagues. The latter felt they were "no longer an integral part of management."

Looking back, Loughrane did not dispute this. He had, after the buy-back, concluded that the agency *couldn't* make it "without either doing a merger or bringing in from the outside, which heretofore never worked, two or three all-stars to rekindle the flame." Thus, his secret meetings, not only with creative stars, but also with possible "agency partners"—or mergers. "I've done a lot of things that nobody around here has ever known," he said later. "I had no one to communicate to. The people I had to play with, the situations and the fiefdoms, were already in place." And they were not Loughrane's team.

"If you're in charge of a big company and your next in line are all independent, that's hard to communicate with. Because they don't give a shit about me and my point of view. All they care about is *their* point of view.

"So particularly if I want to do anything radical, particularly if I want to change the company, particularly if I was looking for other people, particularly if I was looking for other ways of doing business, the last people I want to talk with are the people on this goddamn row! What, are you *mad*? This gang couldn't keep anything secret for more than four seconds. I didn't even tell the board."

Which explains why the directors were dumbfounded when, in April 1986, they were asked to approve a mega-merger (in fact, a sale of the agency) because Doyle Dane Bernbach was "dead in the water."

* * *

Roy Grace stayed just long enough to collect on his Long Term Incentive Award. Neil Austrian had created the LTIAs in 1980 to lock in a handful of executives. The first round of the five-year awards would pay off at the end of 1985, when each participant would receive a windfall of hundreds of thousands of dollars.

The agency had, from 1980 to 1985, pumped $7,874,000 into funding the LTIAs. In the same period, about $13,000 covered the company shares awarded to everyone else on their key anniversaries. So pathetic was the contrast that anniversary awards became a joke that eroded employee loyalty.

On January 30, 1986, Roy Grace announced at a press conference the opening of Grace & Rothschild. He did it with a swift kick in DDB's groin.

"The energy and the focus of larger agencies is toward mindless growth, and not toward turning out a better product," said Grace, adding that DDB "is more interested in the bottom line than in the product it produces."

Grace had informed Loughrane that he was leaving only the night before, though he worded his bombshell as "two weeks' notice." Loughrane, caught unawares, asked Grace to withhold an announcement. "It's a very important thing, losing a creative director. I want to make sure we have a chance to talk to our clients, and I have a chance to talk to everybody in top management here, and figure out how we're going to handle it."

Loughrane believed Grace had agreed. Instead by 10 a.m. next day, the press was calling, following up Grace's conference. By noon, clients began calling Loughrane. "Roy and Diane [Rothschild] had been calling our clients, telling them." In the late afternoon, Loughrane addressed a meeting of the agency's top managers and creatives.

"We don't know what we're going to do for a creative director," he told them, "but I've asked Bob Gage, who certainly doesn't want it, to step in as acting creative director. He has all the credentials so far as the outside world is concerned."

At which point, John Noble walked out of the meeting, having told Loughrane before it began, "If I don't get the creative director job, I quit." A few days later Noble, who had been a candidate for termination in an earlier DDB bloodbath, was named executive creative director of Doyle Dane Bernbach. No one had ever envisioned him as a possible heir to the Bernbach mantle, and in fact he'd be gone soon after the mega-merger.

* * *

The agency's profit picture deteriorated in 1985 as advertisers cut budgets, new business failed to take up the slack, and disinflation put an end to years of soaring media costs that had fattened agency coffers. Payroll was reduced by another fifty jobs. As a cost-cutting measure, Loughrane recommended an end to the expensive Long Term Incentive Awards program. But not before setting up a second round, designating 32,000 shares for himself, and 18,500 for Bob Pfundstein. Vice chairman-general manager Arie Kopelman was down for 6,000; exec VPs for 5,000; research director Ruth Ziff for zero.

Unhappiness at perceived inequities in the upper echelons soon paralleled fears of job losses in the lower.

* * *

The new round of LTIAs, like the first round, would pay out in five years—unless there was "a change in control," in which case it would vest immediately. Board members did not expect any such change. They still had confidence that the agency could "make its own way" under Loughrane and Pfundstein. So they generously voted to give both men one hundred percent of their units when the first round came due at the end of 1985. Technically, the two didn't qualify for the payout, because profits of their division—corporate—hadn't met the requirements of the complex formula underlying the plan.

But what the hell, these were the guys running the company now. Quibbling over a formula could poison the waters.

The poison came a few months later, when round two vested, thanks to an upcoming "change in control."

* * *

Bob Levenson described John Bernbach as a *kochleffl*. The Yiddish word, literally a "cooking spoon," metaphorically connotes a person who stirs things up, makes things happen. It was John Bernbach who brought the mega-merger about, by being his usual affable, social, convivial, getting-around self. Attending a cocktail party given by Ted Voss in January 1985, John met Keith Reinhard, CEO of Needham, Harper Worldwide.

"We struck it off at once," John recalled. They chatted in a cocktail party way about the problems their two agencies faced in a world of shrinking business and disinflation. Before the party ended, they agreed to talk again. Perhaps after he returned from a business trip to London, said Reinhard. Ah, but John was going to London, too. They made a date to meet in London.

John briefed Loughrane, who gave his blessings. Reinhard, after all, was a creative star, up there with the Burt Mannings, the Mal Macdougalls, the Jay Chiats. And Doyle Dane Bernbach had talked merger with Needham when Bernbach was alive. It hadn't come off then, but now the managements of both agencies had changed, and so had times. Both were actively seeking merger partners.

So John and Reinhard met in London later in January, and decided, as

Neil Austrian had earlier, that the two agencies were "remarkably compatible" in their philosophies and cultures. (In actuality, the combining would prove as difficult and unnerving to the two staffs as any other merger.) Certainly, the geographical fit was good. Needham strong in its home town of Chicago; it had never succeeded in New York. Doyle Dane Bernbach, a great New York agency, didn't even have an office in Chicago. Internationally, Needham's strength lay in the Far East; DDB's in Europe.

For all their apparent good fit, the two agencies dropped the subject in mid-year, distracted, perhaps, by other possibilities.

In December 1985, John lunched at the Helmsley Hotel with his BBDO counterpart, international head Willi Schalk. They chatted about their children's schools and other domestic topics. Then Schalk told John he'd been hearing "all the rumors going around about mergers—everybody's talking to everybody else." If Doyle Dane Bernbach was serious about a merger, BBDO would like to talk "before you do anything else." Schalk didn't tell John that BBDO was already talking to Needham, nor did he know that DDB and Needham had talked.

John reported the exchange to Loughrane. They hauled out the Redbook, listing agency clients, and found massive conflicts between BBDO's and theirs. The only possible arrangement would be a holding company, under which the two agencies would operate separately, independent of one another.

An alluring concept. Doyle Dane Bernbach intact, but under the wing of a strong parent with deep pockets and managerial skills. And so, in mid-January of 1986, when business resumed on Madison Avenue after the annual indulgences of the holiday season, John lunched with Schalk again, expressing the hope that talks could begin in earnest. Chairman Roy Grace hadn't yet announced his departure, but he was out of the loop on this and every other possible structural change.

* * *

Details of the talks that followed are not part of my story. Suffice to say the power belonged entirely to BBDO, which toyed alternately with thoughts of doing a deal with Needham and with Doyle Dane Bernbach. Neither of the anxious-to-be-acquired agencies suspected it had competition for BBDO's hand. Willi Schalk gets credit for sparing either rejection, by proposing a union of the two. Happily, the two fell into each other's arms, relieved not to be left behind to their own clouded destinies.

Thus, the so-called "big bang" mega-merger of the three agencies and their holdings. The agreement was announced on April 28, 1986. "Awesome," *Advertising Age* editorialized, "Positively awesome." The participants "have made advertising history by simultaneously combining, not two, but three brilliantly creative organizations under one corporate roof . . . a watershed moment in advertising history." The press, like Doyle Dane Bernbach's board before its last meeting, still assumed all was well with the agency, and so perceived the three-way merger as a "positive, cocky approach bespeak[ing] an admirable go-for-it resolve to be No. 1."

The parent company would be called Omnicom. It would oversee three distinct companies. BBDO, the source of its strength. DDB Needham Worldwide, the merger of two troubled agencies. And Diversified Agency Services, a catch-all of the many specialized and regional agencies and subsidiaries collected over the years by the three major players.

In a stroke they would form the largest agency group in the world. Their supremacy lasted for two whole weeks. Then the Saatchis out-banged them by purchasing Ted Bates Worldwide, thus forming an even bigger agency group, and striking terror into the hearts of agency people everywhere.

* * *

Doyle Dane Bernbach's board found the mega-merger proposal considerably less than awesome when it came before them on the nights of April 24 and 25. Members were enraged when Loughrane and Pfundstein presented a torrent of data, leading to the conclusion that the mega-merger was essential because the agency was "dead in the water."

Mac Dane pointed to prior forecasts of a bright outlook for the DDB Group. "I was surprised," he said later, "at the quick turnaround that we couldn't make it on our own."

"It wasn't a merger proposal," said Ned Doyle. "It was a buy-out." He'd always believed the agency could be turned around by the right person, and he'd believed that Loughrane was the right person. Loughrane broke his heart. In Doyle's words, "He was a complete disappointment. He never did anything."

Board member Neil Austrian, always a proponent of combinations, agreed with Loughrane on the strategic need to merge, but faulted his failure to keep the board informed until there were no options. He believed that, "had the board some other options, this deal never would have happened."

Austrian, the numbers wizard, stormed against the proposal's valuation of DDB shares. Directors who had barely been civil to him since the Saatchi episode of 1984 now rallied 'round him. At the end of an emotionally exhausting meeting on April 24, the board followed Austrian's advice and rejected the mega-merger, unless and until it provided a higher exchange ratio on DDB shares.

(The Saatchis' intelligence network picked up on the secret goings-on, and overnight the British takeover masters sketched out an offer of $30 per share for the stock. The offer contained so many contingencies that the board rejected it out of hand.)

Through the night of April 24, bankers and lawyers crunched numbers, and came up with a slightly-improved ratio for DDB shareholders. "Not as good as it should have been," commented Austrian later. "We sold the business for no premium. For no premium. We *sold* it."

With heavy hearts and feelings of utter powerlessness, the shrimp board voted to approve the submergence of the legendary Doyle Dane Bernbach into the unknown entity of DDB Needham Worldwide.

* * *

The resentment felt by the directors toward this unexpected denouement turned into near-apoplexy at a board meeting in May 1986, called to wrap up the second round of the Long Term Incentive Awards before the "change in control." (The actual mega-merger awaited approval by shareholders of the three agencies at meetings scheduled for late August.) Loughrane and Phundstein claimed 100 percent cash on their performance units. They recommended zero for the other participants. Why? Because only Corporate's profits were higher than the base year set in the plan. The payout would give Loughrane $900,000 and Pfundstein $600,000.

"Nobody else was getting a dime," Joe Daly remembered. "Now how in hell can Corporate make bonuses when none of the divisions made *their* numbers?" The answer was a technicality. The base year happened to include a write-off of $3 million in accounts receivable on the Victor Technology business, "so no matter what you did, you're going to make money corporately," explained Daly.

Austrian reminded Loughrane and Pfundstein that they'd received full corporate bonuses on the last round, when the board waived the write-off while it voted for the payout. "Then Victor didn't count," shouted Austrian. "Now you say it *does* count. You can't have it both ways!"

The directors, who had been roused to fury against Austrian two years earlier, now boiled with anger against his chief opponents of that time. Those men had assured them they could make it work, and had instead "sold them out." They voted with Austrian to reject the second-round LTIA payouts to Loughrane and Pfundstein.

Whereupon the two men threatened to bring immediate suit, an action certain to torpedo the mega-merger. Through a night of heated telephone calls, Doyle Dane Bernbach's wise old advisers—lawyer Josh Levine and accountant David Zack—weighed in on the side of pacification. Tempers cooled. The possible consequences of a lawsuit at this stage were too awful to unloose. The board met again on the following day and approved the payouts to Loughrane and Pfundstein.

But the episode left, in Daly's words, "such a terrible taste," that the two men became pariahs on the executive floor. They were cut out of the agency's memo stream, excluded from meetings, isolated from daily events. And on the day after shareholders approved the mega-merger, Loughrane and Pfundstein were stripped of their building keys and ID passes by DDB's office services manager and a security guard.

There had been bad endings a-plenty in the Doyle Dane Bernbach management saga, but this one took the prize.

* * *

The upbeat tone of the mega-merger announcement on April 28 only briefly diverted DDBers from fear for their jobs. Downsizing continued through the summer, shrinking the payroll from 750 to 600, as prelude to the upcoming shareholder approval meetings. Management of the merged agency must be allowed to begin without blood on its hands.

Anger built among DDBers with the growing perception that they had been abandoned. Whose agency would this be, anyway? Where were their leaders? Loughrane and Pfundstein had "sold them out," taken money from the LTIAs, and won five-year contracts with Omnicom to manage the catch-all group, Diversified Agency Services, leaving DDBers to the mercies of strangers. Oh, sure, John Bernbach would play a major role in the merged agency, but few DDBers had even met the peripatetic international head.

Their new CEO would be Keith Reinhard, a 51-year-old Indiana Mennonite who was Needham's CEO and creative star. Surely he'd bring his own style and his own trusted people. (DDBers, an irreverent lot, groaned when they read copies of the homiletic memos Reinhard wrote weekly to his staff. Compatible cultures? Hardly.) Whatever the long-term outcome, the agency would never again be theirs, would never again be Doyle Dane Bernbach.

Still, not one of the talented city kids nurtured by Bernbach had proved to be a strong creative leader. Was that happenstance? Might that in some subterranean way be the result of Bernbach's inability to cede power? Whatever, this was the price.

* * *

Current and former employees filled most of the seats in the Time-Life auditorium on August 28, 1986, when Doyle Dane Bernbach shareholders met to vote on the mega-merger proposal. Tension and unhappiness were reflected in their faces. From the podium, the words came out formalistically—analytic, legalistic, financial, complete with charts and tables. Cut and dried and unsatisfying, until adjournment was called for, and an agency alumna asked if she might make a statement. Yes, of course.

Paula Green, the copywriter who had, among many other early DDB triumphs, created the Avis "We try harder" campaign with Helmut Krone, took a microphone and spoke spontaneously, from her heart.

"I come here out of love and honor and respect for the three great people who founded this agency, an agency that gave us courage, that put all of us on the way to our own ways, that allowed us to grow. I come here to celebrate them, and to hope that this new agency is in every way a reflection of Bill Bernbach, Ned Doyle, and Mac Dane . . . [and that] the traditions continue even though the name may change."

The room erupted in loud applause. The moving message had restored humanity, and memories, and ideals. Maybe things would be okay after all.

* * *

Joe Daly was asked to speak at a gathering of the agency's international managers and creative heads, soon after completion of the mega-merger.

"I'm the oldest guy here, and I've been in this joint for 37 years," he began, "so you might like to know what I think about the merger.

"You've heard all the pro forma, how much money we're going to make that we weren't going to make, and you've also seen what a great geographic fit this is. And if you think that's why we did the merger, I want to tell you one thing: Bullshit! We did it to get Keith Reinhard into this job."

The group cheered the truth of Daly's words. He repeated them often in the months ahead, even as Needham people gained control over various departments, and more DDBers bit the dust. He re-phrased his statement, proudly boasting:

"We decimated an agency to get one guy."

Daly, of course, meant that Doyle Dane Bernbach had decimated Needham Harper Worldwide.

Funny, it felt just the opposite to the troops and alumni of Doyle Dane Bernbach.

◆ ◆ ◆

Epilogue

"Don't let it be forgot/That once there was a spot/For one brief shining moment that/was known as Camelot . . ."—Alan Jay Lerner

"There's an Irish song with a great line,'" mused senior VP John Curran, on the day that Doyle Dane Bernbach disappeared into DDB Needham Worldwide Inc. "'What's won is won/what's done is done/and what's lost is lost and gone forever.' The fucking company is dead!"

On that, there was universal agreement among DDBers. Whatever became of DDB Needham, their Doyle Dane Bernbach had vanished, leaving them with a profound and bitter sense of loss.

Keith Reinhard would later admit that he had "naively expected" DDBers to like the merger, to say, "What a great idea." He had assumed they would gladly don T-shirts touting "DDB Needham: The New Creative Force." But that kind of boosterism, like Reinhard's folksy staff memos, was a total turn-off to hip DDBers, who touched up the lettering to read, "The New Creative Farce."

The clash of New York irreverence and Midwest homespun reverberated for many months, confounding the forecasts of "cultural compatibility." It would be mid-1988 before the turbulence moderated sufficiently for the New York office to win its first new client. (In contrast, the undiluted Needham Chicago office won new business galore.) It would be mid-1989 before the *New York Times* declared that "after three years of turmoil, [the DDB-Needham merger] is starting to pay off."

By that time, many more DDBers had gone. Bob Pfundstein was gone too, from his high position at Omnicom's Diversified Agency Services. Barry Loughrane would resign at the end of 1989, without comment. The two men who supposedly had "sold out" the agency had ended up with more of the swag, but little future in the company they helped make happen.

* * *

Every step along the way to mega-merger and a year or more beyond brought laments of "Bill Bernbach must be spinning in his grave." The creative rivalries of Marvin Honig, Bob Levenson and Roy Grace. The inability of the post-Bernbach CEOs, Austrian and Loughrane, to pull the place together and get it moving again. The perception that "every man for himself" had become the dominant value. After the mega-merger, the worry that the merged agency might not survive the turmoil long enough to start winning new business.

John Bernbach never doubted. On top of the heap, he confidently predicted, from the day of the Big Bang, that in its new incarnation DDB would exist "in perpetuity."

Meanwhile, *Advertising Age*, the bible of the industry, ran a striking four-page article titled "The Bernbach Fantasies," in which Bill Bernbach was placed with John Keats, Ralph Waldo Emerson, Winston Churchill and Shakespeare.

"Bill's been elevated to saint," muttered his old art director, Bob Gage. "He's up there, floating above us."

So Bernbach had indeed pulled free of his agency's reputation and soared into advertising history's stratosphere. His family had the $20 million. His adored son John buzzed happily around the globe as president of the new agency, second only to the man the merger turned out to be about, Needham Harper's creative star, Keith Reinhard. And the industry had seen that Doyle Dane Bernbach *could not* survive without Bill Bernbach.

Spin in his grave? What could have been more *perfect*?